The American Surfer

Routledge Advances in Sociology

For a full list of titles in this series, please visit www.routledge.com

17. Agricultural Governance
Globalization and the New Politics of Regulation
Edited by Vaughan Higgins and Geoffrey Lawrence

18. Challenging Hegemonic Masculinity
Richard Howson

19. Social Isolation in Modern Society
Roelof Hortulanus, Anja Machielse and Ludwien Meeuwesen

20. Weber and the Persistence of Religion
Social Theory, Capitalism and the Sublime
Joseph W. H. Lough

21. Globalization, Uncertainty and Late Careers in Society
Edited by Hans-Peter Blossfeld, Sandra Buchholz and Dirk Hofäcker

22. Bourdieu's Politics
Problems and Possibilities
Jeremy F. Lane

23. Media Bias in Reporting Social Research?
The Case of Reviewing Ethnic Inequalities in Education
Martyn Hammersley

24. A General Theory of Emotions and Social Life
Warren D. TenHouten

25. Sociology, Religion and Grace
Arpad Szakolczai

26. Youth Cultures
Scenes, Subcultures and Tribes
Edited by Paul Hodkinson and Wolfgang Deicke

27. The Obituary as Collective Memory
Bridget Fowler

28. Tocqueville's Virus
Utopia and Dystopia in Western Social and Political Thought
Mark Featherstone

29. Jewish Eating and Identity Through the Ages
David Kraemer

30. The Institutionalization of Social Welfare
A Study of Medicalizing Management
Mikael Holmqvist

31. The Role of Religion in Modern Societies
Edited by Detlef Pollack and Daniel V. A. Olson

32. Sex Research and Sex Therapy
A Sociological Analysis of Masters and Johnson
Ross Morrow

33. A Crisis of Waste?
Understanding the Rubbish Society
Martin O'Brien

34. Globalization and Transformations of Local Socioeconomic Practices
Edited by Ulrike Schuerkens

35. The Culture of Welfare Markets
The International Recasting of Pension and Care Systems
Ingo Bode

36. Cohabitation, Family and Society
Tiziana Nazio

37. Latin America and Contemporary Modernity
A Sociological Interpretation
José Maurício Domingues

38. Exploring the Networked Worlds of Popular Music
Milieu Cultures
Peter Webb

39. The Cultural Significance of the Child Star
Jane O'Connor

40. European Integration as an Elite Process
The Failure of a Dream?
Max Haller

41. Queer Political Performance and Protest
Benjamin Shepard

42. Cosmopolitan Spaces
Europe, Globalization, Theory
Chris Rumford

43. Contexts of Social Capital
Social Networks in Communities, Markets and Organizations
Edited by Ray-May Hsung, Nan Lin, and Ronald Breiger

44. Feminism, Domesticity and Popular Culture
Edited by Stacy Gillis and Joanne Hollows

45. Changing Relationships
Edited by Malcolm Brynin and John Ermisch

46. Formal and Informal Work
The Hidden Work Regime in Europe
Edited by Birgit Pfau-Effinger, Lluis Flaquer, and Per H. Jensen

47. Interpreting Human Rights
Social Science Perspectives
Edited by Rhiannon Morgan and Bryan S. Turner

48. Club Cultures
Boundaries, Identities and Otherness
Silvia Rief

49. Eastern European Immigrant Families
Mihaela Robila

50. People and Societies
Rom Harré and Designing the Social Sciences
Luk van Langenhove

51. Legislating Creativity
The Intersections of Art and Politics
Dustin Kidd

52. Youth in Contemporary Europe
Edited by Jeremy Leaman and Martha Wörsching

53. Globalization and Transformations of Social Inequality
Edited by Ulrike Schuerkens

54. Twentieth Century Music and the Question of Modernity
Eduardo De La Fuente

55. The American Surfer
Radical Culture and Capitalism
Kristin Lawler

The American Surfer

Radical Culture and Capitalism

Kristin Lawler

Routledge
Taylor & Francis Group
New York London

First published 2011
by Routledge
711 Third Avenue, New York, NY 10017

Simultaneously published in the UK
by Routledge
2 Park Square, Milton Park, Abingdon, Oxon OX14 4RN

Routledge is an imprint of the Taylor & Francis Group, an informa business

First issued in paperback 2012

Typeset in Sabon by IBT Global.

Library of Congress Cataloging-in-Publication Data

Lawler, Kristin.
The American surfer : radical culture and capitalism / by Kristin Lawler.
p. cm. — (Routledge advances in sociology)
Includes bibliographical references and index.
1. Surfing—United States. 2. Surfing—Social aspects—United States.
3. Subculture. I. Title.
GV840.S8L38 2010
797.3'2—dc22
2010020636

ISBN13: 978-0-415-87489-2 (hbk)
ISBN13: 978-0-203-83875-4 (ebk)
ISBN13: 978-0-415-81147-7 (pbk)

Dedicated to Ellen Willis

Contents

Acknowledgments

This book began as my dissertation, as the capstone to my graduate school career. Many, many people helped me along the way. In fact, everyone I'm about to thank should probably be held somewhat responsible for any problems with my argument or the evidence I provide for it. (Kidding.) I am deeply grateful to my dissertation committee for their help and support during the process of conceptualizing and writing this study. To Stanley Aronowitz: I attended your class my first day of graduate school. My mind was set on fire and I knew my life had changed forever. I'm happy to say I've never looked back. To Bill Kornblum: Your kindness and generosity are beyond words. It was an honor to be your research assistant; watching you, I feel like I gained a Ph.D. in research skills, professionalism, and just how to roll. To Phil Kasinitz: I'm so honored to have been able to work with you. You've been gracious and helpful and your reading improved my manuscript immeasurably. I'd also like to thank Patricia Clough for being so freaking brilliant and for turning me on to psychoanalysis, and Sharon Zukin for teaching me some incredibly important lessons about doing cultural research. And Dean Savage: You helped and supported me from day one until the very last. Thank you.

Quite simply, I have no idea what I would think about anything if I hadn't entered into a fifteen-year conversation with labor theorist Jonathan Cutler, whose incisive insights continue to keep me sharp. You are the reader and the audience, always. Michael Roberts, scholar of labor and rock and roll, is my good buddy and the smartest surfer I know. You are too cool, my brother. I'm proud to say that the three of us constitute an original and totally *radical* school of thought. Thank you, Penny Lewis and Miriam Greenberg, for being warm, wonderful friends, whip-smart interlocutors, and for always keeping me honest. Your comments on early chapters of the dissertation were extremely valuable.

My new colleagues at The College of Mount Saint Vincent have been more professionally and personally supportive than any new professor has a right to expect. To Alfred D'Anca and Omar Nagi, my fellow sociologists and friends, I am grateful for the laughter, great conversation, and real sense of community that characterize our vibrant little department.

Ron Scapp has mentored me in professional life in ways I can never repay, only pay forward. Thank you for your unconditional support and brilliant guidance; I am grateful too, for all the collaboration we have to look forward to. And to my smart and fiery students at the Mount, I am thankful for the opportunity to witness you develop in your capacity to think about the world. You remind me daily of the transformative power of critical thinking; I think you guys also keep me young. Last, to Charles Flynn, the Sisters of Charity, and Mount Saint Vincent as a whole; being part of an institution dedicated to the principles of the liberal arts and social justice animates my work and my life.

I owe thanks also to my wonderful editor, Ben Holtzman, who had faith in my project and nurtured it along before heading back to academia himself; Max Novick took over and has provided sound, supportive guidance ever since.

I want to thank my parents for training me in the intellectual life, one dinner table conversation at a time. From my activist mother, I learned empathy and passion. My father, the attorney, taught me the power of reasoned argument. I like to think I turned out a pretty good mix. And you both taught me how to write.

My most intense gratitude is reserved for my own family. To my husband, Stephen, who honest to God always just assumed I would actually do this. Your faith in me carried me when my own had run dry. You are my oceanic feeling. And to my children, Lucas and Callie. It's the two of you who remind me every day that life is like a wave—magical and momentary and inviting one's full attention and presence. I didn't begin this project until after I had children; I think I needed to be your mom before I realized what I was put on this earth to do—love you guys, and bear witness to how precious it all is. Thanks just won't cut it for that one.

This book is dedicated to the late Ellen Willis. My greatest hope for it is that it might be worthy of its dedication.

1 Radical

Surf Culture, Image, and Capitalism[1]

Radical. (rad e kuhl) 1. of or going to the root or origin, fundamental. 2. thoroughgoing or extreme; *a radical change in policy*. 3. (slang) excellent, cool (from Southern California) *radical waves, dude.*

"Dreams are psychical acts of as much significance as any others: their motive force is in every instance a wish seeking fulfillment . . . here we have the most general and the most striking characteristic of the process of dreaming: a thought, and as a rule a thought of something that is wished, is objectified in the dream, is represented as a scene, or, as it seems to us, is experienced."

Sigmund Freud, *The Interpretation of Dreams*[2]

One of the 1963 film *Beach Party*'s opening scenes finds a caricatured "famed anthropologist" surreptitiously observing a group of teenage surfers on the southern California coast. The academic, Robert Sutwell, can't hold back a prurient giggle as he observes the scantily clad teens surf, rub lotion on one another, and speak a foreign lingo. "It's fascinating," Sutwell tells his assistant, "how similar these people are to the other primitive tribes we've studied." To the assistant's protest that they're just "normal American teenagers," the professor replies, "teenagers, yes; normal, no. They're a true subculture. They live in a society as primitive as the aborigine of New Guinea."

The movie makes Sutwell's point over and over again, with a bongo drum soundtrack behind images of parent-free teenagers surfing and dancing wildly around neo-Polynesian huts and bonfires. In his work on "Behavior Patterns of the Young Adult and its Relation to Primitive Tribes," the professor is posing the question that animates the present work: what is the significance of the image he's seeing? Through his eyes, the surfers appear as a form of the return of the repressed in modern society. And importantly, the surf kids are the only "primitive" culture that, in all his years of observing, turn him on enough that in the course of the film he ditches his "square" look, loosens up, learns to surf, and finally romances his sexy assistant, MaryAnn.

There are two facets of "significance" at work in the professor's response to the surf image, and in mine. The first involves what the image means, what it *signifies*. The second is a question of *historical* significance—what it produces, what its historical effects have been. In examining the image of the surfer in twentieth-century American popular culture, I want to investigate the significance of this image in both senses. Given the ubiquity of the image of the surfer in American pop culture, the relative absence of this kind of analysis within Cultural Studies is striking.

There are a few important exceptions. Several see the surf image in terms similar to the ones articulated here,[3] but each one points to the more customary view of the surf image as deeply conventional. Typical of this trend is the work of Kirse Granat May. In her study of the California image in popular culture, May attributes the mass popularity of the 1960s surfer image to the attempt by Americans to "resolve by denial the problems that emerged in the sixties with a more satisfying and less threatening picture of its youth." The 1950s image of the juvenile delinquent, the brooding "hood" riding a motorcycle in black leather, and all the nail-biting over America's youth that the image's prominence represented, was repressed and transformed into the happy, smiling, blonde, tanned, wholesome surfer gang.[4] Now, it's true that the movie's stars, Mickey Mouse club and American Bandstand teen idols Annette Funicello and Frankie Avalon, were certainly far less threatening than James Dean or Marlon Brando had been. In fact, the movie makes a running gag of the earlier images—the hapless Eric Von Zipper, JD ("dat's for juvenile delinquent"), and their motorcycle gang are now the object of ridicule, not worry. *Beach Party*'s teenagers never get into any "real" trouble, and Annette's biggest objective in the movie is getting Frankie to "think of [her] as a wife."

However, even this sanitized image of American youth contains elements that are counter-cultural within the context of postwar America. It's not at all clear that mainstream acceptability characterizes the surfing image in the film.[5] The kids hang out at Big Daddy's, a beat café straight out of Greenwich Village, where they gyrate wildly to surfer Dick Dale's screaming, insistent guitar riffs—Dale's music was organic to the California surf scene in a way that the Beach Boys, for instance, were not—while drinking beer and smoking pot. Even Frankie Avalon is seen smoking and then passing a joint! And the *actual* surfing subculture on which *Beach Party*-type images were based was constituted by teenagers and young adults who very explicitly saw themselves as different from, and at odds with, postwar American culture. As we'll see, there's quite a bit of evidence that far from being a safe alternative to juvenile delinquency, the American surfer signified a threat to moral discipline from the start.

Beach Party was no anomaly; the surfer kids observed by Professor Sutwell had a lot in common with many other celluloid and print surfers. In fact, as I will argue, in its every incarnation, the content of the surfer image has remained largely consistent. As the present work will lay out, decade after decade, the image has signified freedom: *from* work, from scarcity, from the restrictions of traditional gender roles, and *to* live spontaneously with joy and within a profoundly pleasurable ecological and subcultural connection. It's also always symbolized the transcendence of the imperatives of modern rationality in favor of a more "primitive," libidinal relationship to the world.

If the classical sociological theorists such as Marx, Weber and Durkheim have one commonality, it's their attempt to theorize the alienated, disconnected life that capitalism, work, and modern life condemn us to. What unites so many of the different moments of the surfer image is precisely its invocation of the transcendence of this social disconnection, in addition to the ecological and psychological disconnection the overcoming of which it also suggests. In the image of the surfer, we see the *connections*—the Zen connection to the moment and to nature that is the precondition of riding a wave, the social connection of subculture members who spend their time floating together on the ocean and "talking story" (and partying) on the beach—that contemporary (still overworked and alienated) members of society all too often find absent in their lives. The fact that the image has had such a wide and durable appeal means that it tells us something important about the fantasy life of the masses of people who respond to it.

It tells us that American mass fantasy is, at least in one enormous respect, quite countercultural. From the perspective of what I argue is most repressive about contemporary society—the cold logic of capital according to Marx; the Protestant work ethic and instrumental attitude to the lifeworld, including nature, that Weber lays out; the capitalist time-sense as discussed by E. P. Thompson; as well as the regime of contemporary gender roles criticized by feminist authors—the image of the surfer is countercultural through and through.

In making this argument, I lean for my definition of "countercultural" on the work of Jock Young, Herbert Marcuse, and Theodor Roszak. For Young, countercultural lifeways oppose what he calls the "formal, official values of the workaday world" in contrast to the "subterranean values" that oppose them. In his 1971 study of *The Drugtakers*,[6] Young deploys the psychoanalytic distinction between pleasure and reality principles elaborated in Marcuse's *Eros and Civilization*[7] to bring the difference into sharp relief. The formal work values, or what he calls the "ethos of productivity" consist of: deferred gratification; planning future action; conformity to rules; routine and predictability; instrumental attitudes; and the moral valuation of hard, productive work. On the other hand, the subterranean values are: short-term hedonism; spontaneity; ego-expressivity; novelty and excitement; activities performed as ends in themselves; and disdain for work.

Young's operational definition of counterculture—the resistance to work, and the embrace of freedom, play, and connection with nature—is reminiscent of Theodore Roszak's 1968 argument in *The Making of a Counter Culture*.[8] For him, the counterculture is a lived critique of what he calls the "technocracy," which is characterized above all by the "myth of objective consciousness." This myth is the idea that the subject and object of knowledge and action can be totally separate, that the subject can and should observe and act without any connection to the object—a particularly Western mind-body dualism that the many facets of connection embodied by the image of the surfer actively counter.[9] Objective consciousness is a technical rationality emphasizing quantity over quality, objectivization over connection, the technique, the machine, over the person—a dominating logic that Roszak considers a form of "open warfare upon joy," and that Max Weber tells us is the foundation of bourgeois culture. Nothing is left to be, nothing is valuable in itself, all matter, all life, has value only to the extent that it produces. Everything, all nature and every moment, must be dominated and put to work. The image of the surfer, as I hope this book will make clear, embodies a powerful archetype of opposition to this cold, dominating logic.

But it's not just thematically that the image of the surfer and the counterculture are linked. Their affinity is most explicit in the mid-century representations of surfing, in which images of beat culture and hippie counterculture are very clearly invoked. The image of the surfer is one of very few popular representations that carry these characteristics of mid-century counterculture forward into the present day—long hair, pot smoking, connection to nature, primitivism, a focus on leisure, and the strong female and feminized male. And in fact, the image of surfing contained these themes long before the counterculture emerged.

In order to make this point, the image of the surfer will be read throughout this book, against the backdrop of the negative reactions to it by those groups responsible for enforcing the Puritan-style discipline—pro-work, anti-spontaneity—on which, Max Weber tells us, capitalism ultimately depends: from Calvinist missionaries in Hawaii, to school authorities in Southern California, to those today who want the beaches, like the people, to *work* (as trash dumps, as oil-producing spaces, as commercial harbors) rather than just to *be*.

But we'll hear from Calvinists and their more contemporary descendants only to provide a relief against which to examine our real object, the image of the surfer, throughout its *commercial* dissemination during the twentieth century. The fact that while surfing has been repressed by the forces I'm calling Puritans and neo-Puritans, it's been broadcast and amplified by commercial forces, is key to my argument that the most frequently recurring popular culture images endure precisely because they tap into our deepest, most "primitive" desires for freedom and connection. Both sides understand the lure. Puritans know that cultural images that encourage liberation are compelling and contagious and spread undisciplined, spontaneous activity; which is why they work so hard to shut down the channels that broadcast them. Furthermore, advertisers surely know that appealing to dreams, to desires, moves people as well. Knowing this is their business.

This brings us to the second facet of the significance of the American surfer—its historical impact. Purveyors of popular culture broadcast fantasy images precisely because they understand their appeal—they know that in responding to these images, people tend to act collectively. That is, if the images are successful, they inspire people to buy the same thing all at once (without a meeting, no less). If the fantasy images deployed by advertisers and other purveyors of profit-driven popular culture fail to have this effect, they're generally abandoned. That's why the image of the American surfer is so important—as we'll see, it's been a consistently prominent figure in commercially-driven popular culture. If it hadn't been successful in moving people to act—to buy a record, a car, a movie ticket, a Hawaiian vacation—it would have been abandoned long ago. As the present work will show, the image of the surfer is ubiquitous precisely because it has so consistently been successful in the appeal to people's dreams, the stock in trade of manufacturers of consumer culture. But ultimately consumer action is not the only kind of collective action that tapping into subterranean desires can inspire. As we'll see, these desires have tended to overflow the collective buying that the advertisers work to channel them into.

A clear example of this dynamic is the fact that the commercial use of surfing has inspired far more at the level of collective activity than just mass shopping. As this book will demonstrate, the number of people joining the "tribe" of free-living surfers has tended to increase exponentially with increases in the prominence of the image. Images of early twentieth-century Hawaiian surfers inspired mainlanders to flock to Waikiki Beach, and inspired young people to drop out of interwar society and emulate the Hawaiian "beach boys" on the California coast. This coast, much of which was still wild at the time, had been opened up by Henry Huntington's Pacific Electric Railway. Huntington had lured customers onto his trains and out to his new beach resorts with surfing demonstrations put on up and down the coast by famed Hawaiian beach boy George Freeth. Depictions of the subculture developing on the pre-WWII Southern California beach planted California surfing in the American popular imagination and prepared the way for a whole nation of young people to be inspired to participate in surf culture once the novel and then the film *Gidget* immortalized the postwar Malibu beach shack gang. Today, inspiration for the massive growth of surfing comes from a growing crop of journalistic coverage including a new column in the *New York Times* devoted entirely to the growth of surf culture in New York City; documentary films like *Riding Giants*, *Step Into Liquid*, and *Surfwise*; entire cable television stations like *Fuel TV*; surfer characters in film and television fiction; and of course, advertising. Again and again, we will see how commercial forces, which were using the image of the surfer to make profit, unwittingly helped to build and grow the surf culture itself.[10]

So images that tap into mass fantasies inspire mass collective behavior—both consumer and sub- or countercultural behavior.[11] Insofar as they are responses to popular images of freedom like that of the surfer, both kinds of behavior (buying a car you identify with the surfer, or dropping out of the workaday world and taking up the life of a nomadic surfer in fellowship with others) are constituted at heart by the attempt to make the fantasy image real. It is this collective attempt on the part of a mass public that characterizes the social and historical impact of images like that of the surfer, images that *inspire*. The question becomes: is this fact of more than passing significance? That is, does this effect matter politically, in terms of *real* opposition to the very alienation that the surfer is seen symbolically to transcend?

It's become common among progressives, especially in the wake of Thomas Frank's 1997 book *The Conquest of Cool*, to believe that since counterculture is frequently an effect of the commercial impulse of capitalism, it must be politically meaningless. That is, since cultural rebellion is not incompatible with the success of the commercial arm of capitalism, then this so-called "rebellion" must be part of what keeps the system of exploitation going.

Frank's argument joins a long line of left critics of cultural radicalism as politically insignificant. Most seminal of these is the work of the Center for Contemporary Cultural Studies in Birmingham. Birmingham took the British working-class youth subcultures they famously studied seriously as cultural resistance, but ultimately saw this resistance as a "symbolic" solution to the real problem of class subordination, and thus as incapable of social transformation. Frank's work certainly falls within this hallowed tradition on the left of seeing cultural resistance as in one way or another epiphenomenal to "reality," that is, economic reality. (David Brooks, in *Bobos in Paradise*[12], shares Frank's basic conception of the symbiosis of the logic of capital and cultural radicalism because he similarly underestimates the social transformations wrought by the counterculture; in his work, they are reduced to a set of frivolous habits of the rich.)

What's new is Frank's challenge to the co-optation theory central to Birmingham as well as to the Gramscian and Althusserian Marxism by which they were inspired. For Birmingham analysts like Dick Hebdige and the editors of *Resistance Through Rituals*, even the symbolic resistance mounted by young punk rockers, mods, and teddies, was inevitably subject to the impotence supposedly caused by co-optation—capital's appropriation of rebellion in advertising as one more means to generate profit, to fold opposition squarely back into the system of working and buying—and diffusion into mass culture.[13]

Frank makes an alternative case, using American advertising and its most forward thinkers to demonstrate that far from being a threat that capitalists felt the need to co-opt, the counterculture was embraced as a massive opportunity. The counterculture of the 1960s was actually welcomed, and even fomented, by capitalists, who had already been getting pretty hip and countercultural themselves. Frank's argument, that countercultural sensibilities are central to contemporary capitalism rather than a challenge to it, is a convincing refutation of co-optation theory (as is the history recounted here of commercial surf images inspiring the growth of the surf subculture). In fact, though, as we'll see, the history of surfing and its image in popular culture tells a story that's more complex than either the theory of co-optation or Thomas Frank's critique of it can fully account for. It may just be the case that the reciprocal relationship between consumer culture and oppositional subculture, or counterculture, is precisely what gives each one its subversive potential.

It's worth quoting the late great Ellen Willis at length on this point. Arguing against

Feminist

> standard leftist notions about advanced capitalism—that the consumer economy makes us slaves to commodities, that the function of the mass media is to manipulate our fantasies so we will equate fulfillment with buying the system's products," she asserts that "these ideas are at most half true. Mass consumption, advertising, and mass art are a corporate Frankenstein; while they reinforce the system, they also undermine it. By continually pushing the message that we have the right to gratification *now*, consumerism at its most expansive encouraged a demand for fulfillment that could not so easily be contained by products; it had a way of spilling over into rebellion against the constricting conditions of our lives.

She goes on to say that

> the history of the sixties strongly suggests that the impulse to buy a new car and tool down the freeway with the radio blasting rock and roll is not unconnected to the desire to fuck outside marriage, get high, stand up to men or white people or bosses, join dissident movements. In fact, the mass media helped to spread rebellion, and the system obligingly marketed products that encouraged it, for the simple reason that there was money to be made from the rebels who were also consumers. On one level the sixties revolt was an impressive illustration of Lenin's remark that the capitalist will sell you the rope to hang him with.[14]

Frank's analysis similarly sees cultural rebellion as an important effect of capital's consumerist push—but thus, as without real significance. Willis's argument that consumerism fosters rebellion, and that this rebellion is "real," points us in another direction—toward Daniel Bell's classic reading of twentieth-century capital as internally rent. For him, *The Cultural Contradictions of Capitalism* consist precisely of the fact that capitalism inevitably generates opposition to the very Protestant work ethic at its heart. A "new capitalism of abundance" emerged in the 1920s with the advent of mass advertising. Preaching an "ethic of consumption—of hedonism, pleasure, and play," this new capitalism transformed the American social structure such that by the 1950s, "the culture was no longer concerned with how to work and achieve, but with how to spend and enjoy." But capitalism still needed work from people, in addition to consumption, so the "new capitalism continued to demand a Protestant ethic in the area of production—that is, in the realm of work—but to stimulate a demand for pleasure and play in the area of consumption . . . on the one hand, the business corporation wants an individual to work hard, pursue a career, accept delayed gratification . . . and yet, in its products and its advertisements, the corporation promotes pleasure, instant joy, relaxing, and letting go. One is to be 'straight' by day and a 'swinger' by night."[15]

A question emerges: in our postmodern, globalized era of the ever-increasing proliferation of images and the growing importance of their consumption to the production of profit (not to mention subjectivity), is this analysis of capitalism as rent by contradiction hopelessly outdated? I am, after all, tracing a history of a pop culture image from the late nineteenth century through only the early 1970s, and arguing that this history contains insights applicable to the contemporary period. But perhaps the "dangerous" cultural resistance to the imperatives of capital to which Bell and Willis refer is just a thing of the past—certainly, images of surfing continue to proliferate and to inspire more and more surfing all around the world, and still the fortunes of the American (not to mention global) working class have been pretty grim for quite some time now. It's my contention, though, that the post-1973 period constitutes a successful counterattack by capital on what had become an increasingly affluent and undisciplined American working class—another salvo in the dialectic of class struggle and the contradictory nature of capitalism, but not an overcoming of it.

In this contention my work is primarily influenced by that of Harry Cleaver and the tradition of Autonomous Marxism in which he works. In "*Crisis of the Keynesian Era*,"[16] Harry Cleaver demonstrates that the post-1973 period is largely an effect of capital moving from a Keynesian "welfare-warfare" American strategy to a new strategy of crisis and austerity. This change in strategy took place as a direct result of the mass rebellions unleashed during the 1960s, when the American working class broke the postwar wages-for-productivity deal (itself a reaction to the mass uprising unleashed by Depression-era austerity) and pushed up wage rates and transfer payments while simultaneously refusing work discipline on the assembly line, on campus, and in the home—a cultural rebellion that capital took seriously as class struggle, even if so many leftists still refuse to. Of the uprising and its aftermath he asks, "What were the 1960s and 1970s, if not a simultaneous explosion of both autonomous needs and of the refusal of capitalist work? What are the 1980s, if not a renewed capitalist offensive to contain the explosion of needs, to roll them back through a vicious attack on consumption . . . ?"[17]

It's my belief that although the prospects for effective resistance to capitalism may be far more bleak in the post-1973 period of neoliberal globalization, at least one of the potential conditions for the possibility of this resistance—the desire for freedom and libidinal connection and commercial culture's incessant playing to it—still swirls under the surface. The contours of our era, especially capital's ability to leverage concessions from the American working class through (among other things) threats of outsourcing, do make it seem as though the class struggle is over and won, and capital's dissemination of images of freedom no longer constitutes a profitable playing with fire. However, the analysis of twentieth-century capital and culture put forth here looks at a dynamic that transcends different periods of capital's strategy—the Gilded Age, Depression-era austerity, and postwar Keynesianism—and, I propose, may just turn out to transcend the long-running contemporary globalized beat-down that the working class is suffering under a new regime of aggressive neoliberalism in the context of the eradication of national boundaries.[18]

So, inspired by Bell's analysis, I contend that commercially broadcast images of freedom, like that of the surfer, have historically inspired collective leisure activities that implicitly and explicitly challenged the alienation of life centered around work and eternally deferred gratification. And although it's popular among progressives to dismiss this kind of mass countercultural activity as meaningless to the transformation of "real" economic realities, I argue that employers and those who speak for them have always known that cultural values around work and rationality are central for the reproduction of the system as it is.

The most powerful contemporary force in subverting these values has arguably been the consumer side of capitalism itself, whether it's successfully pushing surfing, rock and roll, or other forms of freedom, connection, and play. It's my proposal that this dynamic ought not to be dismissed. It is certainly taken seriously by those charged with enforcing work discipline, as we'll see, and I argue that this is a significant indicator that the political potential of both counterculture and the pop culture images that encourage it ought to be reconsidered. In any case, I hope to demonstrate that the idea—propounded by critical scholars from Marx in "The Fetishism of Commodities," to the Frankfurt School and those they've inspired, like Stuart Ewen and Neil Postman, to postmodern theorists of a neoliberal regime of the production of consumer-subjects—the idea that consumerism is the great enemy of the political potential of the working class has been wildly overstated, to say the very least. Who knows what subversive images—playing to the very real desire for freedom, pleasure, connection among people and between people and nature—could produce if they were properly harnessed by progressives and not only by hucksters?

As is argued in this book's final chapter, there is historical evidence that this aspect of consumer society—its incessant tapping into widely-shared desires for leisure, pleasure, and free association—*has* had real political effects, in terms of inspiring what those on the left have traditionally seen as the most "real" of all political formations, the strike. The argument will be made for the efficacy of collective cultural rebellion against repression and domination in all its forms, especially its fundamental economic form—work. But *more than anything*, what examining the double significance of the image of the surfer—the resistance it signifies, the resistance it produces—demonstrates is that there is a powerful desire for connection and freedom, a dream of the good life, that is regularly available to be mobilized. Advertisers know this, and have always mobilized it quite effectively. Perhaps others whose interest is to mobilize collective action in pursuit of achieving a dream of a better, freer life ought to take a page from this consistently successful playbook.

Stephen Duncombe, in his groundbreaking recent work *Dream: Re-Imagining Progressive Politics in an Age of Fantasy,*[19] puts it thusly: "Progressives could benefit by studying dreams more diligently. Fortunately, we have a ready-made laboratory at our disposal . . . it takes the form of something progressives traditionally disdain: commercial culture . . . First, we need to survey the terrain of today's imagination. We need to take apart the current manifestations of dreams, study contemporary spectacles, and understand how the modern manufacturers of consent channel these dynamics. Then we can begin to imagine how popular desires might be expressed in different ways and via different vehicles . . ." In entering this laboratory and studying a major commercially disseminated archetype, that of the American surfer, I join Duncombe in calling on progressives—those who purport to be in favor of workers' victories, environmentalism, and a liberal attitude to gender roles and sexuality—to abandon the dour Puritanism that largely informs the left critique of popular and commercial culture, and embrace the fantasies of liberation and ecological connection that Americans are giving voice to when they respond with gusto to images of surfing (and others). Advertisers know that tapping into these libidinal fantasies is a source of great energy. Progressives who dream of liberation and of ecological connection would do well to ride this wave.

The first chapter begins with what I call the "foundational myth"[20] of the surf subculture and its image: the oft-told story of the leisure and surf-centered Hawaiian culture, and its brutal repression by the very Calvinist missionaries to which Max Weber, in his seminal work *The Protestant Ethic and the Spirit of Capitalism*, refers as the seed of the culture of capitalism. The popular discourse around Hawaiian culture is laid out, especially in terms of the contradiction between what E. P. Thompson calls the natural time rhythm of pre-industrial societies ("island time") and the clock time of rational capitalism. The most popular images of pre-contact Hawaiian surfers are examined to understand their appeal, which is clearly the leisurely fun, natural abundance, and hangup-free sexuality that they evoke.

The Calvinist discourse around ancient Hawaii, as put forth in the memoirs of missionaries like Sheldon Dibble, William Ellis, and Hiram Bingham, is highlighted as an historical example of the opposition of an uptight Puritan morality to the multi-faceted freedom that they too saw in

Hawaiian culture generally and surfing more particularly. We first encounter the cultural contradictions of capitalism when the chapter moves from a retelling of the Puritan point of view, to the diametrically opposed view that beach developers and tourism boosters took of Hawaiian surfing. The chapter moves next to an examination of the central place that the image of the surfer came to occupy in materials designed to inspire Americans to come to Waikiki Beach at the turn of the last century.

At this time, images of native "beach boys" became central to the commercial image of Hawaii—surf instructors, musicians, and gigolos, these beach boys came to define the surfer image going forward. Images of beach boys—in advertisements, promotions, popular magazines, as well as films and novels—that were broadcast on the mainland are examined for their content and their effects. In terms of content, libidinal freedom—from work, to surf, to play all day, as well as more explicitly sexual freedom, including a freedom from rigid masculinity (and the shackles of traditional femininity in the case of the beach boys' sexually liberated surf students), is the clear theme. And in terms of effects, the growth of Hawaii as a tourist destination shows that the lure worked.

These early Hawaiian tourism images became the materials out of which surf culture and its image were built. That they speak in the language of the modern discourse of primitivism, whereby the "primitive" is seen by Westerners as the repository of the pleasures that they are denied in modern culture, is clear. It's also clear that in the case of surfing as in others, the image of the "primitive" becomes a major building block of countercultural formations.

This dynamic is illustrated historically as we trace the images that constitute a second moment of surf culture's "foundational myth"—the group of people who, inspired explicitly by images of Hawaiian beach boys, dropped out of mainstream American society during the pre-WWII decades and took up a happy residence on the (then-deserted) Southern California beach. Surfing all day and plucking giant lobster and abalone from the sea to be cooked on beach fires at night, the image of these surfers again evokes a primitive, connected-to-nature abundance. Another aspect of the surfer image in this incarnation is the constant use of nicknames, (a practice derived from the beach boys) and the always-mentioned inability of journalists sent to profile them to understand the surfers' "strange lingo." This aspect of the image, and the reasons for its allure, are read through Jacques Lacan's work on the essentially alienating aspects of a fixed identity and that of Louis Althusser on the central importance of this identity for the continued subjection of the working class under capital. Once again, we'll see images of feminine males and powerful females living a spontaneous, collective, and ecologically connected life. And in every profile, both those published at the time and in contemporary treatments, a major theme is the surfers' disdain for paid labor as well as their dismissal of the discourse of scarcity central to capitalist crisis in the 1930s. Later, these Depression-era images came to represent yet another primitive "lost paradise" that was the material out of which surf culture in 1950s Malibu was built.

This dynamic is central to our story, because, I argue, these images of primitive freedom appeal to what Freud, in an uncanny connection, called the "oceanic feeling"—the most primitive layer of our unconscious experience, in which the boundary between ego and outside world is nonexistent, and all experience is one.[21] The "oceanic" is a state before alienation, before the mind-body split that founds our separate identity, and the memory of the oceanic propels us, according to Freud, to do everything in our power to get back there. This explains the deep appeal of the images of early surfers in Hawaii and California alike, as well as the political potential that emerges with the increasingly prevalent and growing crop of early photo books of surf culture on uncrowded, unhurried beaches. This potential is addressed using Herbert Marcuse's psychoanalytic reading of the potentially explosive power of memory in upholding what he calls "the tabooed aspirations that reason denies."

The analysis of the 1960s surfer image begins with Tom Wolfe's profile of the subculture in his widely-read essay, *The Pump House Gang*, and his argument that although postwar affluence was giving rise to what he called a "happiness explosion," grumpy leftists refused to take this affirmative culture as politically significant. He implicitly argues, as I do explicitly, for a redefinition of political terms—those *for* happiness explosions on one side, those against on the other.

Next, a reading of *Los Angeles Times* articles on the attempted repression of "surf bums" by worried police officers, parents, and school authorities demonstrates clearly that in no way were surfers seen as clean-cut defenders of conventional values, as an all-too-common misreading would have it. These articles, as well as an exhaustive treatment of articles in the national press, demonstrate convincingly that at the time, surfers were explicitly seen by both authority figures and a mass media audience as part and parcel of the larger youth uprising of the sixties.

In addition to making this crucial historical point, which is generally overlooked in treatments of American mid-century counterculture, the chapter highlights the fact that it was the broadcasting of the subversive image of the surfer all over America that preceded the explosion of surf culture that took place during the 1960s. The 1950s and 1960s images of first beat, then hippie, surfers, are presented to show that the surfer image of that time was consistent with its earlier incarnations—an image of a free, socially and ecologically connected lifestyle, without rigid gender proscriptions and utterly without a decent work ethic. These themes flow through the image of surfers in national magazines, television shows, the genre known as "surf music," beach party films, and novels, all of which the chapter engages to continue to demonstrate that the content of the image of the surfer is freedom, and the effect of its dissemination is to inspire the quest for more free living.

Chapter 5 begins with the discussion of what political philosophers call "The Malibu Surfer Problem,"—the fact that even in the most just distribution of income imaginable, there will always be "free riders" (like surfers) who *just won't work*. The very existence of this discussion demonstrates that by 1971, when the term was coined, the image of the surfer had become identical with the refusal of paid labor and the insistence on freedom and leisure above all else. The content of the discussion points to two possible conclusions: one, made by John Rawls, who coined the term, that these surfers would just have to be excluded from the program of guaranteed annual income that he famously proposes. That is, those who won't work, won't eat—a pretty glaring similarity to our own "unjust" society. For those who dream of living the life of the surfer (a consistently massive group, as the present study demonstrates), the "just" society doesn't have much to offer.

The other possible conclusion is the argument that I take up as the key political *implication* of my reading of the twentieth-century image of the American surfer and its effects: an alternative strategy in line with the historical push of the labor movement for shorter hours of work. This political strategy incorporates the dreams of freedom that the American public consistently demonstrates the existence of; in fact, it requires these dreams for its success. I want to suggest that there is a real potential for leisure subcultures and mass countercultures, and their commercially disseminated images, to inspire people to collectively work less—both an end in itself and (in terms of the price effects of labor supply) a means to an end, higher wages. Like the mass consumer activity that subversive images so often give rise to, this kind of cultural trend requires inspiration, much more than it does the organizing that those on the left and in the labor movement (as well as most of those who study them) tend to see as prerequisite to social change. I call this dynamic the cultural politics of the class struggle, and the image of the American surfer, and the massive popular response to it, can teach us a great deal about the potential of this kind of politics.

With every successive "jobless recovery," I believe it becomes more and more crucial that progressives take this potential seriously. The long-term trend is for more people to be unemployed or underemployed[22], while the remainder "lucky" enough to still have a decent job are pushed to work longer and harder for the same or declining wages. The strategy of shorter hours in the labor movement has traditionally been about sharing the work in the face of unemployment, as well as about pushing wages higher through controlling labor supply. Most important, it's a strategy that *inspires*—something the labor movement has been short on recently—because it speaks to people's real desires for more free time.

In order for the potential I suggest to move beyond pure theory, however, (or history) I believe that progressives need to embrace the role of collective leisure and popular culture in inspiring what Antonio Negri calls the "refusal of work"—the self-activity of the working class that defines it against the imperatives of capital.

Now, it goes without saying that the ubiquity of images that inspire Americans to play rather than work is not a sufficient condition for any kind of social transformation. For every uprising, cultural and otherwise, there are structural and historical factors without which any attempted explanation becomes platitude. My argument, however, is that in tapping into desires on the part of the working class that will inspire people to make purchases, capital is always in the position (still articulated best in the *Communist Manifesto*) of "the sorcerer, unable to control the powers of the nether world whom he has called up with his spells . . ."[23] Whether it's images of surfing beach boys in Hawaii inspiring mass travel *and* the development of a California beach subculture, or Hollywood surf movies inspiring legions of teens to hit the waves, or today's growing coverage of the subculture in all media inspiring a surf culture that's now bigger than ever—there is no question that although the rebel images constantly offered up by consumer culture are certainly not *alone* a sufficient condition for radical social change (or even a bohemian trend), the role of this kind of inspiration in egging on significant collective behavior has to be taken more seriously by those with an interest in grassroots social change. In terms of historical conditions, what has changed is not this fecund dynamic, but the fact that since the early 1970s, capital's attack on the wage through global neoliberal economic policies—union busting, outsourcing, dismantling the welfare state, etc.—has contracted the sense of mass entitlement to which it was a response. But the future remains unwritten, and the surfer is everywhere.

The chapter concludes with a reading of the editorial page of the *Wall Street Journal*, the authors of which unambivalently oppose the cultural rebellion spreading like a virus through mid-century America. Every time a *Journal* editorial mentions the counterculture during its heyday, it is with both moral disdain and genuine alarm. As I assert in the chapter, if Thomas Frank is right, and capital as a whole is in favor of counterculture and its commercial dissemination, somebody should tell the folks at the *Wall Street Journal*. They seem to have been pretty clear about what I'm calling the cultural politics of the class struggle—the potential economic effects of countercultural lifeways.

However, this work is not a straight history of an oppositional culture. Instead, it examines the *image* of the surfer subculture in American popular culture. Our purpose is to understand the *significance* of surfing in the American imagination, not necessarily to understand surfers. The image of the surfer doesn't always tell us much about the complexities of real surfers. It can, however, help us understand the two related issues of the ever-fertile content of mass fantasy, and the (still) contradictory nature of contemporary capitalism. So we look not so much at actual surfers as at their image, and the very different responses it has provoked among three different groups.

First, Puritans and what I call neo-Puritans of every age, united by the will to impose work discipline, who have attempted to repress surfing. Second, the purveyors of popular culture, who have broadcast the image of surfing far and wide, to the tune of billions of dollars. Third, and most important, is the American public,[24] which has consistently responded enthusiastically to advertisements, record albums, and films that have deployed the image of the surfer.

Puritan disapproval will form the backdrop against which we examine surfing's popular culture representation and what it tells us about the utopian, really countercultural content of mass fantasy. If, as we're arguing, the ubiquity of subversive images has cultural and political significance, understanding these images tells us a great deal about the history of, and more important, the potential for collective action in our society. We begin in ancient Hawaii, the image of which provides the primitive, foundational myth that grounds the surfing subculture and its representations, even today.

2 Island Time
Primitives, Puritans, and Hucksters

"Such a disposition leads them to direct all their aims only to what can give them pleasure and ease . . ."

–Captain James Cook[1]

"I'm on Island Time"

–phrase on Hawaiian t-shirts and other tourist souvenirs

FOUNDING MYTHS

Both the original image of the surfer, and the founding story of the surf subculture, come from Hawaii, where surfing is thought to have originated.[2] Just about every book and documentary on surfing begins with the story of a leisurely, surf-centered ancient Hawaiian culture.[3] According to this surfer translation of Hawaiian legend[4] (which had already, of course been decontextualized and reframed by colonial anthropologists), for thousands of years, surfing and surf contests were an absolutely central part of the island culture. Although complex ritual prescriptions governed who could surf on what kinds of boards and at which beach breaks, everyone surfed—royals, commoners, men, women, children. References to surfing are identified in song, in myth, in courtship rituals, and in ritual prayer (for good waves). And during the winter months, when the waves were biggest, a long festival called the Malahiki—sort of a mega-luau—honored the god Lono and consisted of surfing, feasting, dancing, and talking story on the beach. The upshot of the discussion about surfing's place in ancient Hawaii in the surfing literature is the idea that unlike in contemporary society, surfing was not relegated to the margins of the ancient culture, to a realm of "leisure" that can happen only after work is completed. The story of surfing's first home provides a myth of an origin in which—as in the memory of childhood—play was the defining activity of life. Much as in our imagination of other pre-capitalist cultures, work was done only when it was unavoidable. Otherwise, spontaneity, pleasure, and freedom defined the people's lifestyle.

In this story, native culture embodies the antithesis of the Puritan work ethic—predicated as it is on the repression of pleasure that makes incessant work possible. In the discourse around surfing, early nineteenth-century Hawaii is an instance of a culture war, where connection to the earth and one another meets the alienated, disembodied "I" of Cartesian rationality; where flowing with the rhythms of nature meets the dominating and controlling of nature; and where free play and sexuality meet repression and the logic of control. Although this image of precapitalist cultures has been dismissed as a Western romanticization by many postcolonial authors (more on this later), it is substantiated by at least one notable native Hawaiian activist. Haunani-Kay Trask says of her ancient ancestors: " . . . our Native culture . . . was as antithetical to the European developments of Christianity, capitalism, and predatory individualism as any society could have been."[5] This may be because the politics of cultural identity can be just as essentializing as can imperialist fantasy; in any case, the idea that Hawaiian culture was centered around leisure comes from many quarters.

In the American popular imagination, the image of the Hawaiian surfer has evolved but remains consistent with its origin: most often a bronzed, shirtless, barefoot native male, frequently wearing flowers, playing the ukelele, and generally smiling, full of generous "aloha." It's an archetype connoting a pleasurable life, one engaged primarily in play rather than toil, a childlike one in which delayed gratification and future planning are foreign concepts. The natives live instead on "island time"—the eternal present. Like other archetypes of the "primitive," the Hawaiian surfer evokes a *connection* assumed to have been lost in modern society: connection with nature and the "natural" human inside everyone, as well as a libidinal connection to life that translates into easy, hangup-free sexuality. It is an image that's been extremely prominent in American popular culture[6] for over a century. In this chapter, we will trace the history of this image to understand its meaning to different groups; first, though, a little theoretical grounding is in order.

It's in the *Economic and Philosophic Manuscripts*[7] that Marx identifies alienation as the primary wound that capitalism inflicts on the human being: alienation from the moments of our lives, from our fellow human beings, and from the natural world. Under capitalism, the working class is forced to sell its labor power as a commodity. For Marx, what this means is that the human being takes his or her essential, defining life activity—the intercourse with nature, the working-up of the natural world in the image of something that's been constructed first in the imagination, or "what distinguishes the worst architect from the best bee"—and sells it as an "object" outside him or herself. Experience—life—is objectified. This is the fundamental disconnection, between our lives and our activities, the alienation that founds all its other forms. Alienation is the condition of possibility for capitalism to make profit, since profit comes from capital's exploitation of human labor power *as a commodity*, or a *thing* bought and sold on the market. So it follows that what opposes alienation also opposes the central logic of capital. And a popular culture image that taps into our collective fantasy of an undifferentiated, unalienated existence—where life exists only in the moment and entirely *on its own terms*—opposes alienation and thus at least implicitly opposes the logic of capital. Not to mention that in doing so, it inspires people to act (in the way that unconscious fantasy produces action), to bring the reality closer in line with the fantasy. More specifically in our case, the pop culture image of surfing appeals to our primal desires to escape alienation and to return to a state of connected gratification—the state that Freud says we experience primarily, in the libidinal connection and pleasure of our earliest memories, and that we always desire a return to. What the enduring popularity of the image of Hawaiian surfing tells us is that people dream very publicly of living without alienation.

PURITANS

In the writings of Max Weber, the idea that disconnection characterizes our relationship to nature and the moments of our lives under capitalism takes different names but holds an equally central place in discussions of capitalism, culture, and by extension, counterculture. When Theodore Roszak in *The Making of a Counter Culture*[8] identifies "objective consciousness" as the object of countercultural protest, he is leaning heavily on the work of Max Weber. Weber is the preeminent theorist of this objective consciousness, or rationality, that made possible modern capitalism and that largely defines the repression of modern life still. Taking an historical look at the beginnings of our modern, rational capitalism, he found an ascetic Puritanism at its root. But Weber's analysis reminds us that the seed doesn't disappear in the plant that grows; it permeates it.

In his well-worn classic, *The Protestant Ethic and the Spirit of Capitalism*,[9] Weber identifies what he calls the "spirit of capitalism"—the idea, so familiar to us and yet really "so little a matter of course," that the combination of hard work and a compulsion to save and accumulate money characterizes the ethics of the morally upright man. What unites the two, hard work and penny-pinching, is an ascetic avoidance of any behavior that's spontaneous or hedonistic. In this ethic, the good is identified with a detached, calculating attitude toward the moments of one's life and our natural surroundings; the bad or unethical is identified with the "spontaneous enjoyment of life," in whatever forms it takes. This ethic—the privileging of work, thrift, and calculating detachment over play, hedonism, and spontaneity—is still very much central to the culture of modern capitalism. And it remains difficult to inculcate in each new generation, as any elementary teacher will tell you.[10]

The Protestant Ethic makes the case that without this new spirit, capitalism as we know it today—instrumental, world-dominating, committed to limitless growth—would not exist. Weber's famous argument is that this spirit of capitalism is what was left by the harsh ascetic morality of the Puritans in Europe and America once the religious roots inevitably died out. These Puritans, especially the Calvinists, saw the expulsion from the Garden of Eden as the central defining moment of the relationship between God and humanity. In the beginning, we were with God; after the fall, there was an "unbridgeable gulf" between God and man. In a natural state humanity was stained by original sin, low, dirty, disgusting to God. As laid out in one theological tract after another, this brutally harsh interpretation of the Bible saw the "natural" as evil, or far from God. By extension, whatever was Godlike, or touched by the grace of God, had to be as far from natural—as alienated from nature—as possible.

Because Calvinists believed that the gulf between man and God made it impossible for our actions to affect the actions of God—I've been good, now the big guy will let me into heaven, for instance—they were committed to the Doctrine of Predestination, which postulated that because of original sin, man "in a natural state" was eternally damned. As Christians, though, they had to maintain some semblance of a redemption story. So Calvin and his followers agreed that in His "unsearchable" wisdom, the Big Man had decided to draw some folks out of "the state of sin and death, in which they are by nature," and into a state of grace. Saved! Now that every Calvinist was obsessed with proving to himself that he was among those in a state of grace, rather than a state of nature, anything that smacked of "the natural state" became a sign of damnation. In order to assuage their considerable anxiety that their natural desires and emotions were markers of doom, they worked constantly as a method of keeping them at bay. Constant work was a means of taming and cultivating the earth's natural wildness as well as their own. It was the perfect means of *control*, control of dangerous natural desires and control of the luscious, fertile natural world that constantly tempted them into relaxation. Such a terrible psychological affliction these poor folks suffered. We could just feel sorry for them, if they hadn't been so influential.

But the cultural consequences of the belief that the good and the natural are *opposites* haunt us to this day, thanks to how rich and (thus) powerful they became as a result of their bizarre compulsions and incessant work. It is precisely this counterposition of good and natural that animates the spirit of capitalism, to which it gave rise. It's also what makes capitalism such a pox on the natural environment and our natural desires to enjoy the moments of our lives and the material world that surrounds us. As Weber's story makes clear, only when nature and life are devalued can they be repressed and then dominated, used, and polluted.

Modern capitalism sees everything—nature and human life—as something that can be controlled, used, put systematically to work. This attitude—rationality—is, according to Weber, what's essential in it. It was central to building it—constant work and a refusal to enjoy its fruits result, inevitably, in the accumulation and consistent growth of capital—and this rationality remains its core principle. The heart of this instrumental, controlling attitude toward the lifeworld is Puritan asceticism and the opposition between the natural and the good that animates it.

In order to make a case about capitalism and what opposes it using the image of the surfer, we're assisted immensely by the historical record. Because it wasn't just any old missionaries who tried to convert the surfing natives during the nineteenth century—they were *Calvinists*. The Calvinists came to Hawaii in 1821, just after contact with foreigners had both precipitated the breakdown of the *kapu* system of ritual regulation around which Hawaiian culture had been organized, as well as brought diseases to which the natives had no immunity and from which they died by the hundreds of thousands. The missionaries came to convert the much-weakened "savages" to their brand of Christianity, and they were vocal about their opposition to the many "heathen amusements" they were horrified to behold.

Just as consumers of the image of the precontact Hawaiians see the privileging of play rather than work as the culture's defining characteristic, so did the nineteenth-century missionaries and those who told their story. According to historian Gavan Daws, "by New England standards the islanders' style of life seemed unhealthy and sluggish, and Hawaiian women in particular thought work 'rather a disgrace.' Yet when it came to a frivolous diversion such as a hula they would practice energetically in the hot sun for days on end."[11] One missionary, George Washington Bates made an observation about Hawaiian daily life that "there were no busy artisans wielding their implements of labor; no civilized vehicles bearing their loads of commerce . . ."[12]

Another missionary, William Ellis, wrote with astonishment at what happened when the waves got really good: "the thatch houses of a whole village stood empty, and daily tasks such as farming, fishing, and tapa-making were left undone while an entire community—men, women, and children—enjoyed themselves in the rising surf and rushing white water."[13] Apparently, play and joy took precedence over work, which could always wait until the swell died down. Thomas Thrum, in his *Hawaiian Almanac and Annual of 1896*, observes that prior to European invasion, "surf riding was one of the favorite Hawaiian sports. Chiefs, men, women, and youth all participated, and the daily chores were put aside whenever a good surf was running . . ."[14] This characteristic of Hawaiian life was confirmed by nineteenth-century native scholar Kepelino Keauokalani: "expert surfers going upland to farm, if part way up . . . look back and see the rollers combing the beach, will leave work . . . hurrying away home they will pick up the board and go. All thought of work is left. The wife may go hungry, the children, the whole family, but the head of the house does not care. He is all for sport, that is his food. All day there is nothing but surfing."[15]

In less than ten years, Calvinism had established all-too-firm roots in Hawaii. Still, the accounts of the missionaries tell us two things: one, that they faced intense resistance to their moralizing program *despite* the disorganization of postcontact Hawaiian culture, and two, how intensely opposed is Calvinism and the Puritan work ethic to surfing and the attitude to time, life, and pleasure of which surfing is emblematic. Surfing and the traditional dance, the hula, remained important to the natives even after the taboo system had crumbled. It was these aspects, the everyday attitudes and pleasures of the natives, that the Puritans saw as their true adversaries, rather than the kapu system of taboo regulations.

They were formidable adversaries. Hiram Bingham was the head Calvinist missionary on the scene, and his exploits are still celebrated in American Protestant mythology. His 1847 work, *A Residence of Twenty-one Years in the Sandwich Islands*, is "an account of the efforts to raise the Hawaiians from their degradation and barbarism and convert them from their idols, their cruel superstitions, their *unbridled lusts* . . ."[16] And here's his first impression of the Hawaiians: "The appearance of destitution, degradation, and barbarism, among the chattering, and almost naked savages, whose heads and feet, and much of their sunburnt swarthy skins were bare, was appalling. Some of our number, with gushing tears, turned away from the spectacle. Others, with firmer nerve, continued their gaze, but were ready to exclaim, 'can these be human beings?'! . . . can such things be civilized?"[17] According to Leonard Lueras, Bingham was "no doubt describing a covey of laughing surfers—men, women, and children—who'd paddled out to meet the missionary ship Thaddeus."[18]

So Bingham's objectives are clear, as is his view of the Hawaiians. And he complains frequently that his was no easy task. Under the heading of "Heathen Wailing and Amusement," he writes, "while some of the people who sat in darkness were beginning to turn their eyes to the light, and were disposed to attend our schools and public lectures, others, with greater enthusiasm, were wasting their time in learning, practicing, or witnessing the hula, or heathen song and dance . . . How often have the chiefs and people of the Sandwich Islands been represented as easily influenced and moulded to one's will! Their ready compliance was doubtless in reference to that which they had not physical strength to resist. But in respect to the course the Bible marks out, the case was different. The missionaries found that the conflict between the light of Christianity and the darkness of heathenism was no momentary struggle . . . [many] clung with great tenacity to their heathen customs, and their heathen pleasures. Multitudes passed away quickly to the grave before much impression could be made on them, and others resisted for years all the endeavors of missionaries to reclaim them."[19] It seems that the kapu system of regulation was easier to put an end to than were the natives' "heathen pleasures."

Despite the native Hawaiians' cultural opposition, the population came to submit to the foreign domination of capitalism and the religion of

Calvinism. There seem to be several reasons for this. First of all, it's impossible to overstate the effect of mass death and sterilization on the native population. In less than a century, a healthy population of nearly one million was reduced to a sickly one of about 40,000. This astounding scale of devastation paved the way for the population to be dominated in other ways. In the words of Haunani-Kay Trask, "our disease-ridden ancestors" were "confused by Christianity and preyed upon by capitalists," and "were thereby dispossessed."[20]

Second, an intense process of "education" was visited upon the natives. In the same way that American children receive an "education" that socializes them into routine, repression, and obedience to authority, the natives were subjected to similar repression. In fact, Bingham points to the missionary schools as their most successful instrument:

> Our steady aim has been to extend a moral and religious influence over the whole community by means of the widely extended . . . school system . . . it has afforded, to a great extent, by the pen, slate, pencil, and book, a substitute for the pleasure which the people once derived from games of chance, and of skill, and strength, connected with staking property [of which surfing was foremost] . . . it has been our steady aim to bring to bear constantly on the dark hearts of pagans and their children those moral and evangelical truths, without the presence and possession of which the *design of their rational existence* cannot be secured. While our school system does indeed contemplate the disciplining of the mind, and affords important means and facilities for it, it has always contemplated chiefly a *moral* influence over the heart and life . . . [21]

Bingham here makes a clear bifurcation between his and the missionaries "moral influence" and the "pleasure which the people once derived from games . . ." and sports and the gambling associated with them. And he wasn't just talking either. The missionaries were quite concerned to put an end to these "amusements," especially sex, surfing and dancing the hula. Sensuous pleasure, being right in the moment, "losing oneself"—one's detached, rational self, that is—all of this characterizes both true play and sexuality. Calvinists' anti-play ethic had already worked to put an end to all games and sports in England—in Weber's words, they'd "descended like a frost on Merrie Olde England." Their MO in Hawaii was pretty much the same.

The missionaries knew that the sexuality that characterizes play was the true enemy of rationality, control, and repression. They weren't having it. And surfing, especially, had to go. In the words of surf culture historian Drew Kampion, "Not only did these missionaries impose a strict Protestant paradigm on an exuberant people while diseases destroyed their bodies, but they confined them to modest attire, forced them to speak in a new tongue, and discouraged them from casual sex, gambling, and playing in the ocean. Surfing's association with nakedness, sexuality, wagering, shameless exuberance, informality, ignorant joy, and freedom were counterproductive to the church fathers who, curiously, wound up owning most of the land in the islands."[22]

Missionary Sheldon Dibble, in discussing "the evils resulting from all these sports and amusement," in the section of his book entitled "The State of the People While Heathen," says that "some lost their lives . . . some were reduced to poverty, both by losses in gambling and by *neglecting to cultivate the land* . . . but the greatest evil of all resulted from the constant intermingling, without any restraint, of persons of both sexes and of all ages, at all times of the day and at all hours of the night . . . both the chiefs and the people . . . were sunk in a dead lake of pollution—were even below the beasts of the field in utter shamelessness, and in the undisguised practice of every degrading vice."[23]

Although Bingham issued a difficult-to-take-seriously denial that the missionaries had "caused oppressive enactments against surfing," he did comment gladly that "the decline and discontinuance of the use of the surfboard, as civilization advances, may be accounted for by the increase in modesty, industry, and religion," and that "the adoption of our costume greatly diminishes their practice of . . . sporting in the surf, for it is less convenient to wear it in the water than the native girdle, and less decorous and safe to lay it entirely off on every occasion they find for a plunge or swim or surf-board race."[24] (William Ruschenberger replies in his *Narrative of a Voyage Around the World, Vol I–II* that although the missionaries deny that they themselves put an end to surfing, "but they write and publicly express their opinions, and state these sports to be expressly against the laws of God, and by a succession of reasoning, which may be readily traced, impress upon the minds of the chiefs and others, the idea that all who practice them secure themselves the displeasure of offended heaven . . . then the chiefs, from a spontaneous benevolence, at once interrupt the customs so hazardous to their vassals."[25]) Still, Bingham happily maintains that it was the education that did it: "the heathen sports of the nation nearly disappeared . . . with the advent of elementary instruction in reading, writing, morals, religion, arithmetic, geography, sacred song, and sacred history."

What did this advent in instruction look like? Consider this schoolhouse scene, described by missionary Reuben Tinker at Honolulu in 1831, in which both commoners and chiefs were the students:

> the shell horn [has been] blowing early for examination of the schools in the meeting house. About 2000 scholars present . . . with less exposure of health and morals [than a graduation ceremony] for the gentlemen drank no rum, and the ladies were not severely clad. The king and chiefs were present, and examined among the rest. They read in various

> books, and 450 in four rows wrote the same sentence at the same time on slates. They perform with some ceremony. In this exercise, one of the teachers cried out with as much importance as an orderly sergeant . . . and immediately the whole company began to sit up straight. At the next order, they stood on their feet, at the next they "handled" slates or "presented"—i.e. they held them resting on the left arm—at the next order, they brought their pencils to bear upon the broad sides of their slates ready for action. Mr. Bingham then put into the crier's ear the sentence to be written, which he proclaimed with all his might and, a movement of the 450 pencils commenced which from their creaking was like the music of machinery lacking oil. Their sentences were then examined and found generally correct.[26]

In the islands, the Calvinist missions were largely successful, at least for a time. According to Trask, the Hawaiians were taken in by the missionaries' promise of eternal life because they mistook the abstraction of the soul for the body of their people: "our dying people believed that the Christian promise of everlasting life meant the everlasting *physical* life of our nation."[27] This insight is confirmed by the pro-missionary account of Isabella Bird, a British traveler, who writes that "Mr. Ellis . . . mentions that when he preached, the natives, who seemed to be very indifferent to the general truths of Christianity, became very deeply interested when they heard of *Ora loa ia Jesu* (endless life by Jesus)."[28] But it's interesting to note that once they had competition for the souls of the natives, the Puritans' harsh, ascetic repression didn't really stick. In the absence of their traditional culture, the new culture that most appealed to the Hawaiians was less like an uptight schoolhouse and more like a rock and roll concert. The real high point of Christianity in the islands came not with the Puritans, but later, with revivalists like Titus Coan, loud, exciting preachers who Bingham and his buddies looked upon as charlatans. According to Daws, the Calvinists "were a little taken aback to find unseemly physical outbursts associated with spiritual surrender." Of Coan, Daws says that "it was a common thing for him to reduce hundreds of natives at a time to weeping, shouting, and falling. His hearers came to feel the terrible presence of God so strongly that they quivered in every muscle, or wailed in 'tremendous throes' like a 'dying giant,' or broke down with an 'earthquake shock.' Sometimes the fallen lay groaning on the ground for 15 minutes or half an hour after the fight was done."[29] So despite all the instruction and the threats of hellfire, the Calvinists were ultimately defeated by the wild energy they'd worked so hard to repress.

Much the way it happens in the story that Weber tells about European and American capitalism, the religious roots of repression died out and were no longer needed by a capitalism that could recruit its working class easily once they'd been dispossessed from their ancestral lands. Daws goes on to report that "within the Protestant churches themselves, once the excitement of the great awakening had died down, Christianity became a workaday religion, observed as a matter of convention. Christian chiefs [many of whom had been bought off rather than actually converted, anyway] in large numbers backslid and had to be disciplined. Among the commoners . . . statistics for offences against the moral laws remained constantly high . . . Mark Twain, who visited the islands in the 1860s, concluded that sin no longer flourished there in name, only in reality."[30]

Still, as far as surfing went, the damage had been done. By 1892 the anthropologist Nathaniel B. Emerson wrote that "the zest of the sport [surfing] was enhanced by the fact that both sexes engaged in it, [and] when this practice was found to be discountenanced by the new morality, it was felt that the interest in it had largely departed . . ." and in consequence, "the sport of surf riding possessed a grand fascination, and for a time, it seemed as if it had a vitality all its own as a national pastime . . . today, it is hard to find a surfboard outside our museums and private collections."[31] The upshot of contact with Westerners was the decimation of the native population, the end of the kapu system, and the de facto prohibition of surfing.

The contours of this clash are echoed in E.P. Thompson's classic piece *Time, Work-Discipline, and Industrial Capitalism*[32], in which he traces the difficulty that the new capitalist bosses and the Protestant moralizers who were their cultural support had in resocializing English commoners into members of a new industrial working class during the eighteenth century. Thompson, like Weber, sees traditional work rhythms as natural and industrial work-rhythms, dominated by the movement of the new clocks and watches, as imposed, unnatural, and inevitably subject to resistance. Thompson discusses an "older, more natural time-sense" that he says characterizes all pre-industrial cultures. In England, as in Hawaii, the fundamental struggle was all about *time*. Thompson could have been talking about Hawaiians when he cites the characteristics of a natural time-sense: work is done on an as-needed basis, according to the rhythms of nature, and people don't objectify time as something to be used or sold. Instead, they are connected to the moments of their lives, which are to be *lived* rather than *used*.

People had to be *forced* into understanding time as an object to be rationally "used." What comes naturally, what came first historically, is for people to understand life as something to be lived. Thompson's question is: to what extent was the new time-sense not just propounded but internalized? He answers that the industrial working class did internalize clock-time; evidence for this is provided in the conflict that comes up every time capital enters a traditional society. Their sense of time remains traditional, natural, task-oriented when it comes to work; the clock-colonized consciousness of the working class of the developed world exists in stark contrast.

In Thompson's story of how this came to be, it's again the Puritans who provide the cultural foundation for capitalist bosses, in that they preach a separation between the human being and the moments of his or her life. Preachers railed against laziness and pleasure and pushed for people to see the moments of their lives as means to an end rather than ends in themselves. Time was to be objectified and used rationally rather than "wasted." This separation between the self and time made it possible for people eventually to internalize (not without great resistance, though, and not forever) the new clock-time needed by the industrialists to synchronize production. The clock would now subject life's moments to a rational ordering and use.

In many ways, Thompson's work is a friendly amendment to that of Weber. Weber, unfortunately, was too depressed to be dialectical, so we can't look to him to find the potential for transformation. Thompson is a Marxist, so although he traces the conflict-ridden process by which the new working class was eventually broken and made to internalize the rhythms of clock-time, he also makes resistance and the possibility of transformation central to his work. Thompson states that working-class resistance to capital persisted but increasingly took place within the framework of clock time: the fight for shorter hours and overtime pay. But what he ultimately points to as subversive of the bosses and the Puritans is a countercultural embrace of an alternative relationship to time. In his words, "Puritanism, in its marriage of convenience with industrial capitalism, was the agent which converted people to new valuations of time . . . which saturated peoples' minds with the equation, time is money. *One recurrent form of revolt within Western industrial capitalism, whether bohemian or beatnik, has often taken the form of flouting the urgency of respectable time values.*"[33]

It's a basic tenet of psychoanalysis that repressed material, especially our primary memories and experiences (which are "timeless"—ontogenetically and phylogenetically, our primary experience of life is an eternal now), ultimately find their way back to the surface. That's why we have to move from the missions of the nineteenth century to Waikiki Beach at the dawn of the twentieth century. What we find is the original beach counterculture, ignoring clock-time, embracing the primitive, natural time organized by the sun and the ocean's tides, and valuing pleasure over work. This group of men, known as "beach boys," had their image projected far and wide, and wound up becoming the seed of what's arguably America's most durable countercultural form.

The beach boys self-consciously styled themselves in the tradition of the "ancient Hawaiian waterman", "generally claiming to be descended from ancient royalty," according to one early magazine profile.[34] They fully claimed the founding mythology of Hawaiian surfing and used it for their own purpose—to make a little money and enjoy themselves on the beach. These beach boys came to provide the founding mythology of the next incarnation of the surfing beach subculture, in early twentieth-century California. But in one of many examples of the power of alluring, subversive images to inspire the growth of countercultural forms, this only became possible as a result of the dissemination of their image far and wide. And the image was broadcast so widely because, in contrast to the missionaries and planters, the new capitalists who were becoming more and more powerful in the islands were focused on tourism, that is, on "selling" Hawaii. And they knew that if you want people to buy something, you have to appeal to their desire. The tourism promoters used the beach boys to do just that, and a new story began for surfing—a story in which surfing and its beach-living practitioners were no longer the object of elite repression. The Puritans tried to kill surfing. They were unsuccessful, partly because in their wake came not only sugar and pineapple plantation bosses but also hucksters.

During the nineteenth century, the missionaries were not the only ones writing home about Hawaiian culture; a more positive image of the Hawaiian surfer was beginning to generate some publicity on the mainland even as surfing itself was being attacked in the islands. Eventually this alternative discourse—a glorification and broadcasting of the playful, sexual elements of the culture—became the dominant one, once it was enthusiastically adopted by tourism promoters. Even during the dark ages of the nineteenth century, surfing hadn't been entirely extinguished by the Calvinists. In fact, when Mark Twain visited the islands in 1866 during a sailing trip from San Francisco and sent back articles to the Sacramento Union that would later become his book, *Roughing It*, surfing was featured prominently in his account of island life.

> In one place we came upon a large company of naked natives, of both sexes and all ages, amusing themselves with the national pastime of surf-bathing. Each heathen would paddle three or four hundred yards out to sea, taking a short board with him, then face the shore and wait for a particularly prodigious billow to come along; at the right moment he would fling his board upon its foamy crest and himself upon the board, and here he would come whizzing by like a bombshell! It did not seem that a lightning express train could shoot along at a more hair-lifting speed. I tried surf-bathing once, subsequently, but made a failure of it . . . none but the natives ever master the art of surf-bathing thoroughly.[35]

His experience was similar to that of many Westerners who visited the islands and witnessed surfers—beholding the image inspires a try at the activity itself. Twain himself represents another key figure in the drama of Western contact with Hawaii—not the missionary or the boss, but the adventurer.

In fact, Twain's piece is one of over one hundred books and articles about the "Sandwich Islands" that appeared during the nineteenth century and that gave detailed descriptions of the native pastime of surfing. By 1882, surfing had gained enough currency as an image on the mainland to warrant its first political cartoon—the cover of The Daily Graphic features a woodblock of President Grover Cleveland surfing, riding a wave of "republican distrust at fraud."[36] And the visual images that were broadcast to the mainland via drawings and woodcuts in and on covers of the magazines and books that discussed surfing were probably attracting the scoundrels as well. We can see why: most of them feature loincloth-clad men and bare-breasted women, surfing, laughing, posing on their boards, simply having a great time together.

Isabella Bird, the British preacher's daughter, published letters from her travels to Hawaii in 1873 as a book, and her take on the culture is rather ambivalent. Because of this, taken as a whole they give us a sense of several tendencies at large in the islands at that time: native pleasures, Puritan disapproval, and the newly developing hybrid lifestyle of "beach-combers." She described surfing in the remote island village of Hilo:

> The more furious and agitated the water is, the greater the excitement, and the love of these watery exploits is not confined to the young. I saw great fat men with their hair streaked with grey, balancing themselves on their narrow surf-boards, and riding the surges shorewards with as much enjoyment as if they were in their first youth. I enjoyed the afternoon thoroughly. Is it "always afternoon" here, I wonder? The sea was so blue, the sunlight so soft, the air so sweet. There was no toil, clang, or hurry. People were all holiday-making (if that can be where there is no work), and enjoying themselves, the surf-bathers in the sea, and hundreds of gaily-dressed men and women galloping on the beach. It was so serene and tropical. I sympathize with those who eat the lotus, and remain for ever on such enchanted shores.[37]

Although Bird was frequently "enchanted" by the Hawaiians, she is a guest of the missionaries and a more reliable sympathizer with them. In describing a Christian school for native girls, she recounts that

> the Hawaiian women have no notions of virtue as we understand it, and if there is to be any future for this race it must come through a higher morality. Consequently the removal of these girls from evil and impure surroundings, the placing them under the happiest influences in favour of purity and goodness, the forming and fostering of industrious and housewifely habits, and the raising them in their occupations and amusements above those which are natural to their race, are in themselves a noble, and in some degree, a hopeful work, but it admits of neither pause nor relaxation.[38]

This is because of the lazy immorality of the Hawaiians, which the author points out again and again. The women, especially, are not at all diligent:

> It is very curious, too, to see women incessantly enjoying and amusing themselves in riding, swimming, and making leis. They have few home ties in the shape of children, and I fear make them fewer still by neglecting them for the sake of riding and frolic, and *man seems rather the helpmeet than the "oppressor" of woman . . .*

It's likely that the parents were not neglecting their children, but simply looking after them in a more collective, and thus less onerous way. It's interesting to note, too, that since men and women play together, there is less of the oppression of women by men than is found back home. All this is reflected to Bird in their very faces: "Used to the down-trodden look and harassed care-worn faces of the over-worked women of the same class at home and in the colonies, the laughing, careless faces of the Hawaiian women have the effect upon me of a perpetual marvel."[39]

And in her account, this naturally amoral state of the natives combines with the adventurer type of visitor to the islands to form Christianity's biggest opponent:

> The moral atmosphere of Waimea has never been a wholesome one. The region was very early settled by a class of what may be truly termed "mean whites," the "beach-combers" and riff-raff of the Pacific. They lived infamous lives, and added their own to the indigenous vices of the islands, turning the district into a perfect sink of iniquity, in which they were known by such befitting aliases as "Jake the Devil," &c. The coming of the missionaries, and the settlement of moral, orderly whites on Hawaii, have slowly created a public opinion averse to flagrant immorality, and the outrageous license of former years would now meet with legal penalties. Many of the old settlers are dead, and others have drifted to regions beyond restraining influences, but still 'the Waimea crowd' is not considered up to the mark. Most of the present set of foreigners are Englishmen who have married native women. It was in such quarters as this that the great antagonistic influence to the complete Christianization of the natives was created, and it is from such suspicious sources that the aspersions on missionary work are usually derived.[40]

It was this "amoral" type of Westerner, who from very early on had been attracted to the islands to emulate rather than to transform the native way of life that came in droves as the turn of the twentieth century neared. Bird hit the nail on the head when she claimed that the non-Puritan Westerners, many of them fur traders, whalers, and ship captains, were not cut from the same cloth as were the missionaries and the early planters who echoed the missionaries' morality about work. Their attitude toward surfing and the beach culture that had survived the Christian onslaught was markedly different than that of the missionaries had been, and it became the seed of the discourse broadcast by tourism promoters. The hucksters who used images of sexuality and play to sell Hawaii to a mainland audience had one thing in common with the missionaries, though—they understood the intensely subversive power of sex and leisure. Instead of working to keep it under wraps, they broadcast it far and wide.

SURFING'S REVIVAL

As the twentieth century dawned, only a handful of people—all men, both natives and haoles—were still surfing. Board construction and riding techniques had actually regressed to a very rudimentary state. But then as now, the activity and the setting of surfing had massive power to inspire people. So the activity and the beach culture around it grew with the broadcasting of infectious and alluring images of surfing. Hotel construction and Hawaiian tourism promotion began in the first years of the twentieth century, and surfing was a big part of what the promoters were selling. And the missionaries and the sugar planters were none too happy about it. "Despite the grumbling of the powerful sugar planters,"[41] the Merchants Association and the Chamber of Commerce funded the founding of the Hawaii Promotion Committee (renamed Hawaii Tourist Bureau in 1919), which was encouraged by one ambitious promoter, W. C. Weedon, who'd been giving lectures and slide shows on the West Coast in an attempt to lure visitors.

According to the Tourist Bureau, "The time was right! Due in great part to the writings of men like Mark Twain and Robert Louis Stevenson, Weedon drew packed houses on the West Coast, and soon wrote back to the merchants: 'At every point I go, I find people ready and eager to learn more of Hawaii.' He urged them to provide 'some literature which may bear upon the advantages of our islands for rest and pleasure seekers . . . '"[42] (The first brochure included a quote from Mark Twain about the intense lure the islands have always held for him.) Although the businessmen jumped at the opportunity, and began an upsurge in funding for tourist literature that grew exponentially through the twentieth century, the missionaries and planters were deeply unhappy. This was especially true because surfing, the hula, and the image of the free-living, "primitive" Hawaiian—all the things they'd been working to extinguish in Hawaii once and for all—were being used to lure visitors in promotional materials. In the struggle over the future of Hawaii, the Chamber of Commerce and the Merchants Association was on the side of tourism promotion, and the missionaries and the planters were against it. The advertisers and sellers won, and so surfing went from an obscure anachronism to . . . well, surfing.

A major figure in this story of surfing's revival and its relationship to the promotion of Hawaii is Alexander Hume Ford, a mainland American journalist who tried surfing while visiting Hawaii and fell in love. He decided to live in Hawaii for good, surfing and becoming the sport's biggest booster. Ford's life work involved the creation of the Pan-Pacific Union, an organization dedicated to "fostering peace and goodwill among the nations of the Pacific." According to Ford, Hawaii was a great example of many races of the world living together in peace and harmony, and this model ought to be exported. In addition to organizing the conferences of the Union, he founded and edited the Union's publication, the Mid-Pacific magazine. Leaders from every nation contributed to the magazine, which was printed on the presses of the Honolulu Star-Bulletin for 25 years. Ford also organized the Mid-Pacific Carnivals, yearly celebrations that began in 1907. Each carnival lasted for a few days to a week, and included parades, luaus, and exhibitions. The festivities were primarily for tourists, and displayed the islands as being made up of many races and cultures, of which the native Hawaiian was one.

Ford spent much of his life promoting the Hawaiian Islands as a paradise of racial harmony and happy living. And when he promoted Hawaii, he promoted surfing. In many ways, Ford's work promoting Hawaii, especially in the US, initiated the link that forever tied the image of Hawaii to that of surfing, and all the pleasurable harmony that the image of surfing evokes. In fact, in much of Ford's writing, and in the illustrations, photographic and painted, of surfing in his publications, we can see the first instances of a theme that runs throughout the pop culture representation of surfing: surfing as metaphor for a harmonious relationship with the world.

To be sure, Ford envisioned interracial harmony firmly under what he saw as the benevolent leadership of the white man in the Pacific, and much of his work attracting tourists and transplants was explicitly aimed at populating the Hawaiian islands with mainland whites.[43] According to Ford, Hawaii was in danger of becoming "Our Japanese Territory" (the title of an alarmist article he wrote in *Collier's* in 1909), with "the little brown men" quickly becoming the majority of the population, and displacing both Hawaiians from their small holdings and whites from their professional positions after a generation or so.[44] For better or worse, though, when he wanted to lure white Americans to the islands, surfing was his ace in the hole. And his strategy was largely successful.

Ford wasn't the only American nationalist in the islands to extol the virtues of surfing with an eye to luring mainlanders to the islands. Lorrin Thurston, a son of missionaries who was heavily involved in the overthrow of the Hawaiian monarchy and who promoted tourism, among other haole business concerns, through his newspaper (which later became the Honolulu Advertiser), was another. In 1925, Thurston wrote an article in the *Los Angeles Times* entitled "What Hawaii Really Means to Southern California." The article claims that "the life of a Southern Californian has not been fully rounded without a visit to Hawaii," and focuses mostly on surfing, or "coasting on hills of foam" at Waikiki Beach, which is "a sentiment, more than a locality, and such a sentiment! With overhanging palms, and singing-boys, and the witchery of the moonlight on the sparkling waves in the evenings, and open-air dancing on the verandas . . ."[45]

Ford was, however, the most effective in taking advantage of the fact that the moment was right for the promotion of Hawaii to Americans using surfing. He was a nationalist working during nationalist times, and although the still-powerful Puritan families were not in favor of using sex and surfing to promote the islands, history was on Ford's side. The planters themselves were being accused by the American government of not being true nationalists, and were weakened by a crippling general strike by their primarily Japanese workforce—a strike that served to lend credence to the shrill denunciations of growing Japanese influence. Fear of Japanese domination was fueled by Japanese imperial interests, as well as the insistence of the *issei*, or first-generation immigrants, of maintaining their culture, and the fact that by 1920, 40% of the islands' population was Japanese—many of them *nisei*, or second-generation, just coming of age. Fear of Hawaii "going Japanese" was seen by whites on the island as reason to take action. So Ford's efforts to lure whites to Hawaii via the image of the primitive pleasure of surfing ultimately won out over the "grumbling" of the missionaries and planters.

Ford organized the first surfing club, the Outrigger Canoe and Surfboard Club, to "give an added and permanent attraction to Hawaii and make Waikiki always the home of the surfer . . ." The Queen agreed to grant him a twenty-year lease on an acre of Waikiki beach for five dollars a year, and the club was born. Ford was a tireless organizer, promoting the club and giving surfing classes to young people on the beach. Many new Honolulu businessmen were big supporters of his efforts, understanding that his work to promote surfing would benefit their, and his, push to develop Hawaii's tourist economy. He used the newly formed Hawaii Promotion Committee to further his goals. He worked to disseminate tourist brochures that featured surfing as a lure to the islands. And he procured display windows on Fifth Avenue and Broadway in which he displayed pictures of Hawaii, featuring surfers at Waikiki, with text advertising some of the easy and the reduced-rate ship passage that Ford had worked to make possible.

Ford was a savvy organizer, for sure, and it seems he understood the power of mass media to broadcast alluring images. In 1909, he wrote an article extolling the wonders of surfing in *Collier's National Weekly*, one of the most popular magazines in America at that time. In the article, he describes in detail the "supreme moment" of catching the wave, which is "a thrill like none other in the world."[46] The article features several photos of surfing at Waikiki; one notable shot shows five white men standing by the water, their arms flirtatiously above their heads and around the surfboards behind them, their legs crossed at the ankle, wearing abbreviated bathing suits and giant smiles. This was one of many mainland magazine articles that he wrote trying to lure Americans to the islands.

And when Jack London, famous novelist and early celebrity "personality," camped on the beach at Waikiki with his wife Charmian in 1907, Ford made sure they were introduced to surfing. Jack and Charmian's adventures were followed closely by mainland Americans—they were glamorous, adventurous characters, and Charmian had an image as being an equal partner to Jack, beautiful, sexually liberated, and a little wild. Charmian, a writer herself, was prescient in her understanding of the relationship between Ford, surfing, and the promotion of Hawaii. Here is her recounting of Ford's customary discourse:

> Take surf-boarding, for instance. A California real estate agent, with that one asset, could make the burnt, barren heart of Sahara into an oasis for kings . . . Just as the sport was at its dying gasp, along came one, Alexander Ford, from the mainland. And he talked. Surf- boarding was the sport of sports. There was nothing like it anywhere else in the world. They [the Hawaiians] ought to be ashamed for letting it languish. It was one of the island's assets, a drawing card for travelers that would fill their hotels and bring them many permanent residents.[47]

By her account, Ford had succeeded—by 1915, when the Londons returned to Hawaii, Charmian wrote that the Outrigger Club had 1200 members "with hundreds more on the waiting list, and with what seems like half a mile of surfboard lockers."[48]

Jack London loved surfing once he got the hang of it, and wrote home about it in five magazine articles and a fictional story. Especially significant to surfing publicity is his article, "A Royal Sport," from the October 1907 issue of the *Woman's Home Companion*. He included his article in his widely read book of his travels, *The Cruise of the Snark*, and introduced a popular mainland audience to the wonders of surfing, which he called "a royal sport for the natural kings of earth." Ford introduced London not only to surfing but also, wisely, to Irish-Hawaiian surfer and potential poster boy George Freeth. At 23 year of age, Freeth was considered the best surfer in Hawaii and quite a sight, apparently. London was enormously taken with the young surfer:

> Out there in the midst of such a succession of big smoky ones, a third man was added to our part, one Freeth. Shaking the water from my eyes as I emerged from one wave and peered ahead to see what the next one looked like, I saw him tearing in on the back of it, standing upright on his board, carelessly poised, a young god bronzed with sunburn.

London's description of the "royal sport" and its native practitioners helped shape the image of what he called "the natural kings of earth" for generations:

> And suddenly, out there where a big smoker lifts skyward, rising like a sea-god from out of the welter of spume and churning white, on the giddy, toppling, overhanging and downfalling, precarious crest appears the dark head of a man. Swiftly he rises through the rushing white. His black shoulders, his chest, his loins, his limbs—all is abruptly projected on one's vision. Where but the moment before was only the wide desolation and invincible roar, is now a man, erect, full-statured, not struggling frantically in that wild movement, not buried and crushed and buffeted by those mighty monsters, but standing above them all, calm and superb, poised on the giddy summit, his feet buried in the churning foam, the salt smoke rising to his knees, and all the rest of him in the free air and flashing sunlight, and he is flying through the air, flying forward, flying fast as the surge on which he stands. He is a Mercury—a brown Mercury. His heels are winged, and in them is the swiftness of the sea. In truth, from out of the sea he has leaped upon the back of the sea, and he is riding the sea that roars and bellows and cannot shake him from its back. But no frantic outreaching and balancing is his. He is impassive, motionless as a statue carved suddenly by some miracle out of the sea's depth from which he rose. And straight on toward shore he flies on his winged heels and the white crest of the breaker. There is a wild burst of foam, a long tumultuous rushing sound as the breaker falls futile and spent on the beach at your feet; and there, at your feet steps calmly ashore a Kanaka, burnt golden and brown by the tropic sun. Several minutes ago he was a speck a quarter of a mile away. He has "bitted the bull-mouth breaker" and ridden it in, and the pride in the feat shows in the carriage of his magnificent body as he glances for a moment carelessly at you who sit in the shade of the shore. He is a Kanaka—and more, he is a man, a member of the kingly species that has mastered matter and the brutes and lorded it over creation . . . [49]

Quite a different view of the native than the one articulated by the missionaries, to say the least.

In a trope that comes to characterize the surf image going forward, this native form of "lording-over" turns out to be a power without domination. London describes the ethos of the regal native and his sport:

> The whole method of surf-riding and surf-fighting, I learned, is one of non-resistance. Dodge the blow that is struck at you. Dive through the wave that is trying to slap you in the face. Sink down, feet first, deep under the surface, and let the big smoker that is trying to smash you go by far overhead. Never be rigid. Relax. Yield yourself to the waters that are ripping and tearing at you. When the undertow catches you and drags you seaward along the bottom, don't struggle against it. If you do, you are liable to be drowned . . . yield yourself to that undertow.

> Swim with it, not against it, and you will find the pressure removed . . . it will be no trouble at all to reach the surface.

London's impact on the early image of the surfer can't be underestimated. Surf historian Leonard Lueras likens London's effect on surfing to what Hemingway did for bullfighting. In creating a mass-media image of the surfer for the American audience, London paints images that continue to define surfing going forward–a power that comes from yielding, from connecting, rather than from destroying or dominating. And the one who wields this power—modernity's ubiquitous cultural partner, the noble savage. Although London shared with his world-traveling friend Ford an abstract "white man's burden"-style racism, London was even more taken with the native surfer. His Hawaiian surfer fantasy emphasizes a playful but powerful sexuality, a primitive whose lifestyle is totally other to but also (unlike other "primitives") totally accessible to the Westerner.

SELLING THE DREAM: THE BEACH BOYS

The living embodiment of the surfer as noble savage was one Duke Kahanamoku, a figure revered in Hawaii and worldwide, and a man regularly referred to still as the "father of modern surfing." It's no accident that Duke appeared in nearly thirty Hollywood movies, each time appearing as a different nationality but in reality playing the same character—the swarthy, regal savage. But Duke's image was not just Hollywood's creation—it was his own, as well. Duke won the gold medal in the 100-meter freestyle at the Stockholm Olympics, and "afterwards, he was feted like true royalty as he toured Europe and the US giving exhibitions, swimming in meets and earning nicknames like 'the human fish', 'the bronze duke of Waikiki', and 'the swimming duke'." [50] Everywhere he went, "surfing's great ambassador" performed surfing demonstrations and introduced surfing to beaches worldwide. He's still revered in Australia for introducing its citizens, who had just won through civil disobedience the right to swim in the ocean without bathing machines—huge, ridiculous wooden contraptions with wheels that blocked the (fully-clothed) bather from view of the beach—to surfing, a pastime which would come to define the culture of that island nation.[51]

The press was fascinated by Duke and followed him wherever he went, portraying him in terms that, although they might make us cringe today, were, if not politically correct, certainly filled with admiration. During those first decades of the twentieth century, surfing's image was broadcast worldwide via the brown, smiling face of its traveling, world-champion ambassador, the Duke. The Hawaiian pastime took root on every beach that Duke visited, forever altering beach culture worldwide. Duke's influence demonstrates the infectious nature of surfing—when people see it, they want to try it. As we'll see again and again throughout history, the image of surfing has been one of American culture's most inspirational.

Duke frequently told the press, "I'm just a beach boy from Waikiki." And even more than the figure of Duke, the Waikiki beach boy came to define Hawaiian culture in the American popular imagination during the early twentieth century. Beach boys taught tourists, many of whom were frequently-photographed celebrities, how to surf, and thus publicized (and glorified) surfing even more for mainland audiences. The beach boys were the original beach counterculture, defined in the popular imagination by leisure, fun, and sexuality. According to Leonard Lueras, "due to the langorous nature of their hang-loose 'occupation,' and also because of their basically sensuous and fun-loving ways, Waikiki's beach boys early on gained a reputation as partying fools and gigolo-like womanizers. Theirs was a naughty but nice mystique that survives, in a pleasantly laid-back style, to this day."[52]

According to Grady Timmons, oral historian of the beach boy lifestyle, "the first beach boys are thought to have appeared on Waikiki Beach soon after the first major resort, the Moana Hotel, was completed in 1901." Waikiki was largely unknown and undeveloped at that time, and the new hotel depended completely on stateside publicity to lure visitors. "In advertisements that appeared as early as 1906, the Moana was proclaiming surfing and canoeing to be exciting vehicles of sport for tourists." [53] The beach boys were an enormous part of the marketing strategy of the new hotel and the ones that followed, including the giant, luxurious beachfront Royal Hawaiian Hotel, built by the Matson Steamship and Navigation Company in 1927. According to Timmons, "the Royal Hawaiian was the hotel that made the world take notice. Along with Matson's new seven-deck luxury cruiser, the Malolo, it was part of a travel package that succeeded in attracting the very rich and famous . . ."[54] This travel package was advertised with alluring images of beach boys and surfing.

According to Timmons, "surfing and outrigger canoeing . . . were revived in Waikiki in great part due to the beach boys . . . as Charles (Panama Dave) Baptiste used to say, 'hell, if it wasn't for us beach boys, nobody would come to Hawaii.'"[55] Now, beach boys were prone to tall tales, but there is certainly truth to Panama Dave's boast. According to Duke, "As the result of our constantly working the waters off Waikiki during . . . the pre-WWI days, surfing had taken on a new lease on life. Tourists caught fire at the sight of our demonstrations offshore, and they spread the word wherever they went."[56] In tourist brochures, postcards, and advertisements put out by the Matson Company and the hotel owners and developers, the surfing beach boy is a prominent figure. And because Waikiki was so remote, its tourist economy was really built on these images. The companies selling Hawaii needed experiences, and images of these experiences, that were intensely alluring in order to lure tourists to the faraway islands. In the beach boys, they found both.

Big, strong, Hawaiian and part-Hawaiian, the beach boys (really grown men) were members of the Hui Nalu (or wave sliding) surf club, an outfit formed by Duke and some friends in 1911 for Hawaiians, in contrast and friendly competition to the mostly haole Outrigger club. They welcomed tourists, taught them to surf, romancing the divorcees and becoming close friends with the men. They played on the beach all day and drank and played slack-key guitar all evening on the Moana Pier, at the Waikiki Tavern, and in the hotels. According to Timmons, "legend casts them as bronzed watermen with enormous charm, good humor, and musical genius—carefree, partying fools, and ardent womanizers. The legend is surprisingly close to the truth."[57]

The potential consumers of Hawaiian beach life responded with gusto to the images, and to the beach boys once they'd arrived. The tourist strategy was wildly successful in Hawaii. In 1930, the islands saw 16,000 visitors; that number doubled in the decade leading up to the second world war, which ended tourism for its duration, during which the hotels became "r and r" sites for GIs. After the war ended, the party began again, and by 1955 the tourist count was nearly 100,000. In 1959, Hawaii became an American state and jet travel to the islands kicked in for the masses—a quarter of a million tourists came that year. Today, the tourist count in Hawaii is over 500,000 visitors *per month*.[58] Americans (and Japanese) bought what the Hawaii promoters were selling, and we can attribute this fact to the appeal of the images used to sell the beach to tourists. Largely, these were images of free-living, fun-loving surfers to whose party you were always invited.[59]

Not surprisingly, Ford's Pan-Pacific Union was one of the major forces in the promotion of the islands through the use of images of beach boys. Both the Pan-Pacific Press Bureau and Ford's *Mid-Pacific* magazine advertised Hawaii as beach boy central. During the 1930s, the Pan-Pacific Press Bureau disseminated countless photos of beach boys to mainland newspapers and magazines in order to publicize Hawaii to Americans.[60] In them, beach boys are guiding smiling tourists toward happiness and relaxation. In one, a rugged waterman steers an outrigger canoe through wild surf with a confident smile on his face and a woman laughing hysterically behind him, a lei around her neck. In another, a beach boy gives a man a full body massage on a surfboard, while a woman who is presumably the man's wife is perched on the nose. In another, a bronzed, straw-hatted beach boy teaches a buttoned-up, coiffed woman to play ukelele. Another photo depicts a smiling, middle-aged woman with a beach boy on each side of her—one is teaching her to weave a straw hat. With the other, her eyes are locked in a coy, amorous mutual gaze. Many of the Pan-Pacific Bureau's publicity photos for Hawaii featured Duke Kahanamoku, whose image embodied the strong, handsome, welcoming, easygoing allure of the beach boy. And in the mid-1930s, the Pan-Pacific Press Bureau distributed photos of a blond, smiling Tom Blake with surfboards and pretty women, all over American magazines to promote Hawaii.[61] Tom Blake was to become a major figure in the development and promotion of surfing; here we can see a link between the work of Ford and the image of Blake.

The *Mid-Pacific* magazine reprinted London's "A Royal Sport" in two parts in 1915. Surfers repeatedly graced the magazine's cover, and no fewer than forty-five articles on surfing appeared between the years 1911 and 1935. A typical *Mid-Pacific* cover, from January 1915, is a painting of a man, white and not necessarily muscular, but in a bathing suit smaller than a loincloth, surfing, again with the board coming out of the image and toward the viewer.[62] Other covers depicted surfers as more explicitly native, but nearly always strong, muscular, relaxed, and smiling or raising their arms in celebration as they ride the wave.

Advertisements for the Mid-Pacific Carnival, a week-long winter celebration mimicking the Malahiki but engineered for tourists, were made into postcards and posters. One characteristic poster image (from the carnival held in 1917) features two dark surfers in silhouette, riding a soft breaker into shore with palm trees and Diamond Head in the background.[63]

The Hawaii Promotion Committee, which later became the Hawaii Tourist Bureau, was instrumental in linking the surfing beach boy with the allure of the islands. In 1913, the Committee put out a fifty-page booklet full of text and images laying out the history and current conditions of the islands. On the cover, which reads "*Hawaii: The Paradise of the Pacific*," is a photograph of two beach boys surfing: the one in front is clearly a native, and looks openly at the camera as he rides the breaker with ease, his hand casually touching the breaking wave. Behind him is a whiter surfer, in a more crouched, athletic position. The fact that this image is the cover of one of the most widely disseminated tourist booklets on Hawaii says much about the prominence of the beach boy and of surfing in the selling of Hawaii. And although the considerable amount of text in the book features climate, business opportunities, natural beauty, hospitable people, hula dancers, etc., as well as the aquatic sports, photos of happy, speeding surfers are all over the book.[64]

A Hawaii Tourist Bureau magazine ad from the twenties says "Play this summer in Hawaii," under a photo showing a flapper-looking woman in a brief bathing suit and a cloche-like swim cap sitting in an outrigger canoe. She and the dark, muscular beach boy who is next to her, pulling her canoe onto the beach, are looking into one another's eyes, grinning widely. Diamond Head and the Moana Pier are in their background, as are about ten surfers.[65] One famous brochure put out by the Bureau sports an image of a native surfer, crouched down, surfing on a stylized, rapid wave, next to the caption "Hawaiian Islands."[66] A dark, handsome beach boy on an outrigger canoe is pictured on the cover of a 1929 Hawaii Tourist Bureau brochure with an oar in his hand, a flower in his hair, and a scantily clad native woman next to him. Behind them is the unmistakable landscape of Waikiki, defined by the volcanic peak of Diamond Head in the distance.

The cover says simply "Hawaii". The beach boy had by this time become an iconic representation of that one evocative name.

In 1933, the *Honolulu Star-Bulletin* published a book of photos of the islands for the Bureau entitled "*Hawaii as the Camera Sees It.*" Beach boys and surfers are well represented among all the photos, which include shots of colonial buildings, volcanic natural beauty, natives in various traditional outfits, notable visitors, and the American military. On one page, captioned "two happy young people of Hawaii," we see a smiling young woman holding a canoe paddle next to another photo of a boy "sitting on the sand, strumming the inevitable ukelele." One of Franklin Roosevelt's many visits (the Royal Hawaiian was called the Western White House during his presidency) is documented, highlighting the fact that his two teenage sons went surfing with Duke Kahanamoku and were photographed with Duke, a few other beach boys, and an outrigger canoe at Waikiki. On a page entitled "the Tourist's Paradise," we see a shot of a surfboard polo game in front of the Royal Hawaiian. Another page shows three very serious-looking "radio men" crouching in the sand, their equipment before them and behind them, a row of nine native beach boys in the standard pose—lined up against their surfboards, each one emblazoned with the beach boys' name. These photos are all in addition to the usual shots of surfing, with captions like "30 miles an hour on a surfboard" next to a picture of a dark, smiling beach boy.[67]

In 1934, the Hawaii Tourist Bureau commissioned six short films which were made by a Hollywood production company and which were shown before movies in mainland theatres. The films also toured US summertime fairs and expos for several years, and surfing figured prominently. Three beach boys and a beginner are pictured surfing at Waikiki in the title shot of one, "*The Island of Oahu,*" in which the narrator describes surfing: "There is no sport on earth more thrilling than surfriding. It was the sport of kings in the past, and every newcomer to Hawaii today is gripped by the ambition to ride one of these mighty chargers of the surf."[68] Early filmmaker Burton Holmes also put Hawaii travelogues on film; he featured a beach boy surfing in "Happy Hawaii," a short film and slideshow that he took on the road and narrated himself, in a foreshadowing of the technique that started it all in terms of surf movies—more on this in the next chapter. A version of the production was made into a home movie and sold to the public as "*Surfing—The Famous Sport of Waikiki.*"[69]

The Tourist Bureau published *Hawaii* magazine as part of its strategy, and surfing appears again and again on its pages. The cover of a 1929 issue of *Hawaii* magazine is made up drawings of activities that the bureau hoped would lure tourists. At the top of the page is a game of "surfboard polo" with an outrigger canoe and Diamond Head in the background.[70] Surfing, outrigger canoeing, and sailing are featured on a stylized cover of *Hawaii* magazine from 1930.[71] And this strategy has really never let up: the March 2007 cover of the magazine depicts three people—first, a pretty native girl, in the middle, a white woman, and bringing up the rear, a sun-parched native man with a flower in his hair—riding a wave on an outrigger with Diamond Head in the background. These explicitly tourist-geared magazine covers joined the scores of American magazines—*Outing, Sunset, the New Yorker, Popular Mechanics, Vogue, Travel*—that featured surfers on their covers during these same years. In addition to showing off the native beach boy, many of these covers actually depicted women surfing, either in poses of athletic prowess or of blatant sexual titillation. In either case, the women are clearly having fun.

Paradise of the Pacific (now *Honolulu*) began publishing in 1888, and was another magazine published with the intent of drawing well-heeled visitors from around the world. During the nineteenth century alone, the magazine had published eleven glowing, illustrated articles featuring surfing—and that was just during surfing's period of decline! As the twentieth century dawned, the link between surfing and Hawaii in the magazine's pages only became stronger. During the first half of the century alone, the magazine published nearly fifty articles that featured surfing, and surfers frequently graced the cover, especially beach boys. A typical *Paradise* cover, this one from 1928, shows an idyllic beach scene—a surfer holding his board, looking out over the ocean as the sun sets over the tropical island paradise. Another cover shows a typical surfer action shot: a close-up of a strong, dark surfer, crouched over and intent, the wave breaking behind him, the board speeding out of the frame of the picture.

The Matson Steamship Company, which along with its passenger ship concerns, owned the Moana Hotel and opened the Royal Hawaiian hotel in 1927 on Waikiki Beach, also did its part to promote the lure of the islands. Again, surfing images are prominent. The cover of a 1930s Matson Oceanic Line brochure entitled *"Hawaii, Come Ride the Surf at Waikiki!"* shows a boy of about ten getting a surfing lesson from a native beach boy.[72] A 1937 Matson Line magazine ad is a photo with a woman in a red two-piece bathing suit laying, stomach down and legs apart, on the sand while leaning her elbows on a surfboard as the water laps at her toes. Sitting on the board is a Hawaiian woman with leis in her hair and around her neck, wearing a grass skirt. The two women are smiling and talking while a tan, muscular man, his arms folded as if waiting for the women to finish, watches with the toes of one foot perched on the board. It's as if the surfboard functions to connect these three figures: the Western woman, the sexy native male surfer, and the lovely grass-skirted primitive woman, full of aloha. The American woman, although not yet in 1937 sexually liberated at home, certainly seems to be when she's on the beach. It's a sexy picture, and it's another example of the sexual liberation that was being used to sell Hawaii. Successfully.[73]

An earlier, twenties-era brochure put out by the Matson Navigation Company also uses a picture of a beach boy, this time in the act of surfing, Waikiki as his backdrop, to lure visitors. From 1928, a Los Angeles

Steamship Company (which merged with Matson in 1931) brochure cover features an art deco-style painting with two figures silhouetted in the foreground. One is a man, sitting on the sand, playing ukelele, looking up at a woman with an American hairstyle in a more angular version of a hula-style pose. Beyond them in the picture is a massive steamship, a palm tree, and a giant stylized sun bathing it all in orange rays.[74] This ad is emblematic in that the postcards and tourist brochures were often really fine artwork reflecting the tastes of the day—deco in the twenties, realist in the thirties, etc.—by great commercial artists who painted the fantasy image of Hawaii as tropical paradise. This changed somewhat with the introduction of photographs, but these too emphasized the same themes.

An eager, competent young woman in a red bathing suit and cap surfs with a beach boy on the cover of a Matson souvenir passenger list from 1931. And it wasn't just Matson: a brochure produced by the Great Northern Pacific Steamship Company, which ran trips from the Pacific Northwest to Hawaii for a few years prior to WWI shows a smiling, fit white man balancing precariously on what is depicted as a very fast-moving surfboard, which is coming out of the frame of the picture toward the viewer.[75] The lesson is clear: those who wanted to lure tourists to Hawaii used the surfer to do it.

This is true of every tourist concern in Hawaii. A TMC (or "Travel Made Carefree") Tours brochure entitled "Hawaii Calls" has on its cover a drawing of a smiling beach boy playing ukelele under a palm tree with Diamond Head in the background. He's wearing a lei, Hawaiian shirt, and a straw hat with his name, Alika, on it.[76] A Slim Holt Tours brochure cover features a tan, smiling, guitar-playing beach boy wearing a lei, leaning on an outrigger canoe. A Hawaiian Tours brochure depicts a couple surfing at Waikiki. The man is on the board behind the woman, holding her hips, their bodies mirroring one another's as they ride the board.[77] And the cover of a brochure published by American Express in the twenties and titled "Hawaii: The Mecca of Tourists," depicts a young woman with cropped hair and a short red one-piece bathing suit surfing ably on a powerful wave, her arms stretched out and up in a (very feminine) gesture that conveys mastery, grace, and power.[78]

Another tourist brochure, probably from the 1930s, depicts a wealthy couple next to the words "nearby Hawaii,"—because of course, at that time, only for the rich would the five-day one-way boat trip qualify as "nearby." What's interesting about the brochure is what the couple is beholding on the Waikiki beach that beckons to them—tan, muscular men. Five of them in the water surfing toward them. One is sitting on the sand next to where they stand. And in between, three more, standing and carrying an outrigger canoe. As if to make the point more, the male tourist is looking lovingly at his female companion. She, however, is gazing at the beefcake on the beach.[79]

Matson used beach boys to advertise its hotels as well as the ships that brought tourists to them. "Pictorial of Hawaii" was a booklet that was placed in the hotel rooms at the Royal Hawaiian and the Moana-Seaside during the 1930s. Its cover featured a view of the hotels from the water, in which two tourist-laden outrigger canoes ride the surf.[80] Other hotels saw a winning strategy and followed suit. A "tourist guide and handbook" for guests of the Pleasanton Hotel during the twenties or thirties shows on its cover a male surfer riding a fast wave, arms outstretched in the frequently-depicted gesture of the freedom and power that comes with surfing.[81] In the same book, a painting of flappers and beach boys lounging at Waikiki on an outrigger canoe, shaded by palm trees, with Diamond Head in the background, portrays the two flapper women in the foreground with head-scarves and abbreviated bathing suits, staring provocatively, almost aggressively, at the beach boy sitting with them. The flapper in the foreground with the small bathing suit, leaning with her arms out and her legs apart, sits with the beach boy behind her. She's turned toward him so that their eyes are locked in a serious look. The flapper beside her is staring at the beach boy also.[82]

A brochure for the Hana-Maui hotel pictures blue sky, blue water, and a tan man with a giant pink surfboard on its cover.[83] A Willard hotel brochure from the 1940s is entitled "Surf Riding" and depicts three surfers with Diamond Head in the background and a plane getting ready to touch down.[84] The hotels gave out luggage stickers as souvenirs, many of which featured surfing.[85] And restaurant menus, hotel matchbooks, stickers—you name the medium, tourist promoters in Hawaii plastered beach boys and surfing women on it to sell the islands.

A great many of the surviving photographs from surfing's earliest days were taken by photographers who sold pictures to tourists for a living. Souvenir photos and postcards from the early twentieth century have surfers as one of their most frequent subjects. DeSoto Brown, archivist of the Bishop Museum in Hawaii and keeper of most of the early surfing/beach boy images, warns of the possible inauthenticity of some of the commercially broadcast images of surfers in a collection of images he published in 2006: "While he [one of the most successful of the Hawaiian commercial photographers, Ray Jerome Baker] desired to document Hawaiian people and their culture, he also needed to make a living from the photographs he sold, so he was always mindful of what potential buyers might find attractive. Surfing certainly qualified as a saleable subject . . ."[86] Brown repeats this warning whenever he writes text that accompanies commercially sold photos or postcards in his published collections. Now, from the perspective of an archivist of Hawaiian history, this is a reasonable caveat. But from the perspective of our argument, that commercial forces seeking to sell Hawaii as a tourist destination found the image of the beach boy surfer a compelling one in terms of its power to lure people, it's quite significant that the beach boy image was so prominent in commercial photographs.

When people visiting the islands wanted to "capture" Hawaii to represent their experience there, they purchased massive numbers of photos and postcards of surfers. And when photographers wanted to take a picture that would sell, they generally aimed their lenses at the surfing, lei-adorned beach boys.

An early 1900s postcard entitled "Surf Riders, Hawaiian Islands," is a painted copy of two different, often-reprinted nineteenth-century photos of native men in loincloths. One is surfing, the other is standing, staring at the camera with his surfboard held horizontally behind his back.[87] A 1915 photo postcard, captioned "Surfriding at Waikiki," shows eight male surfers speeding along, Diamond Head in the background.[88] Even Mad magazine's cartoon character Alfred E. Neuman got into the surfing action in a postcard dated circa 1910, riding an outrigger canoe at Waikiki with a shark snapping up at him as he grins obliviously. The caption says "I enjoy surf riding at Waikiki Beach, Honolulu."[89] A 1920 postcard shows Duke Kahanamoku and three smiling white swimmers, all lounging on a canoe at Waikiki.[90] A book of twenty postcards entitled "Souvenir of Hawaii" from around 1920 has on its cover the classic view of Diamond Head in the background and four relaxed surfers coming in on a rolling wave.[91] A 1935 photo postcard of Waikiki foregrounds outrigger canoes and a circle of relaxed beach boys, with a few overdressed tourists strolling toward Diamond Head in the background.[92] A ubiquitous postcard reading "Aloha From Waikiki" shows four men and two women riding a leisurely roller.[93] As a matter of fact, "aloha" is probably the text most commonly found on twentieth-century postcards that featured surfing.

The postcard images of beach boys and surfers on the beach kept on coming, decade after decade. Like the other images, these postcards, by the millions, highlighted beach life in Hawaii as the site of the pleasures of surfing, music, lounging, and sexual freedom. And Hawaii was depicted as ever-receptive, ever welcoming to strangers. In the postcards and ads, the vision of the native is animated by the concept of *aloha*, which Timmons describes as "love, freely, spontaneously, and generously given." At its most simple, *aloha* means welcome, and this welcoming, gentle, receptive nature has been identified with the islands and its inhabitants since the beginning of the twentieth century. In the widely disseminated narrative of what happens to a tourist when he or she spends time in Hawaii, the idea is that the person becomes happy because they gain the native feeling of *aloha*.

Aloha is a controversial concept, to be sure, and many Hawaiian activists point to its promotion as one more way that the natives are forced to participate in what Haunani-Kay Trask calls their own "collective humiliation as tourist artifacts for the first world." Others, like Duke Kahanamoku, the "ambassador of Aloha," saw *aloha* as something that the world needed more of, and worked to spread this gentle, peaceful way of being all around the world. In any case, Timmons says that *aloha* was a guiding principle of beach boy life, according to their recollections, and there is no question at all that *aloha* was something both linked explicitly with surfing and used to lure visitors to Hawaii. And the gentle receptivity conveyed by the term has been consciously used by surfers throughout the twentieth century to point to what makes their values unique.

Looking at all these commercially disseminated images of beach boys and surfing tells us two things. One, that the surfing beach boy was considered by the interests promoting tourism to make an extremely alluring image—that's why they're everywhere in this stuff, and why these images were used enduringly, year after year, decade after decade. Second, that these interests were right—tourists were lured en masse to Waikiki by these images. So what was it about the beach boys and surfing itself that was so successful in seducing tourists? Examining the ad images, three related themes emerge. First and most obvious, the surfboard is a classic phallic object, portrayed in most of these pictures as a source of power and pleasure. Second, almost all of the images portray surfing and beach boys within the terms of a certain (nonthreatening) discourse of primitivism, in which the native is portrayed as the home of a natural, unfettered sexuality, surrounded by the total freedom that a landscape of lush, toil-free abundance conveys. And third, many of the advertisements are clearly playing to women, especially newly liberated, flapper-style women participating in the first American sexual revolt that began around the twenties.

Hawaii was selling sexual freedom for women as part of the tourist package. The surfing beach boy was the visual representation of this new sexual freedom, which American women back home were beginning to demand in the new consumer society. In Hawaii, say the ads, your liberation is waiting for you. The images were not only beach boy beefcake—so many of the ads show flapper-style women in poses of power and sexual prowess, it's impossible to miss the fact that women's sexual liberation was a theme that the hucksters were playing to. In fact, many of the ad images show women surfing without beach boys at all. Several photos depict grinning flapper girls with their giant phallic surfboards, linking the urban female's liberatory culture with the beach and surfing.[94] In the vast majority of the images used to sell Hawaii, the mainland female is depicted as powerful, joyous, and sexually in charge; the men are the objects of their desire, tan, muscular, smiling, full of welcoming *aloha,* wearing flowers, and at their service.

The gender dynamics animating the Hawaii image didn't go unnoticed. A front page story in *The Honolulu Advertiser* of March 10, 1926 was headlined, "Beach Boys Sling 'Wicked Hoof' to Win Honolulu's first Charleston Contest."[95] Here we see another explicit link in cultural representations between the urban dance-hall/flapper culture of the mainland and the beach boys' fun at Waikiki. The link was also to the "primitivism" that animated both the dance craze and the fascination with the beach boys: "The real Negro eccentricity that makes the dance the rage of the mainland came to the fore. And when it did, one understood the dance's sweeping popularity."

One useful index of the existence of a subversive phenomenon is how upset defenders of the status quo become about it. And for those opposed—for patriarchal, Puritan, or racist reasons—to the kind of unfettered and unauthorized sexuality hinted at in the ads for Hawaii, what was going on at Waikiki was absolutely *not* alright. For instance, in 1932, noted film actress Dorothy Mackaill was interviewed in an article for the International News Service in the context of an interracial murder scandal in Hawaii. Her take is moralistic and racist, but her description of the beach boys and the Hawaiian lifestyle was broadcast far and wide:

> What can we expect of these people when they see Kanakas openly receiving the attentions of American white women? It is little short of disgraceful to see how some white women lie on the beach at Waikiki, in abbreviated bathing suits and permit the "beach boys" to rub them with coconut oil so they will get a good tan. White women can easily lose all sense of moral balance in the South Seas . . . they encourage the attentions of the "beach boys" all too frequently and then go with them to the luaus . . . [which] sometimes last several days . . .

Of the Hawaiians in general she says disapprovingly, "they are always enjoying themselves with music and eating, leaving work until another day . . ."[96]

In another article in a national magazine entitled *Liberty*, an article appeared in 1932, "A Paradise Gone Mad—Facing the Facts in Hawaii." Under a photo of Duke Kahanamoku carrying a woman on his shoulders while surfing, both of them grinning, with their arms outstretched, a caption reads disapprovingly: "a white girl with a 'surf-board god'—that is, a Kanaka instructor." The picture was a rare instance of bad press for Duke, but a relatively common publication of disapproval for the beach boys' interaction with white women. [97]

Whether the image of beach boy as fun-loving gigolo was projected with a frown or with a wink, mainland women got the message and flocked to Waikiki to enjoy the relaxed, available sexuality that came with their surfing lessons. One beach boy remembers that

> wahines have a thing about it [the water]. Get a woman in the water and something happens. Every woman I ever met wanted to make love in the water. A lady once told me, "when I was 19, you took me tandem. Can you imagine what it was like for me, going to a Catholic school on the mainland, have a man take me surfing? To sit on top of me, on the back of my legs. The thrill I had. Skin to skin. In the water."

The hotels themselves were just an extension of the playground. Another beach boy remembers, "hell, we used to live at the Royal. We were always sneaking up and making it with the girls. My friends and I used to say, 'eh, by the time we get old we're going to have been laid in every room in this hotel.'" In addition to surfing lessons, the beach boys offered their "sponsors" other services, like "lomo lomo" massage, that functioned as foreplay. But most often, the sex came with the surfing. According to Timmons, beach boys as a matter of course packed a small canoe with beer and took women outside the breakers to swim and "fool around."[98]

The allure of the beach boys was not limited to women, however. Whereas the gentle beach boy image was the object of female desire, for men the image was one to be identified with and emulated. As one profile, "Waikiki's Famous Beach Boys," puts it, "There comes a time in every man's life when he desires to run away from the drudgery of the unromantic shop or office and start living the life of that envied creature of manhood—the Hawaiian beach boy."[99] Frequently, when rich men came to one of the hotels, they'd be assigned a beach boy to teach them to surf. One well-known friendship was between millionaire Herb Fox and a beach boy who saved his life in 1937, beginning a lifelong friendship capped by Fox's death in 1962, when he was given a beach boy funeral, his ashes scattered in the ocean at Waikiki.

According to Timmons, rich men loved the beach boys because their attitude was infectious. Of legendary beach boy Chick Daniels, he writes

> Chick was popular with rich men because he kept them laughing and at ease. He also was a philosopher . . ."the way to stay young is to relax all the time," he would tell them. "You people don't have a life. You have a schedule. If you take a day off, you don't know what to do with yourself. Take a day off! Break the schedule!" More instructive, though, was his attitude toward money. Chick was that rare individual who taught the rich how to enjoy wealth. When he sat down with his millionaire friends, he outspent them . . . [100]

This was possible because the beach boys used to make a fortune in tips. Tourists were only too happy to part with large sums of money in exchange for being part of the relaxed surfer lifestyle. Chick Daniels, especially, reportedly could have been a millionaire, since he was the head beach attendant at the Royal Hawaiian hotel. But like all the others, he insisted on sharing and spending his giant tips as soon as he got them. The beach boys' live-in-the-moment attitude to life and money reportedly relaxed the wealthy men, who couldn't get enough of it. At home, these rich white men were trapped by the instrumental, dominating masculinity that was part of how they were "supposed" to be. In Hawaii, their beach boy companions taught them the pleasures of relaxing and just receiving all the pleasures that the world had to offer.

Most Americans were as taken with the beach boys as were the rich, which is why images of Waikiki, surfing, and beach boys were everywhere in mainland pop culture during the first decades of the twentieth century. Although most folks couldn't afford the trip to Hawaii, the rich and famous could, and everybody else tuned in. Then as now, what celebrities did was big news, and was broadcast widely on the mainland. Doris Duke, the tobacco heiress, built a $2 million estate at Waikiki called Shangri-La. She was a lifelong friend of many beach boys, and was frequently photographed surfing and hanging out with her beach boy friends. Cary Grant, often photographed on the beach, was quoted as saying, "My fondest [Hawaiian] memories are of the Waikiki beach boys who tried to teach me to surf . . . I loved those guys."[101] Jimmy Durante was photographed, cigar in mouth, laying on the sand in front of the Royal Hawaiian with three laughing beach boys. Will Rogers traveled to Waikiki in 1934 and was photographed surrounded and serenaded by a band of beach boys.[102] Joel McCrea and Dolores Del Rio filmed a movie in Waikiki in 1931 and were serenaded by Chick Daniels in a famous photo. Actress Leila Hyamas, in a somewhat kinky 1940s photo, was seen getting a *lomi lomi* massage from a beach boy and her husband.[103] Deborah Kerr was photographed in the fifties on an outrigger canoe with Steamboat Mokuahi, the Royal Hawaiian in the background. Another famous photo depicts Shirley Temple surrounded by the Waikiki Beach Patrol, which had become the official organization of the beach boys by the 1930s, with the miniature surfboard they'd given her as a souvenir, marked with the words "Aloha Captain Shirley."[104]

The photos of celebs and beach boys kept on coming through the early twentieth century, especially with celebrity favorite and legendary prankster Panama Dave: Panama Dave and Mickey Rooney playing guitar together. Detroit Tiger baseball star, Hank Greenberg, laughing with Panama Dave. Having a drink with John Wayne, dining with actress Rosalind Russell, posing with heiress Gloria Vanderbilt in Look magazine. Waikiki Beach continued to gain popularity as a haven for the rich and famous, constantly sending images of leisure back to the mainland: Frank Sinatra and Ava Gardner came for their honeymoon, John Wayne came to make movies, Red Skelton arrived with his son who was dying of leukemia—among his son's last requests was one asking to be taught surfboard riding by a Waikiki beach boy. Publicity photos from the 1930s included Mary Pickford, Mickey Rooney, and Eddie Cantor, each one posed with a surfboard.[105]

In prose as well, the press channeled representations of surfing in Hawaii, which became ubiquitous in the culture. Frances Parkinson Keyes wrote about Waikiki in a 1925 issue of *Good Housekeeping* magazine, highlighting the "childlike," playful qualities of the beach boys, who never seem to take themselves too seriously:

> far out to the opalescent horizon stretches the ocean in broad bands of jeweled color—turquoise, sapphire, emerald, amethyst; and curving around it like a tawny topaz girdle presses the hard, firm sand of the shore. The pearly surf, diamond crested, sweeps in with a swift, strong

> surging unlike any sound that I have ever heard before; and balanced in superb symmetry on their surfboards, the beach boys come riding toward land . . . In their leisure moments, the beach boys, who act as lifeguards, array themselves in outlandish costumes and parade along the beach, indulging in all sorts of pranks and buffoonery, their own childlike enjoyment in these pastimes quite as great as the amusement they afford to others. In the evening they gather on the pier and sing . . . before an audience which completely fills the Moana Hotel pleasure pier and the long approach to it, accompanying themselves on ukuleles and steel guitars.[106]

Another typical narrative of life at Waikiki begins the January 1926 *Sunset Magazine* article, "Rough Riders of the Surf." "A Mid-February afternoon—warm, sunny, glorious. Bluest of blue skies, sea of jade and topaz, white beach flooded with sunlight . . . bathers and spectators alike are languid, indolent, steeped in the mellow warmth of the tropic winter sun . . ." The author goes on to describe a more excited bunch, those watching the surfers and the surfers themselves, before stating that everyone who comes to the islands tries surfing at least once because the allure is so powerful once you've watched someone do it.[107] The author of this article describes surfing as exciting and fun; many other popular depictions of surfing are a little more . . . titillating.

One of the earliest widely-read articles appeared in 1914 in *Outing* Magazine. The article, "Riding the Surf at Waikiki,"[108] begins with the author and a guide watching Duke Kahanamoku and fellow beach boy Kahola, "the two best surfers in the islands," heading out to go surfing. Lest the reader miss the erotics of race here, the article's author points out that "Kahola's mighty back makes a warm-colored break on the white sand." Next to be featured in the article is "the pretty Mrs. Neave . . . who came in yesterday on the Tenyo Maru from Frisco, 'just crazy to try surf-board riding.'" These two images—the strong native surfer whose first words in the article are "what's your hurry?" and the pretty "Mrs." ready to take a surfing lesson—are front and center, next to one another, just as they are in so many of the early representations of Waikiki.

The author compares life on the beach to a "Roman Holiday" in which he and his beach boy companion are "a very willing pair of barbarians." Another character on the beach is "Linda," a female beach boy, teaching tourist women to surf and loosen up. After some prodding, Linda is successful in getting her client, "Mrs. Propriety" to take off her bath-wrap, although the latter complains that this is "worse than the front row in the chorus—I feel like an aborigine . . ." In no time, though, Mrs. Propriety is laughing joyfully, relaxed like the rest of the group of women and beach boys. Paddling out, "the pretty Mrs. Neave, watching [beach boy] Makaele, forgets all about her bathing suit. This is one of his specialties . . ." Finally, after the dramatis personae are introduced and the sexual tension established, the author begins to describe, in detailed, really quite romantic language, the "sheer exuberance" of riding waves. In his language, the sea is personified and the surfing male is feminized:

> we hear a distant hail from the sea and, looking back over our shoulders from the top of the next low swell that heaves us up, we make out a fine series of surf charging toward us hot off the reef . . . now the surf has caught us, towers over us. I feel my feet lifted in the air, the board shoots forward, higher and faster I drive till in a sudden white seething I break through the top . . . then, lost for a second in the foam, quick my hands slip back, legs gather up, one foot in front as though kneeling, and I rise head and back together, feel for the balance center, then stand erect . . .

But then as the party sees Duke and Kahola speeding in on a wave, the pleasure of gazing at the surfers once again takes over the article's voice:

> for now the eager visitor will see the finest sight at Waikiki, the last word in surf riding. No race in the world is so beautifully developed as the Polynesian, and these two men are the pick of their race. Without changing a line you could put them into a Greek frieze, but you would have to animate or electrify the frieze to keep it in key with their poised grace supreme in this immemorial pastime of their people. Both are as much at home on the streaming mane of a breaker as a Pawnee brave on the bare back of a galloping bronco . . . we emerge to find their glistening brown bodies against the sky . . .

This goes on and on, until the author's vision is "swallowed by the half-drowned work I make of that breaker because of watching him too long." The author, George Marvin, is a male. But he shares with his female companions the pleasure in beholding the figure of the native surfer. It's an image that everyone can get turned on by equally, both men and women. This is very sexy stuff—and it was only 1914!

In a 1933 article entitled "Riding the Waves at Waikiki,"[109] author Harold Coffin points in a matter-of-fact way to the phenomenon we're outlining: that there are "suppressed desires that urge thousands to the booking offices of the Hawaiian steamship lines," and that if we were to "analyze them . . . we would probably discover that every other person had ambitions having to do with a Hawaiian surfboard." The photos that illustrate this article are typical in that both men and women are depicted with equal frequency, and that the women are looking just as powerful and joyful as are the men.

A lengthy 1940 fictional story in *Collier's* entitled "Waikiki Mirage"[110] is told in the third person, but the reader is clearly meant to identify with Virginia, the young female protagonist, who lives such a vibrant fantasy life that it's difficult sometimes to distinguish between what's going on in her mind and in the story—but that's exactly the point. Waikiki is the setting of this fantasy, the story of which revolves around a beach boy that she falls desperately in love with at first sight. This first sight comes during a hula lesson, in which her teacher tells her "you don't need lessons, dear. You seem to do the hula instinctively." She meets Mike when "a dark, handsome young man leans in the doorway . . . he had a gardenia behind one ear." When Virginia asks her hula teacher who he is and what he does, the native woman replies, "swims, fishes, and surfs, mostly." To this Virginia enthusiastically replies, "a beachcomber!" and sets off to follow him, thinking excitedly, "a beachcomber. A derelict . . ." and fantasizing about his past, which she assumes to be wonderfully sordid. She finds him "standing at the entrance to the Outrigger Club with a surfboard under his arm" and sets off to learn to surf, exhorting her nervous, soon-to-be-dumped boyfriend "in a fierce voice" to "live dangerously! Why if I were a man . . . I'd fight and I'd cross the ocean in little boats and I'd fly airplanes upside *down*!" The adventuress carries the day and the two are off to go surfing.

Shortly, both Virginia and her boyfriend wipe out, and Mike, in a classic surf-lit trope, rescues the starry-eyed girl. A kiss ensues, and later more fantasizing, this time about marrying into a native family: "divested of her bathing suit, Virginia was standing quite naked in the center of the room saying dramatically, 'your people shall be my people . . . '" Because Virginia is an "intense girl" with lots of moxie, her fantasy comes true by the time the story ends with Mike telling her that "we're going to have a very adventurous and romantic life together . . ." The drawing accompanying the story is a visual representation of what's depicted in "Waikiki Mirage"—a wild, strong female, riding on a surfboard, caressing the biceps of the dark, smiling man on her board with the flower in his hair, who gazes lovingly at her.

WAIKIKI IN THE MOVIES

The Waikiki romance story with the strong female protagonist was wildly popular in the press, and became so on the big screen as well. Hollywood gave the people what they wanted, reliably broadcasting a collective fantasy on the silver screen. In 1922, movie star Betty Compson filmed *The White Flower* at Waikiki and although the silent film is impossible to find now, a publicity still from the film has Betty, in cropped hair and abbreviated bathing suit, posing coyly in front of four dark Hawaiian beach boys and their boards, the peak of Diamond Head in the background. And although Duke is not in the photo, one of the beach boys is posing in front of his board, clearly marked "DUKE" at the top, in a clear nod to the recognizability of the name and its identification with Waikiki.

Gidget wasn't the first studio film to initiate a beach craze—according to DeSoto Brown, "the US went through a Hawaiian craze in the late 1930s, which was initially inspired by the popularity of a Hollywood musical called *Waikiki Wedding*, released in 1937. Most of the film was made on sets at Paramount Pictures, but a few location shots did make their way into the final edit . . ."[111] These shots depicted Diamond Head in the background of many scenes. And the opening credits are shown in front of images of swaying palm trees and several scenes of ten or more surfers, rolling in together on the back of a gentle Waikiki wave.[112] A publicity still for the film was taken in Honolulu, with Bing Crosby singing and playing ukelele on the Waikiki sand with three of the most famous beach boys of the day, who also played "natives" in the film.

The film counterposes the traditional rhythms of chanting, tom-toms and swaying hips in native ceremonies, which are featured, in Hollywood-style big song and dance numbers, throughout the film. We'll deal with the problematic portrayal of the natives as smiling, dancing, and kind, if a bit silly and superstitious, below. In the meantime, one striking counterposition in the beginning of the film is quite telling. The first scene is of a traditional wedding, replete with hula, drums, liquor, leis, and (in retrospect, almost maniacally) smiling faces. The portrayal may not be "accurate," but the native ceremony is certainly portrayed as alluring. And the "haoles," Crosby and his buddy, are not only invited, but are honored guests. This scene of love, happiness, and Western/native friendship, animated by relaxed music and overtly sexual dancing, is followed jarringly by a far less appealing, quite opposite image, also peopled predominantly by native females: dejected-looking native women on an assembly line, a clock behind them, following the unnatural rhythm of the factory with "Imperial Pineapple" emblazoned on their shirts.

The very next scene illustrates the way that the film gets the angles right in terms of the relationship between Hawaii's commercial promotion and appealing to women's sexual desire. The portly, somewhat grumpy president of Imperial Pineapple is in his office, Diamond Head visible out his window. His son is chiding him for paying Crosby's character, ad man and beach bum Tony Marvin, for just coming up with promotional ideas and never actually spending any time at the office: "You let him lounge around all day on his boat like a beach-comber." To which his father replies that if he were forty years younger and had such great ideas, he'd hang out at the beach all day too. "Hell, I'd do the hula," laughs the old man.

Although Crosby's beach bum character is a sailor rather than a surfer, the effect is similar. His character is a combination of beach boy and ad man, and the film makes clear that the role of both is romancing women, appealing to their desire and linking this desire with Hawaii in the popular imagination. The film's dramatic tension is provided by the fact that Tony's big idea—to have the "Pineapple Girl" beauty contest winner come to Honolulu for "three weeks of romance" and write home about it in a syndicated column, thus linking Imperial Pineapple with the romance of the islands in the minds of women, who of course do all the grocery shopping at home. Unfortunately for the company, Pineapple Girl Georgia Smith is unhappy and wants to go home. Her complaint? "I was promised three romantic weeks in Hawaii and I'm not getting them."

In addition, she's dictating a negative review of the islands to comic relief Martha Raye to send home for her column. It's not only the president of Imperial Pineapple who's upset at this turn of events—he's visited by a group of Honolulu's biggest businessmen, one of whom tells Georgia sternly that, "your syndicated impressions of the island will be read by 50 million people. If you say you don't like it here, we may as well close up these islands!" This is a nod to the fact that by this time, running the factory efficiently was not enough to be a successful capitalist. The suits in the film are actually only portrayed as concerned with "image" and sales; the selling side of capitalism had definitely come to carry the day culturally.

The Chamber of Commerce types decide that the only way to fix the situation is to find Tony Marvin and have him give her the romance she wants. Of course, a caper ensues and ends with true love *and* good publicity. In a nice enactment of the Hawaiian dynamic, the Western woman has an incredible power. If her sexual desire isn't satisfied, the suits are screwed. If she gets what she wants, her satisfaction will be publicized and the sellers of the image of Hawaii will make a fortune from other women throwing their money after the shared fantasy. And the suits have to go to Tony Marvin to get their desired outcome—a character who fuses the adman and the beach bum, and who is explicitly characterized as being very connected to the natives. He speaks their language, wears flowers around his neck, and is comfortable in their world. In addition, before Georgia can get the romance she wants, she too has to symbolically drink the "ona pua" and get dressed down in a revealing grass skirt and flowers by native women. After the musical number that accomplishes this, they look at her approvingly and say, "now you a real Kanaka wahine (native woman)!" Once she "goes native," she can experience true sexual satisfaction.

"Blue Hawaii" is the song that runs through Waikiki Wedding's plot. And like "Sweet Leilani," another of the songs sung by Bing Crosby in the film, it was a massive hit on the mainland and part of the Depression-era Hawaiian craze. In fact, "Sweet Leilani" became Crosby's first song to sell over a million copies, and won the 1937 Oscar for best song. In the film, the Hawaiian music is also linked with female sexual desire. Tony's first attempt to woo Georgia is to serenade her outside her window. Before singing, he cries, "for romance, and Imperial Pineapple!" It turns out that Martha Raye's character is inside the house instead of Pineapple Girl. As she listens to "Blue Hawaii," she stretches out languidly on a divan, becoming increasingly relaxed and ready. And lest the viewer miss the erotic effect of the typical island music, she comes out and yells, "when those guitars go boo-eee, I'm a gone woman!" She then runs out the grass hut door, jumps into the arms of Crosby's best friend and fellow lounge-about, and kisses him.

The "boo-eee" sound is known as "slack-key" guitar, for how the strings are played, and is a sound unmistakably associated with Hawaii. Another major broadcaster of the Hawaiian beach boy surfer image and all its connotations was the music industry, within which the Hawaiian loosely tuned "slack-key" guitar style became a massive hit. Slack-key makes a musical sound that became, and remains, the sound of Hawaii to mainland ears. And this style of music originated with the beach boys, whose singing and playing in the evenings was as much a part of the Waikiki experience as were their surfing lessons during the day. Grady Timmons quotes a son and nephew of early Hui Nalu members: "music was almost a preferred means of communicating. When they sang together, they were together, spiritually. And the songs. Some happy songs, some dirty songs, some serious songs, some sad songs. Song meant a lot to them. When they weren't out surfing, they'd be sitting around singing."[113]

According to Timmons, the old Moana Hotel Pier "stood at the heart of the beach, reaching out some three hundred feet toward the reef," and on Sunday evenings the beach boys played and sang on its far pavilion to enormous audiences. "People jammed the pavilion, lined the walkway, or sat along a seawall that ran toward Diamond Head. Others straddled surfboards in the water or gathered on rafts, the men drawing straws to determine who would bring drinks from the beach . . . the songs were delivered in elaborate harmonies." In 1944, composer Johnny Noble was interviewed in *Paradise of the Pacific* magazine and described how central these (often drunken) song sessions had been to the tourist experience: "these Hawaiian beach boys seemed to weave a spell of the real Hawaii over the assemblage. Tourists and local residents alike sat quietly while they listened, enchanted, to the island music that stirred the heart . . . the boys had no set program, for it was all informal, but they would play and sing song after song, a surf of melody."[114]

Although the Moana Pier was closed in 1930, the popularity of beach boy music spread exponentially, in Waikiki and on the mainland. It became known as "hapa-haole" music—Hawaiian music put into a Western pop structure and sung in English. The sound is a compelling evocation of the beach context in which it was produced—hearing the slack-key guitar, one can almost feel the tropical breeze, hear the waves, and feel the relaxed, languid pace of life on the beach at Waikiki. Hapa-haole garnered massive national attention when Albert (Sonny) Cunha performed Henry Kalimai's "On the Beach at Waikiki" at the 1915 Panama-Pacific International Exhibition in San Francisco, attended by 17 million people. The following year, hapa-haole songs sold more records than any other musical genre. The genre's massive popularity kept up for decades, and in 1935 Harry Owens, the orchestra leader at the Royal Hawaiian hotel, recorded "Sweet Leilani," and it became a number one hit. Bing Crosby sang the song in Waikiki

Wedding, and Owens won an Oscar for best song. Although the music wasn't used quite as explicitly as was surfing to promote tourism to Hawaii, the images that accompanied the hapa-haole craze in the states mirrored ones we've seen in advertisements already. And the Hawaii Tourist Bureau's celebrated radio show, "Hawaii Calls," was syndicated internationally and broadcast all over the world for forty years beginning in 1935. The show was broadcast from the beach at Waikiki and featured the live hapa-haole sound, interspersed with stories from the beach. A publicity photo for the show has the radio equipment and hosts down in front of several smiling native beach boys, their boards upright behind them.

In the early part of the century, it wasn't just recorded or radio music that people listened to—many songs became popular because Americans played them in their homes, from sheet music. According to DeSoto Brown, "the sheet music market was a busy one, and printed pieces competed for sales on crowded racks the way magazines do today; thus eye-catching cover illustrations could be crucial to success."[115] Not surprisingly, what Americans went for on the sheet music racks were often alluring depictions of Hawaii, and frequently these included images of surfers. A cover for sheet music from 1937 for a piece called "What Are the Wild Waves Saying" depicts four outrigger canoe riders on a big Waikiki wave. The two in the back appear to be native beach boys, with a white couple, more relaxed, in the front. The sheet music cover is a painted version of a publicity picture disseminated by the Pan-Pacific Press Bureau at that time.[116] Even Santa Claus wasn't immune to getting sexed up and surfing in Hawaii. In 1949, the music to the popular Christmas song "Mele Kalikimaka" was published with a painting of a grinning, singing, ukelele-playing Santa surfing in on a wave, clad in nothing but his fur cap, black boots, and a red and white kerchief as a loincloth.[117] And the sheet music for the 1951 hit "Sunshine, the Beach Boy" has on its cover a painting of a smiling, guitar-playing native beach boy with a straw hat foregrounded next to another picture of an attentive beach boy staring up at a beautiful woman in a bikini. They are under a palm tree, readying an outrigger canoe for a ride.[118] For decades, in fact, the fascination with Hawaiian music refused to let up on the mainland: a record from the 1960s entitled "Waikiki Swings: Today's Top Hits from Hawaii" features music by Don Ho, Sonny Chillingworth, and others of "Hawaii's Greatest Recording Artists." The cover shows five young, smiling, bikini-clad girls hanging out of a VW bus along with three surfboards.[119]

The happy gigolo beach boy image, as well as the very song, "Blue Hawaii," remained popular for decades after "Hawaiian craze" of the 1930s. In fact, as jet travel began opening up the islands to more and more tourists, the craze, and the beach boy image that went with it, only intensified. In 1961, Elvis Presley inaugurated his Hawaiian film trilogy with *Blue Hawaii,* featuring the same song that had been so popular in *Waikiki Wedding* (its pre-release title was *Hawaii Beach Boy*). In the film, Elvis is Chad

Gates, a wealthy haole boy returning home from two years in the army. All he wants is to go back to surfing and hanging out at the beach shack with his beach boy friends, and romancing his beautiful and strong native girlfriend. Chad's parents want to welcome him home and into the career they have planned for him, a managerial job at the pineapple company his father runs. His mother wants for him to become "responsible" and to stop hanging out "with those dirty native beach boys." She also harbors a blatantly racist disdain for his girlfriend. Chad refuses what his parents are offering and instead takes a job as a "tour guide," giving surfing lessons to (according to the trailer) "gals with more than scenery on their minds."

In the meantime, the viewer is treated to plenty of beach boy musical numbers, featuring slack-key and rockabilly music, and plenty of shirtless native men, swinging their hips and singing happily along with Elvis in tight swim shorts. In the end, Elvis marries his sweetheart and becomes successful on his own terms, using the beauty of the islands and his own sexual allure to found a tour guide company, partnering with his girl and employing all his beach boy friends. He suggests a contract to his father and his father's boss, in which his company would arrange for the hundreds of Great Southern Pineapple company employees to have their annual sales meetings in Hawaii. "You could bring them over here, show them how we grow the fruit, process it, let them get a first-hand taste of Hawaiian sunshine and then go back to their territories and sell like they've never sold before."

His commercial business uses sex and the allure of the "traditional Hawaiian way," including hula, torches, luaus, and surfing, to sell Hawaii and become rich. His parents represent the uptight industrial wealth of Hawaii; Elvis and his friends represent the sex- and surfing-driven pleasure associated with the commercial selling of Hawaii, as well as the race-mixing intermarrying that's become part of the island character and that Chad's mother can barely tolerate. The libido side of the story, represented iconically by Elvis, wins over its other: Chad's father finally tells him, "I'm proud of you," while his mother is forced to suffer through the interracial wedding—reminiscent of the classic image of Hawaii as paradise of racial harmony—that happily ends the gigolo success story.

THE LURE OF THE PRIMITIVE

Another one of American culture's most famous beach boys remains James Michener's fictional Kelly Kanakoa. Michener's novel, *Hawaii*,[120] was published in 1959 (the same year that jet travel to the islands began and tourism exploded) and was a massive bestseller. Like all of Michener's famous novels, it's over 1,000 pages long and is the product not only of a gifted fiction writer but also of an arduous research process. Although it's a work of fiction, the author captures some complexities of the beach boy that

Grady Timmons' oral history doesn't; nostalgic boasts about the good old days have their limitations. Specifically, the issue that Michener delves into with his beach boy character is the complexity of the sexual politics of the Western/native interaction. The majority of the images that we've examined thus far have been animated by a certain discourse of primitivism that has always been the dark companion accompanying European modernity's triumphant march. This discourse views the "native" as the physical home of a certain natural, unfettered sexuality which is the polar opposite of the Puritanism that founds so much of the modern world's dominant culture. The fact that so many of the images that lured Americans to Hawaii depicted native life this way shows that modern Americans were incredibly taken with the fantasy of "primitive" sexuality. What does this mean?

The last chapter of the novel, in which we're introduced to Kelly (short for Kelolo), is entitled "The Golden Men," in reference to a concept so named by "a group of sociologists in Hawaii" to mean a cosmopolitan man at home in both east and west, both a businessman and philosopher, and both a modern American and a man in tune with "the ancient and the Oriental."[121] Golden Man Kelly is a compilation of all the classic beach boy attributes: tall, muscled, bronze, handsome, generally dressed in a sarong or bathing suit, wearing a straw hat or a flower in his hair, hanging out at the beach all day, playing cards and singing songs with the other beach boys. He's also directly descended, he says, from a Hawaiian king. He's fluent in "degenerate pidgin," which is "a requirement for a beach boy," and, to complete the picture of the iconic beach boy, he's a wonderful singer and player of classic "slack-key" guitar. In fact, when a nightclub singer from New York points out to Kelly that a song he composed on the beach and gave away, "The Rolling Surf," is a huge hit on the mainland, and says, "you ought to sue the dirty bastard!" Kelly couldn't care less.[122]

These fictional early twentieth-century beach boys are on the payroll of the beachfront hotel—"tourists instinctively loved [them] for the Hawaiians reminded them of an age when life was simpler, when laughter was easier, and when there was music in the air."[123] The beach boys would get assigned as surf instructors and guides for divorced and widowed women who came ashore on the Moana Loa, a thinly disguised Matson Line cruiser. As we're introduced to Kelly, he's giving a young mainland divorcee, Rennie, a surfing lesson that's emblematic of what the beach boy does, and of the close relationship in popular representations between Waikiki surfing and sex.

> [Rennie] was excited by the exhilarating motion of the sea and felt that she would never be able to rise and stand on the board . . . but when she felt Kelly's strong arms enveloping her from the rear she felt assured, and as the board gathered momentum she allowed herself to be pulled upright, always in Kelly's stout arms, until she stood daringly on the flying board . . . Instinctively she drew Kelly's arm closer about her,

> pressed backward against him, and reveled in his manliness . . . [they kiss underwater and then] when their board was well separated from the others . . . his adept hands began their explorations beneath her new bathing suit. Sighing, she whispered, "is this part of the standard instruction?"[124]

Whereupon the two retreat to Rennie's hotel room and begin a sexual affair that lasts the length of her vacation and that renews Rennie's spirit and self-confidence. The charge for surfing instruction appears on her hotel bill, but everyone's clear that the payment is really for something more comprehensive.

At one point, Rennie asks Kelly where he lives and he demurs, saying dismissively that, "it's nottin." Rennie asks, "you mean, your ancestors were kings and you have nothing for yourself?" Kelly claims that he's happy just having his guitar, his surfboard, and a "cute wahine like you." This back and forth is a theme with beach boys and their charges—the question, "what kind of life is this?" comes up with several different "wahines." Although the women take great pleasure in their vacations, they are unable to comprehend that surfing, sex, and music could be "enough." Kelly occasionally has his doubts, too, since the women he meets are always bringing it up:

> Once or twice as the year . . . skipped away, Kelly had fleeting doubts which he shared with [fellow beach boy] Florsheim: "whassamatta me? Takin' care of lotsa wahine . . . where it gonna get me?" But such speculation was always stilled by the arrival of some new divorcee or widow, and the fun of working it around so he got into bed with them, while they paid the hotel and restaurant bills, was so great that he invariably came around to Florsheim's philosophy: "Mo bettah we get fun now, while we young."[125]

This dynamic is especially apparent in the encounter between Kelly and the client that Michener has him spend the most time with. In the relationship between Kelly and Elinor Quigley Henderson, a widowed friend of Rennie's, a great many of the facets of this complicated relationship between two diametrically opposed conceptions of "success" come to light. Elinor is a New Englander, a descendant of the one missionary who came to the islands, was disgusted by what the other early missionaries were doing, and abruptly left. Elinor says that she has

> "been haunted by Hawaii ever since I read my great-great-great-grandfather's secret journal . . . he wrote a prophetic passage about the Hawaiian of the future . . . 'the Hawaiian is destined to diminish year by year, dispossessed, distraught, and confused.' He must have had you in mind, Kelly."

Elinor says that she intends to write a book about the islands now and call it "The Dispossessed."

When Kelly protests that he has everything he wants, Elinor replies that his people have neither land, nor money, nor even their own gods. Kelly "laughed nervously and began to say something but fought back the impulse, for he knew it would lead to peril . . . Instead, he wagged his finger in Elinor's face and said, 'You'd be surprised at what we Hawaiians have. Truly, you'd be astounded.'"[126]

Elinor has far more awareness about Hawaiians—their history, their oppression—than any of Kelly's other clients. Significantly, she spends her time with him and takes surfing lessons, but never sleeps with him. At first, it seems that she's refusing to project her sense of the "primitive" onto Kelly. When they first meet, for instance, Elinor correctly ascertains that he is smart and educated, and tells him that he isn't "required" to talk pidgin to her any longer. In this way, Elinor is able to see him as a more complex character than can the other "wahines."

Still, her view of him remains a projection of her notion of the "primitive." All the women project their own desires and issues onto Kelly in their own ways. Elinor, for her part, can't see Kelly, or his people, as anything but deluded victims of the agency of the white man. It's her way of clinging to a sense of power that she doesn't feel in her actual life. When Kelly attempts to prove to her that Hawaiians "have" quite a bit, even after all the colonial horrors and humiliations, he takes her home to see his mother in a somewhat shabby but large estate, filled with friends and music and tropical abundance. He introduces them: "Muddah, dis wahine Elinor Henderson, Smith. Muddah's Vassar." Kelly's mother is a graceful, regal, "well-bred" descendant of Hawaiian royalty, with the best American education, and yet, when Elinor asks what Kelly's mother did when she came home from Vassar, Kelly replies that "in the hot afternoons she sang, and was good to the Hawaiians, and wasted her money. What else?' Elinor began sniffling, and after a while said, 'I'm bitterly tangled up, Kelly.'" Elinor can't see Kelly's or his mother's lives as the result of their own agency, or as in any way equivalent to her own. Kelly is heading back to the hotel to sing "for a friend." Elinor is incredulous that he sings "his life away" for free. Kelly asks rhetorically in response who Elinor thinks is happier, his mother "or the women you know back home?"[127]

The confused Elinor does learn to surf but Kelly's main lesson is, for the most part, lost on her. The fact that as Kelly became better acquainted with American girls, "he felt sorry for them" because they had so little enjoyment back home, is impossible for her to comprehend. She can't see enjoyment as the measure of a life. At one point, she goes to the library to check on Kelly's ancestry. The librarian, Lucinda Whipple, is a missionary descendant who is overjoyed to see a Quigley in the islands. She invites Elinor to the yearly anniversary of the missionaries' arrival, where each ministers' name is called and his descendants stand for applause. The fact that Elinor accepts the invitation tells us that she's not as divorced from

Hawaii's missionary roots as she might like to believe. That evening, Kelly asks Elinor about the book she wants to write about Hawaii.

> "You still determined to call it The Dispossessed?"
> "More than ever." "Who do you think the dispossessed are?" Kelly taunted.
> "You. Who else?"
> "I thought maybe at the mission society you discovered that they were the real dispossessed," he argued.[128]

Kelly's more nuanced reading, especially of the failures of the Calvinist missionaries (most Hawaiians, he says, are Catholics, Mormons, or Buddhists), is lost on Elinor. In her worldview, there simply can be no victories for "the dispossessed."

Elinor insists, too, on seeing the power relationship between the gigolo and his client in the same terms as that between the imperialist missionaries and the Hawaiians—the powerful act, the powerless are acted upon, used, and thrown away like trash. When she finally admits to Kelly that she's falling in love with him, he pulls her close to him suggestively but she refuses, saying that she thinks it's "immoral" and "disgraceful" the way mainland women "use" the beach boys for their own pleasure. For all her enlightened sensibilities, she still refuses to allow the possibility that she and Kelly are equals.[129]

Elinor takes pride in "always sid[ing] with the dispossessed," but she misses the strategy by which the landless beach boy uses the opportunities at hand to forge a life for himself that he can enjoy. Selling white women their primitive fantasy allows him a life of leisure and pleasure on the beach, a life that revolves around surfing, sex, music, friends, and family. Her deep Puritanism blinds her to the utopian possibilities in this "cheap" market hustle—she's far too earnest to be able to judge life on the basis of happiness or pleasure. The beach boys, on the other hand, can take pleasure in their marketable allure. The astute Florsheim understands the dynamic well.

> "I t'ink dis one t'ing berry punny . . . allatime New York dey got pitchas wid' colors 'Come to Hawaii!' An' dey show dis rock wid wahines, grass skirts, flowahs in de hair, wigglin' de hips like to speak, 'You come to Hawaii, mister, we gonna screw till you dizzy . . . but de punny t'ing, it ain' so easy to ketch a wahine on dis rock. It ain' dem mainland kanakas has de good time ovah heah, it's de wahines. You know what I t'ink, blalah . . . I t'ink mo bettah dey get you 'n' me on de pitchas."

Florsheim, laughing, flexes his muscles and poses, staring out to Diamond Head in a classic beach boy travel poster trope, and says, "Kelly blalah, we de real attraction."

Not Elinor. She is in some ways as imperialist as any of the other whites Kelly encounters—her imperialism just has a softer touch (which can be worse—at least the early colonizers saw the values of Hawaiian culture as a force to be reckoned with). Kelly wants her to see that despite all the horrors caused by whites in the islands, his culture still allows him to live in the moment, for pleasure, even under difficult circumstances. But Elinor, like his other clients, only sees what she wants to see. She never learns the existential lesson he tries to teach her, and in a nice piece of poetic justice, Elinor is washed away by a tsunami that hits the island as she and Kelly are lounging on a deserted beach. As the wave carries them over the island, Elinor wraps Kelly's hands around a tree branch—although he's unconscious, he grips "as if by instinct." Saving Kelly keeps her from saving herself, and she is washed out to sea. She's unable to existentially "ride the wave" of life in the moment, so it drowns her. She's still a missionary do-gooder at heart, whose final act is to save the poor, downtrodden Other. Kelly goes on to live many more happy moments—in fact, he winds up getting rich and famous as a singer, again selling the primitive fantasy to mainlanders who want a piece of the life he's got—but Elinor resists the imperative of the islands to relax and enjoy just as her ancestors did. She resists until the bitter end—her last thought is, "this cursed island!"

Elinor is still seeing the native/Western relationship through lenses that cast the imperialists as full of male, dominating power, and the native as "dispossessed" because they are without this power—that is, feminized. In important ways, her position echoes the critique of the discourse of primitivism laid out by writers like bell hooks in her seminal essay *Eating the Other*[130] and Marianna Torgovnick in her 1990 book *Gone Primitive*.[131] For both authors (as for Elinor), the white Western fascination with the exotic Other is tantamount to a form of cultural rape. One entire chapter of Torgovnick's work is dedicated to debunking Freud's concept of the primitive as his own projection of unrepressed, non-Victorian sexuality onto indigenous cultures to whom this projection has done generations' worth of violence. Since the present work is using some of the insights of psychoanalysis to argue for the utopian possibilities of a countercultural identification with images of primitive sexuality, let's follow Torgovnick and examine Freud's notions of the significance of what he calls "primitive" sexuality.

In discussing civilized, or modern life, Freud points to the "curious" phenomenon of moderns believing that "uncivilized" or premodern life was somehow better, happier, and more free than modern civilization. For psychoanalysis, the "primitive," unconscious layer of the psyche is the home of all the desires, sexual and aggressive, that get repressed when we become "civilized" or socialized beings, so that society can function without falling apart under the pressure of these powerful, primary drives. But according to Freudian theory, these drives can never be fully repressed in the sense that they can be made to disappear. The energy of drives, or instincts (which for Freud were always either libido or destrudo) can be rerouted to a different object but must always expend itself on something. In a repressed society that's narrowed down sexuality from its original, polymorphous perverse state to the genital, heterosexual, legitimate form of sex that serves the propagation of the race, most of our sex drive goes unsatisfied and gets rechanneled, or sublimated, into aim-inhibited libido such as friendship and affection or into cultural activities such as art or literature—brought "higher" than the genitals, as it were.

And under the pressure of the "mutual primary aggressiveness" against one another that constantly threatens civilization with the violent breaking of civilized social bonds, civilization, through the Oedipus situation, turns the human aggressiveness that so threatens it back onto the human being in the form of a super-ego, which takes up all this aggressive energy and turns it inward, punishing the ego, or self, with guilt and anxiety. In these ways, civilization uses complicated forms of repression to inhibit the primary desires that threaten it. And to some extent, it's been successful. But sublimated sexuality, and aggressiveness turned to guilt, just don't satisfy the way the full sating of a primal desire does. So in civilization, in addition to being guilty and anxious, we're profoundly unsatisfied sexually.

And although in *Civilization and its Discontents*,[132] Freud identifies the aggressive drive as the greatest threat to civilization, it can be argued these days that aggressiveness gets far more satisfied in modern society than does sexuality. In *Eros and Civilization,* Marcuse identifies this as a dangerous dynamic whereby Eros undergoes not only the repression made necessary by the scarcity inherent in the "reality principle," but a surplus-repression that functions to turn the body from an instrument of pleasure and intercourse with nature and one another, into an instrument of alienated labor under what he calls the "performance principle." Under this, the historically specific reality principle that characterizes capitalist society, Marcuse says, Eros undergoes such an intense level of repression that it becomes unable to hold back or "bind" aggressiveness—and Freud posits Eros as the only force with this capacity. In a sense, the only thing stronger than hate is love, and when love, or libido, is so repressed in modern society (so that people can work, under the domination of the performance principle), hate and aggressiveness are unleashed on a disastrous scale. So in Marcuse's style, it can be argued, against Freud's conclusions but straight out of his theory, that it's really sexuality that suffers such brutal repression in modern society, and it's really sexuality that threatens to explode through not society itself, but modern, rational, repressed, and increasingly violent, capitalist society.

So our primal sexuality constantly writhes under the surface of our civilized morality. Puritan types of every generation rightly fear it, and know that when it's unleashed, it can overwhelm all attempts to tame it. It can be argued that this is what happened during the sixties, and that since the seventies the appetites of the working class have been beaten with the stick of increased working hours and lower real wages—a more demanding performance principle. In any case, though, what happens to the repressed sexual material that we're encouraged to feel so guilty about? Well, one thing, among others, is that it can get projected onto others, exotic Others, to be exact. In *Eating the Other,* bell hooks looks at the way in which white Westerners appropriate the culture of people of color to "add spice to the bland European experience."

The exotic Other is imagined to have a capacity for pleasure that repressed Europeans have come to lack. The Others are sought after for experiences, sexual and cultural, that are imagined to open the white-bread bores to greater, fuller pleasure. And although this new relationship between modern European and Other may seem more progressive than older patterns of slavery or overt, brutal racism, the fascination with the "spice" of the Other is just another way in which the powerful group uses the powerless group for their own purposes, in this case a screen on which to project their own repressed desires, and a body which they can dominate, "have" as part of a story in which the Western continues to be the masculine dominator and the Other is feminized, weak, taken. The old story of domination and subordination has put on new clothing but hasn't really changed a bit.

Similarly, Marianna Torgovnick analyses the fascination with the "primitive" as a projection that does violence, symbolic and actual, to the peoples all around the world so labeled and objectified by the Western gaze. And clearly the images of Hawaii and surfers increasingly seen by Americans on the mainland were so powerfully alluring precisely because they tapped into just this discourse of primitivism, in which the consumer could indulge fantasies of pleasure denied in their "real," capitalist world, through contact with the dark, fun-loving, free Other. Torgovnick is right that the West—"psychologists and imperialists, socialists and capitalists, liberals and fascists, share the same assumptions"[133] about the primitive. These assumptions are generally "that primitive beliefs and social relationships sometimes are . . . seen as equivalent to the 'oceanic': to a dissolution of boundaries between subject and object and between all conceived and conceivable polarities. Western thinking frequently substitutes versions of the primitive for some of its deepest obsessions—and this becomes a major way in which the West constructs and uses the primitive for its own ends."[134]

Fair enough. (In our case, this is certainly substantiated with the image of the surfer, which is nothing if not "oceanic.") But is it possible to imagine that there could be another outcome of the Western fascination with the Other besides just exploitation and domination? If the Other is seen as having agency too, and the coming together of the two, Western and Other, is seen as two forces (with differential power, sure) colliding with indeterminate outcome, we might see the discourse of primitivism as a dynamic rather than just a one-sided pounding. Michener's beach boy, Kelly, has quite a good life (as does his "dispossessed" mother) and it's precisely the primitive fantasy, or more specifically, his exploiting the primitive fantasy that gets him a life of pleasure, fun, sex, and material abundance. Can a person really do better than surfing all day and drinking, playing music, and having sex every night? Michener's story is fictional, but he wants us to see that feeling sorry for Kelly the way that Elinor does is its own form of imperialist fantasy.

Similarly, Tom Wolfe, in his 1970 essay, *Radical Chic*,[135] skewers the Upper West Side rich white liberals who indulge their own fantasies of liberated aggression and sexuality by bringing a bunch of Black Panthers to Leonard Bernstein's apartment one night for a fund-raiser. The Panthers obligingly pose for the white folks, playing the role of primitive—as more in touch with their instinctual desires, as more satisfied, as dangerous and wild and free—by giving their audience what they want. In return, the white folks throw money at the Panthers like there's no tomorrow. Wolfe makes plain that it's the white people who are getting played here, not the African Americans on display. They are making a tidy profit, serving their own collective political purposes, by allowing the whites to project their fantasies onto them. Through Wolfe's straight-shooting eyes, the Panthers are savvy, not pathetic or exploited. In fiction and in nonfiction, it's certainly not outside the realm of possibility that the Other is smart enough to use the primitivist fantasy to its own advantage.

Maybe what hooks and Torgovnick identify as such a damaging fiction is not *necessarily* quite so damaging. The primitive fantasy does at least seem to give the objects of the fantasy something to work with. And perhaps the fantasy is not such a fiction, either. All projection aside, what about reality? That island culture was less repressed than mainland culture, that Hawaiian culture was more sexual and less uptight and without a work ethic? Why else would the Calvinists have worked so hard to beat the natives out of their languid, leisurely ways? To get them out of the water and into more constricting apparel? And why else would Hawaiians themselves, even today, after so much repression, colonization, and decimation of the native people and ways, why do they still speak approvingly of "island time"—more leisurely, less rushed—as opposed to the unnaturally forced rhythms of "mainland time"?

Far more important than the truth value of the primitive fantasy, though, is the significance of its allure. Whether or not it's a fair portrayal, or to what extent beach boys like Duke and Kelly played up the portrayal for their own purposes, is beside our point at some level. The fact is that there *is* a more primitive level of sexuality that gets repressed in the course of "civilized" life, and that for better or worse, this sexuality is what's being projected with the image of the Hawaiian surfer. And this sexuality is precisely what threatens the capitalist order in which everything is made to work rather than to be. It's intensely alluring, as the wide resonance of these images makes clear, because freedom and sexuality are so counter to the alienated routines of everyday life. It's for this reason that an identification with the image of "the primitive" has been so enduringly linked with countercultural sensibilities throughout the twentieth century. This link is especially apparent when we trace the outlines of the surf subculture in America.

To do this properly, we need to leave behind our desire to debunk fantasy as untrue or as damaging, and just examine its contents. What we see will tell us a lot about the potential to subvert what Weber's Puritans have built. There's really no way to verify levels of psychic repression one way or another, after all. So let's agree with Marianna Torgovnick that images that speak primitivism tell us more about the West and its desires than about the so-called "primitives" themselves. We are telling a story about America, after all. We know the images were popular, and their popularity and the growth of their use in commercial culture is an index of how they tapped into American desire. When we look at these images, they tell us several things. First, the commercial forces that deployed them to sell Hawaii understood their appeal and pushed the image of Edenic freedom—sexuality and play—that defined them. And second, people want freedom. How do we know this? Americans responded massively to these images, buying the products, which included Hawaiian tourism, that they were intended to sell. This response tells us that the fantasy that surfing was part of is a fantasy that's widely shared. A fantasy that people will *take action* to *make real*. People who are interested in social movements are not used to seeing consumer action as "legitimate" collective action; it's the argument of this book that it is.

In arguing for the politics inherent in surfing, the important point is that surfing itself, independent of the traditional cultures that it leans on, does oppose the subject/object dichotomy, the distance from nature, and most importantly, the relationship to time and work that characterizes modern rational culture. What surfers call "the stoke" is precisely what Freud called the "oceanic feeling," a feeling he describes in *Civilization and Its Discontents* as the peace and joy of utter wholeness, connectedness—a feeling that we all had once, in the pure undifferentiated pleasure of the infant feeding at the breast, and that remains in our unconscious, as memory and desire. The West has imagined members of primitive cultures as being more oceanic—surfers, on the other hand, describe themselves explicitly this way.

The native Hawaiian surfer was, at the dawn of the twentieth century, an iconic image of the primitive, of everything that urbanized, industrialized Americans felt they'd lost with all their technological "progress." Living in cities—and suburbs—where space was rationally mapped by a grid and in which time was completely colonized by clocks, Americans were fascinated by the lure of the free leisure time and wild space inhabited by the Hawaiian surfers. Americans projected their repressed—that is, fun-loving, sexual, languorous, leisurely, premodern—fantasies onto (among other things at that time) the figure of the Hawaiian surfer. So these images tell us less about what Hawaiians were really like, of course, and more about what was repressed and desired among turn of the century (and beyond) Americans. It can be argued that the image of the surfer has, from the time of this revival on, represented the return of the repressed in modern society—the other of control (of self and nature), the opposite of the Protestant Ethic, the antithesis of alienation. And when the repressed returns, it makes some big waves.

THE PRIMITIVE AND COUNTERCULTURE

Bohemians in general and surfers in particular have always exhibited a fascination with the primitive, and in the case we're examining, this fascination transcends the Hawaiian context of surfing and follows the sport and the subculture to the coast of California and its popular culture depictions. Surfing is a key example of the dynamic whereby the fascination with the primitive is a building block of countercultural forms. The history of surf culture makes the point that an embrace of the Other of modern rationality and repression builds an alternative, life-affirming culture—a counterculture. Torgovnick and hooks both point up this link, between bohemian sensibilities and primitivism, in a disapproving way. A more favorable look at the significance for the development of American counterculture of a fascination with the primitive is laid out in Norman Mailer's classic but much-maligned essay, "The White Negro."

For Mailer, the imitation of the primitive subverts domination rather than upholding it. People solve problems with the tools available to them, and the discourse of the primitive is enduringly available to Westerners. It runs deep. So it's not such a surprise that when members of Western culture desire to live in a way that opposes the rational, instrumental domination of time, nature, and sensation, they look to the so-called "primitive" for some inspiration. Among these, Norman Mailer has been the most influential. And for all his insensitivity, he's right about what countercultural types are doing when they embrace what they see as primitive. Torgovnick and hooks aside, it's not all bad.

In 1959, Mailer writes an essay in *Dissent* called "The White Negro" that attempts to explain the meaning and potential of "Hip." For Mailer, the American Negro is the embodiment of the primitive—the wild, the sexual, the "immature"—and hipsters are those who, wisely, imitate the Negro. In his words:

> Probably, we will never be able to determine the psychic havoc of the concentration camps and the atom bomb upon the unconscious mind of almost everyone alive in these years . . . It is on this bleak scene that a phenomenon has appeared: the American existentialist—the hipster, the man who knows that if our collective condition is to live with instant death by atomic war, relatively quick death by the state as *l'univers concentrationnaire*, or with a slow death by conformity with

> every creative and rebellious instinct stifled (at what damage to the mind and the heart and the liver and the nerves no research foundation for cancer will discover in a hurry), if the fate of twentieth-century man is to live with death from adolescence to premature senescence, why then the only life-giving answer is to accept the terms of death, to live with death as immediate danger, to divorce oneself from society, to exist without roots, to set out on that uncharted journey into the rebellious imperatives of the self . . . So it is no accident that the source of Hip is the Negro . . . [because] any Negro who wishes to live must live with danger from his first day, and no experience can ever be casual to him, no Negro can saunter down a street with any real certainty that violence will not visit him on his walk."[136]

By necessity, according to Mailer, "the Negro" lives in a constant present, without alienation from his body or from the moment. This is what makes imitating this figure so countercultural. The essence of modern society is precisely an alienation between mind and body, between subject and object, between self and moment. All instrumentalization (of people in labor, of nature for industry) and domination is predicated on this alienation. It's the most fundamental piece of modern economic life, as Max Weber worked to show us. Clearly, Mailer is projecting a fantasy onto the figure of "the Negro," just as the Hawaiian image was a projection of European fantasy. The point for us is that the rejection of this alienation, and the embrace of the kind of existentialism that Mailer advocates, is the key to the building of a counterculture. That is most certainly the case for surfing in America, a bohemian subculture which combines a fascination with the primitive with an activity that both partakes of a nature-imposed rather than clock-imposed time rhythm *and* necessitates a complete absorption in the moment and in nature in order to do it.

For Mailer, the political potential of Hip, for white and black, lies in the fact that the "White Negro" or "hipster [who had] absorbed the existentialist synapses of the Negro . . . may come to see that his condition is no more than an exaggeration of the human condition, and if he would be free, then *everyone must be free*."[137] This is only likely to happen if "the Negro emerges as a dominating force in American life." The relationship of the civil rights and black power movements to the tremors that rocked Square society during the sixties and seventies, makes the essay seem pretty prescient indeed. Perhaps it's still the case that when a certain existentialism—a living entirely in the moment, with courage rather than security—when this frame of mind becomes dominant in American society, freedom becomes possible on a larger scale than just for the avant-garde. In any case, Mailer's idea that an embrace of the "primitive" relationship to time and the body is the essence of American counterculture is illustrated by the emergence of a surfing counterculture out of just this kind of embrace of primitivism, the moment, danger, thrill, physical pleasure, and freedom. This link between primitivism and counterculture can be traced both analytically—images of the primitive convey an embrace of pleasure and a rejection of the opposite of pleasure, work, and American counterculture involves a rejection of the repression of work above all else—and also historically in the case we're looking at, among others.

But before we examine the history of this link in the context of surfers, we need to point out something that Norman Mailer, in his defensive masculinism, couldn't see. Mailer was so insistent that Hip be Manly that he disavows what every red-blooded American authoritarian patriarch type knows in his gut about bohemians, beatniks, and hippies—they're *queer*. Or at least, very feminized characters. We can't look to Mailer to make explicit the radical sexual politics that we've seen in the link between the primitive and the bohemian—he's too defensive, even if he does include "homosexuals" on his approved list of social deviants. But if we want to understand the *content* of repressed sexuality, we have to return to Freud. For classical psychoanalysis, the primal layer of erotic energy is what Freud called "polymorphous perverse"—we want sexual pleasure from everything, on and in all parts of the body. Only later does a gendered version of "legitimate" sexuality get put on this original layer. Still, in our uncivilized erotic instinct, all of us have both masculine and feminine desires. We all want to be boys *and* be girls. Deep down, we're all perverts.

The primitive sexuality depicted in the images we've seen of surfing from Hawaii are overwhelmingly "polymorphous perverse" in just this way. The images don't just depict sexual freedom within a regime of compulsory heterosexuality where girls are nurturing and boys are dominating. The images are radical precisely because of their gender-bending nature. In fact, if there is one thing that is more apparent than anything else in the images of surfing and of beach boys that were broadcast from Hawaii, it's the great pleasures of transcending traditional barriers of gender identity. Like the native women who dominate some of the earliest woodcuts depicting surfing, the flapper-style women are depicted with the phallic surfboard in positions of pleasure and power. And the men—or "boys"—are heavily feminized. Sexually submissive to the tourist women, posing on the beach, performing pretty songs, wearing leis in their hair, smiling, living for pleasure, without planning or control, and, above all, surfing. In all depictions of surfing from any era, the quality of "yielding" power to the wave, of the non-depletive "dance" of surfing, of the centrality of the "wipe-out" or having the wave throw you around, all the feminine imagery associated with surfers, should not be missed. In other words, in surfing, girls rule. Similarly, the feminized sexuality that comes through in images of surfing men is one of its biggest draws, for men who miss out on feminine, receptive, in Jack London's words, "yielding" physical pleasures in regular, patriarchal life.[138]

Then as now, queer is dangerously compelling. The allure of these images has inspired collective action: people flocked to Hawaii, chasing the image that had so tantalized them. But even more: groups of men were inspired to try to reproduce the life of the beach boys on the California coast starting in the first decades of the twentieth century. They became the seed of a massive, global subculture of surfers—a subculture animated by values and norms that are ultimately contrary to the dictates of objective consciousness, to the work ethic, to all Puritan morality, and to the alienating logic of capital. It's in this translation, of repressed instinct into subculture, that we can see the effective politics of pop culture images developing. Because, as Stanley Aronowitz points out in a friendly corrective to Marcuse's theory in *Eros and Civilization*, repressed instinct is not itself a sufficient condition for the possibility of social transformation. (This point is implicit in Mailer's argument as well). In an essay pointing up the subversiveness of popular culture in addition to its domesticating qualities, Aronowitz ends by arguing that the possibility of liberation depends not on instinct but on culture:

> Whatever possibility exists for the rise of autonomous political and social perspectives among the recent generations of workers must be ascribed to those *pockets of resistance against the prevailing forms of society*, rather than to the latent, liberatory content of the instinctual structure . . . young people develop beliefs and desires for social action that counter those that have been handed down from above . . . the question of whether young workers will rebel against the authority relations of the workplace depends largely on the question of whether they have developed the modes of social life that counter the prevailing culture.[139]

That's why it's so key that these images didn't remain at the level of fantasy: they inspired subcultural activity aimed at living the fantasy. Next we must turn to the youth culture that was built from the material of unrepressed libido in all its forms that we've seen in the image and activity of the surfer. We'll see the way in which the purveyors of popular culture continued to use the surfer to play to the desire for pleasure, even if it meant being a class traitor to their neo-Puritan brethren. Just as neo-Puritans of every era rightly fear, this free sexuality, Eros, when unleashed, has no tolerance for the discipline of work. The more mainland popular culture broadcast the allure of the image of the surfer far and wide, the more young people *did* come to develop "the modes of social life" counter to the "prevailing culture," otherwise known as the repressive work-discipline that capital demands. In the early decades of the twentieth century, groups of people who'd been inspired by the Hawaiian fantasy of primitive pleasure and freedom came to form the foundation of the surfing subculture on the mainland.

CA specifically

3 The Oceanic Feeling
Surfing's Lost Paradise

One of several important ways that popular commercial culture (which includes *all* cultural production aimed at making a profit) accomplishes the collective behavior its purveyors aim to inspire is by tapping into the power of *memory.* The cultural impact of nostalgia—the memory of and desire for a lost Eden—is considerable, and it's particularly prominent in the image of the surfer. In psychoanalytic terms, we're all shaped fundamentally by a sense of paradise lost because our most primal memories involve the total connection between self and other, between inside and outside, that characterizes the original, oceanic feeling. Whether it's the experience of connection and gratification that characterizes the womb, or the baby nursing at the breast, or even a phylogenetic, cellular memory of early life forms in the ocean, what is *original* to the personality is the oceanic feeling of connection and plenitude. Unconsciously, we all continue to be driven by this memory, this desire to return to what is symbolized so powerfully by the ocean.

In constantly alluding to a lost Paradise, images of surfing exude the promise of redemption, of a return to the oneness with the world that Freud calls "oceanic." (It's striking that surfing is an enduring, massive presence in American life—and it's constantly overlooked as such. Sort of like the unconscious, which is also a massive presence in life but tends to go unacknowledged and unexamined except by psychoanalysis.) Early California surf images are some of the most prominent and meaningful representations of lost paradise in the American popular imagination. Partly this is because they've been so widely disseminated by the commercial forces that are clear about their appeal.

Surf culture on the beach at Waikiki was fed by the commercial promoters and journalists who understood its appeal and used it to make money selling newspapers, tickets, tourism, and anything else they could think of. The same dynamic was taking place on the beach in California, where commercial promoters used surfing to promote and to sell. In 1907, George Freeth, the "bronzed mercury" of whom Jack London had written while on the beach at Waikiki, was brought to the California coast by Henry Huntington, who was the first major commercial developer there. Huntington was developing beach resorts and laying the Pacific Electric railroad to take people there—so he had quite a bit of money riding on the success of the beach as an attraction. At Redondo Beach, Huntington hired Freeth as a lifeguard, swim instructor, and to "walk on water." Freeth gave surfing demonstrations at Huntington's new beach resort, the massive "Redondo Plunge." This beachside pool could hold 2,000 swimmers at a time, and it's estimated that Freeth introduced the wonder of surfing to thousands upon thousands of visitors, in addition to the millions of readers of the California and national papers that breathlessly followed Freeth's every move. And Freeth surfed all along the California coast, just as a newly mobile population was taking advantage of its ability to go to the beach. Freeth continued working for beach resorts up and down the coast, in San Diego and Ocean Beach, advertising the resorts with great success by using the compelling image of surfing. Once again, commercial forces found that surfing had a powerful attractive force to the masses, and could be successfully tapped into to inspire people to act collectively—in this case, just like at Waikiki where Freeth started—to head to the beach. Freeth died at thirty-five of complications from the Spanish Flu, after a heroic career as lifeguard, dramatically saving scores of swimmers and boaters from sure drowning at sea.

It was left to Duke Kahanamoku and Tom Blake to continue the work that they'd shared with Freeth, which included well-publicized feats of heroic lifesaving. But it was surfing, and not lifeguarding, that in both cases was picked up by commercial promoters, for its intrinsically alluring properties. Tom Blake is considered the founding father of California surf culture, in part because he was the quintessential surfer—the link between the ancient Hawaiian culture he idolized and the surfer counterculture that he inspired—and in part because of his tireless activities promoting surfing in the mass media. And like the experience of early surfing's other major promoters—Ford, Kahanamoku, Freeth—he didn't have a difficult time. For these men, their desire to spread the "stoke" of surfing (and the innovations in ocean lifesaving that came from surfers, especially Blake) took form at just the right historical moment, when they rode the wave of commercialized popular culture's ascent in modern life.

TOM BLAKE

In terms of concrete historical connections, the figure of Tom Blake is a key conduit between early twentieth-century beach boy culture (and the ancient Hawaiian culture that inspired it) and the California surf subculture that began to form in the twenties and thirties and exploded into American pop culture in the fifties and sixties. A legendary figure, Blake personally innovated most of what's associated with surfers to this day: he was the first to experiment with making better surfboards, revolutionizing board design in the process with lightweight materials and the fin; he was the first to build waterproof camera housing and inaugurated the tradition of surfers documenting themselves and their friends; and he was the first among countless surfers to come to write a book on the history and pleasures of surfing. In addition, his sun-bleached, rumpled personal style became the prototypical beachcomber look, still in effect today.

As the oft-told story goes, Blake was a young boy from Wisconsin who went to see a movie one night in 1920. The newsreel that played just prior to the film showed a surfing Duke Kahanamoku doing an exhibition for rapt audiences who'd never seen surfing before. In a serendipitous turn of events, in the very same movie theatre the night that Tom Blake was watching the Duke newsreel, Duke and some friends, who'd happened to be in town, had ducked into the theatre to see themselves on the screen. Blake was incredibly taken by Duke on the screen, and was simply over the moon when he ran into him after the show. He introduced himself, and within a short time had moved to California, and later to Hawaii, to surf and swim full time.

Blake—blond, tan, handsome—became one of Hawaii's most accomplished surfers and revolutionized the sport by inventing a "hollow board" that was far lighter and more maneuverable than previous surfboards. (He also promoted its use for lifesaving, for which it was widely adopted, as well as inventing and promoting other devices, such as the lifesaver, that revolutionized water rescue.) He got the idea from an ancient board at the Bishop museum (more evidence for the fact that the twentieth-century development of surfing depended on a reverence for primitive Hawaiian tradition.) He was also a great promoter of surfing. He'd published articles about surfing in the *Mid-Pacific Magazine* and *Paradise of the Pacific* in 1930, and in 1935, he published his book, *Hawaiian Surfboard*,[1] which traced the ancient and more recent history of Hawaiian surfing and described aspects of the surf culture for readers on the mainland.

In the same year, he published photos of surfing in Hawaii in *National Geographic*[2], accompanied by a few thousand words that he'd also submitted. The spread featured a now-legendary photo of a smiling, shirtless Blake standing with six boards that he'd built, several of them more than twice his height. Also featured was a photo of Amelia Earheart, waiting for flight weather and riding an outrigger canoe with a friend and two beach boys, an oar in her hand and an ear to ear smile on her face as the canoe speeds down the face of a wave. Many of the photos are of women, as a matter of fact, in typically powerful poses with captions like "Girls as well as men enjoy the sport." Blake also had articles appear in *Popular Mechanics* and *Popular Science* over the next two years.

All this publicity coincided with Blake being in California to follow in Duke and George Freeth's footsteps by promoting the spread of surfing. Blake was on a year-long tour to, among other things, show lifeguards on both coasts the value of his new hollow board for lifesaving purposes, as well as to introduce beachgoers to the pleasures of riding for sport. Blake became a celebrity, known as "Ye Olde Beachcomber," and his easygoing, in-tune-with-nature lifestyle became forever linked with surf culture. This easygoing surfer lifestyle is broadcast in all Blake's work. In *Hawaiian Surfboard*, he wrote that "someone expresses my sentiments very well in these simple lines:

> 'along the shore I wander, free,
> a beach comber at Waikiki,
> where time worn souls who seek in vain,
> hearts ease, in vagrant, wondering train.
>
> A beach comber from choice, am I,
> Content to let the world drift by,
> Its strife and envy, pomp and pride,
> I've tasted, and am satisfied.'"[3]

Blake's book, articles, and appearances are largely credited with providing the inspiration for the California beach subculture that took hold on the coast between 1935 and 1942. Although the imperatives of war would interrupt the growth of the surfing life temporarily, this was just a small blip in a trajectory of surfing that had begun in ancient Polynesia, been resurrected at Waikiki, and exploded in California.

Blake is a concrete link both backward and forward in surf culture. He's a white man, inspired by a beach boy, who develops a reverence for ancient Hawaiian culture *and* creates the outlines of the California subculture that references it—in large part precisely because of his work, *Hawaiian Surfboard*, and his promotional and innovative activities. Although the first printing of *Hawaiian Surfboard* was very limited, the book was extremely influential because of who read it. It's been said of the Velvet Underground that only ten people bought their first album, but each one of them started a band. The impact of *Hawaiian Surfboard* is similar. It wasn't exactly a bestseller, but many who did read it moved to the beach and gave birth to the surfing counterculture in California. These young (mostly) men were hugely inspired by Tom Blake, in whom primitivism and counterculture came together and were broadcast for all to see. Consider this passage:

> Waikiki Beach has been kind to me. The native Hawaiians have been kind. I have had the honor of riding the big surfs with these Hawaiians—I have sat at their luaus—watched their most beautiful women dance the hulas—I have been invited into their exclusive Hui Nalu surfriding club—a club for natives only. I have held the honor position (bow seat) riding waves in the outrigger canoe—the honor position (holding down the outrigger) on the sailing canoe. I have been initiated into the secrets of spear fishing far out on the coral reefs.

> I have learned much from these people.
>
> Acquaintances in the States have asked me why I bury myself in the Hawaiian islands. The reason is because I like it. It fits my nature, it is life's compensation for a nature such as mine. I like it because I can live simple and quietly here . . . I can dress as I please, for comfort . . . I can keep one hundred per cent sun tan here the year around, rest and sleep for hours in the wonderful sunshine each day.
>
> . . . I like it because of the natural beauty of everything here, the very blue sky, very white clouds, very green mountains, clothed in foliage to their ridges. My greatest pleasure in life is through my eyes so why should I stay around Main Street or Broadway? The coco palms waving in the clean trade winds, the colors of the water on the coral reef, greet my eyes each day as I near the beach and when the giant waves of the Kalahuewehe surf are breaking white, far from shore, it means royal sport is waiting and I actually break into a run to get to the Outrigger Club, don trunks and get out my favorite surfboard of teak wood. I like the opportunity of studying and seeing the great mixture of races gathered here, each one retaining many of their old customs of eating, dress, and living. I pick a custom or two from each race to use at my convenience. Perhaps it is the Buddhist religion of the Chinese—the poi eating and surfriding of the Hawaiians—the raw peanut eating of the Filipinos—the happiness, enthusiasm and appreciation with which the Japanese meet their daily duties. . . . [4]

All value judgments aside about the white fascination with ancient Hawaiian customs, or about "picking a custom or two from each race to use" at his "convenience," this passage is one of many examples in the book of the link between Western appropriation of the culture of the "Other" and the building of a counterculture. In the words of Blake biographer Gary Lynch: "Tom Blake is the obvious link between the ancient South Pacific watermen and the twentieth-century Anglo watermen . . . he understood and adopted the aloha frame of mind . . . at the same time Albert Einstein was finishing his accepted e=mc2 theory, Tom Blake was carving 'Nature=God' into the sandy bluffs of what is now Malibu . . ."[5] And Drew Kampion says of Blake: "vegetarian and pantheistic, he was the prototype for an emerging lifestyle."[6]

Both his view of the natives and his personal image are prototypical of the early California surf culture. His admiring words about Hawaii were widely disseminated at the time, as were some of the photographs he took of Hawaii's rolling waves and smiling natives. The most striking of his photos are several in which two or three young Hawaiian fellows are climbing up the thin, swayed over stalk of a palm tree. They look like a graceful hybrid of human and animal, natural and simple as can be. Clearly, this is how Blake saw, and admired, the natives.

The photos of Blake himself that were widely circulated during the 1930s and 1940s in the American popular press are quite striking as well. For one thing, a look at these photos shows how influential Blake's style was on the California subculture that he helped to grow and document. Bleach-blond, tousled hair, tan, healthy skin, wearing light-colored, baggy, simple clothing—Blake epitomized the relaxed, carefree look that is associated with the beach to this day. Another theme that ties together the photos of Blake is that we see again the typically feminine proclivity of surfers to preen and pose for the camera, and the camera's love for surfers, especially the commercial camera. Blake was in dozens of Hollywood movies early in his career, and the photos attest to this. He knows how to affect a striking pose, and he does it quite a bit in the surviving photos that document his life. This can't be seen as accidental, either: the self-portraits that he took just after filming his first feature in 1922 are classic, artistic and erotic celebrations of the grace of the (practically nude) male body—on the beach, of course. And a few of the photos taken of him in Hawaii in 1926 are artfully staged nudes. According to Gary Lynch, who interviewed Blake extensively about each of the surviving photos, "discreet nude photographs were fairly common among surfers of the period. Nude photos of Duke Kahanamoku have even surfaced in the surf-memorabilia market."[7]

As the inventor of many of the most significant lifesaving innovations in history, which were immediately taken up by the Coast Guard and lifeguards, Blake got more press than the average surfer, except maybe his good friend Duke Kahanamoku. All over the country, newspaper articles chronicled his countless competitive swimming and surfing wins and the successful use of his inventions, and photos of Blake surfing and paddling were used in the advertisements for his hollow boards (in which the word "pleasure" is repeated over and over again).[8] That the items were featured as being "Genuine Authentic Tom Blake Approved" shows what a celebrity "Ye Olde Beachcomber" had become.

In this way, his essentially bohemian outlook was broadcast far and wide as synonymous with the surfer lifestyle. And it's important to note that his bohemianism embraced popular culture as a means to spread the joy of surfing. The original surf bum was neither anti-competition, nor anti-commercialism, nor anti-mass media. In fact, just the opposite—he saw all of it as toward the greater glory of surfing, or God. Blake was the organic intellectual of the early surfer, making explicit and circulating their reverence for ancient Hawaii, and for nature, and their disdain for "normal" ways of life. According to Tommy Zahn, a protégé of Blake's and a famous fifties surfer in his own right, "Tom has seen it all. He was the most significant link between Hawaii and US mainland surfing—much more than George Freeth or Duke . . . in his lifetime, Blake has emerged as a bona fide cult figure . . . one aspect of his lifestyle was . . . giving yourself more time, more *freedom*—and freedom is a big part of what Blake is all about. His life was not . . . cluttered up with all the garbage of the basic nine to five trap . . ."[9] Blake once said that "my own philosophy is embodied in these few lines:

> 'what god has given to the earth,
> Let them the earth enjoy,
> And by the grace of god,
> Let not my hand destroy.'"

Blake exhorted his readers and friends to "settle for what harmony we have and enjoy it, and consider the magnificent potential of body, mind, and thought. For heaven on earth is a state of consciousness."[10] These were the countercultural ideas—based on a fascination with the pleasure of the primitive, a connection with nature, and an insistence on the extraordinary in life—that were disseminated with Blake's image. Did they turn people on? Did they ever.

Blake himself was quite aware of his affinity with the counterculture. Later in his life, he explicitly reached out to its members, writing in his 1968 tract, *Voice of the Wave*:

> A graybeard surfrider presents some "way out" ideas for the younger generation to contemplate: there is more than meets the eye to the deep water swells as they march majestically across the sea, to the silent drums of the atom . . . the surf rider has this going for him and he experiences a peculiar joy and inner satisfaction in putting this force to work under a board. This may be because that force is a spiritual, a divine force that has been in production by nature or God for a long time. why say nature or God? Just this: over the years, the close association with waves of all kinds, coupled with a religious background, has convinced this old surf rider that nature is synonymous with God . . . the same formula applies to all things; each has a bit of the divine power to sustain it; be it an atom, a wave or man. For proof of this nature is god concept, we have but to analyze a wave. Its water molecules are composed of atoms of a specific kind . . . each water atom, and there are billions in the smallest wave, is a model of order, harmony and rhythm; thus the atom becomes a key point of reference to logic, to right action, in judging the wave as well as all problems in life. Is it any wonder then, that the surf rider gets such satisfaction from riding a wave? For the brief period of the ride, he has this god-given energy going for him, instead of passing by him . . . ancient Hawaiian tradition tells us they felt likewise . . . [11]

So Blake not only had an affinity with the counterculture that we can see in hindsight, but in 1968 he moved expressly to link his own ideas, and surfing itself, with the "way out" values of the counterculture. Later, he wrote *Voice of the Atom*, probably over about 10 years, a metaphysical tract along the same lines, which was published in 1988.

A handwritten jotting from 1968 reads: "When I was a young man, I fell from social grace, or rather was pushed into deep water. Thereafter I became a rebel of the society that had so taken advantage of a well-meaning youth. I soon found that deep water supports a rebel, if he has the will and ability to swim . . ."[12]

THE HALCYON DAYS

The beginning of nearly every book and documentary about surfing begins with two founding myths: one, the story of the surf-centered culture of the ancient Hawaiians, and two, the story of what Drew Kampion calls the "halcyon days," the "seed culture" of pre-*Gidget* California surfers. Because the latter group modeled themselves on the former (as interpreted by the beach boys, who were invoking their own mythic past by deploying the image of the Hawaiian waterman and claiming to be descended from Hawaiian kings), the two cultures look extremely similar. The smiling faces, the absence of images of paid employment, the Hawaiian signifiers, the somewhat deviant sexuality, and, of course, the image of the "natural"—natural abundance, the ocean, and its barely-clothed denizens. This neo-primitive culture came to occupy a very large place in the American imagination, and a mythical one in the surf subculture itself.

Both of the founding stories are essentially tales of a perfect paradise, lost. (Crowds and development are said by surfers to have spoiled both Waikiki and Southern California; this is why the surf safari to far-flung beaches continues to be a major part of surf culture. The search for the perfect, uncrowded wave has never let up.) Both have been invoked in pop culture for commercial use, and in both instances the commercial dissemination of these stories has formed the inspiration for a new countercultural group. In essence, the inspirational, mythical California images portray a life without alienation—the alienation of individual identity, of rigid gender expectations, and between human being and nature.

The press in the 1930s and 1940s did seem clear that these surfers were consciously modeling their lives on their own founding mythology—a hybrid story made up of ancient Hawaiian kings and twentieth-century beach boys. The relationship between the Southern California surfers and the Hawaiian beach boys, especially, is made explicit in nearly all of these articles. The surfer life is depicted as one of primitive simplicity, consciously harkening back to the islands. By 1954, the subculture had grown so large that the Los Angeles Times was proclaiming that "San Onofre [Is] Fast Turning Into Another Waikiki." "San Onofre enjoys the reputation all over the world not only as the surfing capital of the west coast, but also as the Waikiki of the mainland. This latter claim is based upon the Polynesian type of life at the San Onofre surfing colony and its great similarity to the colorful existence of the beach boys of Hawaii." Because many of the

San Onofre surf club members "cannot commute daily from their homes," when the waves are "humping," "most of the club's members sleep in their panel trucks or in the back of their passenger cars on specially constructed beds or in their sleeping bags on the beach. The panel trucks are a work of art, in some cases rivaling the craftsmanship of expensive house trailers . . ." The author describes the club's amenities: "rest rooms and dressing rooms, several grass shacks which are used for mid-day siestas and evening luaus, and a surfboard storage rack," and goes on to describe a typical early evening: "dinner is cooked over open fires on the beach or on stoves in the trucks.

> After the dishes are washed and put away, the colony gathers around a huge bonfire for an evening of song and dance. Soon the melodious plinking of ukeleles and the strumming of guitars interrupt the monotonous sound of the waves lapping against the shore. An occasional impromptu Polynesian dance by one of the girls is met with ear-splitting war cries by members of the male population. On weekends these luaus gather momentum and many times last all through the day and night and into the next day, until the participants fall asleep or until a run of big surf brings them back to reality. The basic dress at San Onofre is the Hawaiian-type bathing suit, or cutoff levis or white pants. Shoes are unheard of, day or night. Beach towels wrapped around the waist in sarong style are worn by the men in the evening or during the day when their trunks are wet. Out on their boards they will wear almost anything, from coconut hats to seaweed leis. Most of the members have Hawaiian or English nicknames by which they are commonly known. In fact, many members do not know their fellow surfers by any name but Hammerhead or Hi-ho Silver or the Viking.[13]

Also, all the California surfers prided themselves on making the pilgrimage to Hawaii at least once a year, if not more. The identification with "native" life was nourished over the years and decades by the constant traveling between California and Hawaii by Tom Blake and the others. According to Drew Kampion, "stowing away to Hawaii became a right of passage for surfers right up until the era of $75 airfares in the early sixties."[14] And according to Craig Stecyk, in the evenings, "surfers tended to congregate at clubs like the Hula Hut, the Club Zamboanga, the Hawaiian Paradise, Sweeny's Tropicana, the Coconut Grove, and the Holo Holo, that specialized in true Hawaiian music."[15] In making yearly and twice-yearly pilgrimages to Hawaii (where a parallel subculture was flourishing all over the islands), playing Hawaiian music on ukeleles on the beach, hanging out in thatched beach shacks, living on the beach for weeks at a time, and espousing the concept of *aloha*—a feminine, yielding, welcoming, free love—as a guiding principle of their lives, they were invoking a mythical past from which to launch their own countercultural challenge to the man in the gray flannel suit. So just as these early surfers have become central to surfing's founding mythology, they were using the power of memory and primitive desire in deploying their own founding mythology. For these surfers as for the generations that came after them, ancient Hawaii provided a cultural touchstone, a (largely imaginary) social location from which to ground their own lifestyles and implicitly oppose those of mainstream American life. From very early, like other incarnations of the compelling image, these surfers gained popular attention far out of proportion to their actual numbers.

A prominent characteristic of the popular press coverage of these early surfers is that the photos of a group of people riding on one wave far outnumber photos of any individual surfer on a wave. Surfers were presented to the public as a collective basically as soon as they became one on the California coast. Much of the earliest press coverage of the California surfers had covered them in their capacity as lifeguards—the only profession that allowed them to basically live on the beach and surf whenever the waves were good. They were usually described as dashing heroes, and in many of the photos that accompanied the brief stories, the early surfer look comes through: men, on the beach, standing in front of their surfboards, tan, strong, frequently laughing, and nearly always photographed as a group.[16] For instance, a photo spread in the *Los Angeles Times Sunday Supplement* during 1931 entitled "Riders of Sunset Seas," features a Tom Blake photo of four male surfers about to catch a wave. This is certainly similar to the images of the Hawaii beach boys, much of whose pleasure in life was depicted as coming from their tightly-knit group, singing and drinking together, hanging out at the beach together, etc.[17] What's reflected is what Roy Rosenzweig calls a working-class ethos of collectivity—made up of countercultural values of mutuality, solidarity, and rowdy fun, which are in stark contrast to the Puritan work ethic and competitive individualism encouraged by the bosses.[18]

One of the earliest journalistic articles devoted to surfers was published in the *LA Times* in 1911, and in it, we see the gender politics that have defined surfing from the start. Entitled "Venice Girls Ride Surf-Boards With as Much Skill as Boys,"[19] the article hails the "dauntless young suffragettes . . . [who] seem bound that no mere man shall beat them at anything." Two photos depict "Miss Frances Guihan," called "commodore of the surfboard fleet," or the "new bevy of girl riders." She's wearing a short-sleeved dress, quite abbreviated for the mainland of that time, paddling her board in one shot, looking focused and powerful, and in another, posing joyfully with the board, nearly twice her height. She is the quintessential pre-flapper of turn of the century America. Another *LA Times* article from 1912 entitled "Riding Surf-Board Thrills: George Freeth is Teaching Girls at Redondo, Pretty Miss Says it is Best Sport in the World,"[20] features a photo of a grinning young barefoot woman in a skirt pulled up above her knees, pulling powerfully on a fishing rod on which she seems to have a big bite. The article focuses on the young women's proficiency with all ocean sports, but surfing is identified as the most difficult, thrilling, and impressive to watch. "The exciting Hawaiian sport, surf-board riding, so easy for the native Hawaiian and so difficult for the American, has been taken up by some of the summer girls here, and judging by their perseverance they mean to master the feat or die in the attempt. These girls are probably the only women in the country who ride the surf board, and but few men have learned the art of handling the board." The majority of the article, under the heading, "Requires Nerve," focuses admiringly on the physical grace, power, and bravery of the young women. No shrinking violets, these.

A 1919 article discussing the growing popularity of surfing and also mentioning Freeth features two photographs, each one featuring both a man and a woman surfing with equal proficiency.[21] Another 1923 article features a large photo of "dainty dancer" Helen Pachaud "engaged in a playful stunt with a surf-board," upon beholding which the closest lifeguard apparently fainted. Pachaud is grinning mischievously as she balances, one leg in the air behind her, on a surfboard, most of which is up in the air.[22] Another example is a 1934 full page photo of "Miss Patricia Sousa, daughter of Mr. and Mrs. John Philip Sousa of LaJolla," who is shown smiling out at the water, carrying her surfboard with ease and grace, under the headline "Surf Rider Awaits Tidal Wave."[23] In a 1939 ad for a Blake custom surfboard, reading, "Hawaiian Paddle Boards," the image we see is of a strong, laughing blond woman paddling a board nearly three times her height. The board is at a forty-five degree angle to the ad copy, conveying a sense that the woman is paddling without fear down a steep water hill.[24] A 1940 *Life* magazine article, "Surf Riding on California Beach is a Favorite Summertime Sport,"[25] features photos of Nana Wigton, "24 and a Los Angeles model," bodysurfing. The danger of the sport and the skill necessary to master it are the themes of the piece. And puff pieces featuring Hollywood stars and socialites during the 1920s and 1930s, like "How Southern California's Most Photographed Girl Keeps Her Figure,"[26] feature now-familiar to us images of strong, smiling, surfer women. One especially powerful image depicts the woman surfing with her arms in the air, fists clenched and smiling. Over and over we see that from the start, the image of surfing has included an image of a joyful, powerful female.

And one or more happily feminized males. One of the biggest articles was published in the *LA Times Sunday Magazine* during 1937. Entitled, "Surfboards, Ahoy!,"[27] the article cites the Hawaiian influence on the California "boys" who practice the "fastest-growing sport" of surfing: "it was the Hawaiians who really developed surfing"; they are characterized as "a natural, pleasure-loving race" who've inspired the surfers. The article is accompanied by a set of very large photos taken by surfer/photographer Doc Ball. The one at the top features three surfers riding in graceful, ballet-like poses, two of whom are riding just next to one another. One is looking down at the water, his arm resting on the shoulder of the other surfer, who is gazing at his friend, his own arms in a graceful pose. The surfers themselves certainly approved of these depictions—in Doc Ball's own *California Surfriders*,[28] we see a photo of the surfers looking at this very article in the newspaper, enjoying their own image.

Always highlighted is the intensely compelling nature of surfing. This theme is the angle of a 1944 *National Geographic* piece entitled "Surfboarders capture California,"[29] consisting primarily of some of Doc Ball's most dramatic photos, accompanied by breathless captions. It's also the major theme of "Surfboards, Ahoy!" which calls surfers "addicts" and states that "Once the surfing bug bites them, most ordinary, sane citizens go just as goofy over the sport as Dr. Ball. Lawyers abandon their cases, doctors leave their patients and husbands desert their wives when the "grapevine" reports that the big waves are running." According to the article, "surfing gives a feeling of freedom" and because of this, it's "gaining recruits every day." And then, "this thrilling sport takes . . . a firm grip on the lives of its devotees!"

Its image was taking a firm grip on the imaginations of its beholders, too. It seems that what was so compelling about the surfer was, when you get down to it, that he (or she) symbolized the joy and freedom of libido. Consider this poem, entitled "Surf-Board Rider," and published in a 1939 issue of *American Mercury* magazine:

> Dark, against the drapery of blue,
> Cresting the darker waters of the sea,
> Straight as a mast that leans against the wind
> He comes, a god incarnate riding free! . . .
>
> . . . His is the exultation of the flesh,
> The bold transfiguration of the dust,
> A carnal stronghold for the joy of life
> Which crests adventure and at last is thrust
>
> Against a climax when the waters pour
> His gay assurance out upon the shore.[30]

Here we see once again that the image of the surfer in all his (here nearly divine) glory is quite a turn-on. The language of "thrust" and "climax," and the imagery of "flesh" and the "carnal," are linked with the concepts of adventure, the joy of life, and, most importantly, freedom. It's the archetypical image itself that demonstrates the existence of a link between freedom and sexuality in the human psyche, and the tabooed hope that a life centered around the pursuit of libidinal pleasure is actually possible. The surfer represents, quite simply, the "stronghold for the joy of life."

THE REFUSAL OF IDENTITY

Another theme that's common to every piece of newspaper and magazine coverage of the new lifestyle is a discussion of the "strange lingo" that the surfers use. In every article, the journalist mentions a few words that are incomprehensible to the common reader and have to be decoded by the writer (often erroneously, in fact). One that's always mentioned is the surfers' habit of calling a big wave a "humper" and excitedly yelling "hump up!" or "humper!" to one another when one is spotted on the horizon. A 1942 article on the California surfers in the *Christian Science Monitor* weekly magazine is actually entitled "Humper!"[31] and its main hook is the surfers' strange lingo, incomprehensible to the outside world. The article conveys the idea that the language mirrors the incomprehensibility of the activity and lifestyle of the surfers, focusing on the great danger involved in surfing the "mighty giants" that "crash" into the shore. Surfers are portrayed as being more difficult to pin down and understand than are other, "regular" folks. An aspect of the unusual lingo that's always mentioned is the fact that the surfers refer to one another by nicknames only, and that many don't even know one anothers' "real" names.

In this depiction, surfers are not only refusing conventional gender identity; they are refusing to be identified at all. In discussing the role of schools and other ideological institutions in reproducing the working class, Louis Althusser traces the role of identification in the development of the submission to authority that's necessary for becoming an obedient worker. In these institutions, people are taught to be good (that is, obedient) subjects, and to believe that their desire to be "good" comes from the inside, from the individual consciousness of each subject. Althusser's assertion is that

> all ideology hails or interpellates concrete individuals as concrete subjects, by the functioning of the category of the subject . . . [in other words] ideology "acts" or "functions" in such a way that it "recruits" subjects among the individual (it recruits them all), or "transforms" the individuals into subjects (it transforms them all) by that very precise operation which I have called *interpellation* or hailing, and which can be imagined along the lines of the most commonplace everyday police (or other) hailing: "Hey, you there!" Assuming that the theoretical scene I have imagined takes place in the street, the hailed individual will turn round. By this mere one-hundred-and-eighty-degree physical conversion, he becomes a *subject*. Why? Because he has recognized that the hail was "really" addressed to him, and that it was "really him" who was hailed (and not someone else).[32]

So the (always already interpellated) subject (and his or her subjection) is the condition for the effective reproduction of a docile working class—a bourgeois ideology is carried by a subject with a consciousness, who can be named and whose ideas are in accordance with his practices. He or she is "authentic" in this way. In Althusser's words, the individual

> *is interpellated as a (free) subject in order that he shall submit freely . . . [and] freely accept his subjection*, i.e. in order that he shall make the gestures and actions of his subjection "all by himself." *There are no subjects except by and for their subjection.* That is why they "work all by themselves."[33]

So what does it mean when a subculture is represented—as surfing always has been—as being made up of members who don't know one another's "real" names and certainly refuse to give them up to outsiders? We saw that the Waikiki beach boys were known to their clients and to the mass media (and generally to one another) not by their "given" names, but only by the nicknames that emerged within the context of their playful subculture—Panama, Steamboat, Chick, Splash, Curley. On the Southern California coast, beginning during the Depression and continuing through mid-century and on to contemporary representations of surfers, this is the case as well. In fact, every notable surfer of the prewar and interwar era was known by a nickname: Whitey Harrison, Doc Ball, Straightoff, Nellie Bly, Frenchy, Peanuts, Doaks, Swarts, Hoppy, Hammerhead, Birddog, Scobblenoggin, Gooseneck—you get the picture. This is just a sampling of the names encountered in photo captions from Doc Ball's archive of the 1930s and 1940s, and the nickname tradition is absolutely ubiquitous in all popular culture depictions of surfing to come. Althusser reminds readers that all of this takes place in a capitalist society, that is, in the context of the class struggle. We can see the refusal to be "named" as a refusal of the *subjection* that makes working-class reproduction as (as alienated, exploited workers) possible.[34] For surfers to go by funny nicknames is "irresponsible" and "inauthentic" to the extreme—because it's a sign that they are refusing to be pinned down as responsible subjects, whose "identity" can be isolated, understood, and categorized. They are refusing to give the Man an affirmation that yes, it was "really him who was hailed."

We must return again to the fact that this characteristic of surfers has been broadcast far and wide throughout the history of surfing. According to our theory, this can be explained by the fact that commercial forces broadcast images that they sense have a widespread allure, and so there is a sense among these forces—advertisers, filmmakers, tourism promoters, journalists and the newspaper publishers who want their stories to sell papers and lure people to the beach—that something about the insistence on nicknames is appealing to the masses. Why the allure? Well, when Althusser says that "there is no ideology except by and for subjects," (ideology being a representation of an imaginary relationship to the real world), he's leaning for his discussion on Jacques Lacan's psychoanalytic theory.

In *The Mirror Stage as Formative of the Function of the I,*[35] Lacan uses the metaphor of the mirror to identify the foundation of "identity." Our earliest experiences of "reality" don't involve a coherent "I" or identity to whom those experiences happen. First of all, our primary experiences are characterized by Freud's oceanic feeling—a oneness between the inside and the outside—but also, what we originally experience is fragmentary. We never see our "selves," that is, our primary experiences don't involve a self. Instead, they involve colors and sounds and touches, pieces of hands and feet and bellies and a little bit of the nose, other faces, and, especially, sensations. In the course of development, Lacan says, at some point we (symbolically) look in the mirror. We begin to "see" ourselves as a unitary being, a single identity that encompasses all of the things in the mirror that move at our mental command. But the key point for Lacan is that this identity is always alien to us at some deep level, because it didn't originate from inside us, but remains an *image* "put on" from the outside. It becomes internalized, certainly, but it always chafes us because it's not *really* us, it doesn't accord with our primary (or primal) experience.

It's alienating, too, because although this identity is supposed to encompass who we truly are, in our essence, it necessarily excludes something of what we hope, desire, or experience. This is because all identity is founded on difference. For instance, in order for me to assert my identity—the content of my "I"—I have to invoke something *other* than "I"—something different. For instance, "I am a woman." Well, this is true, but what about all the experiences I've had in which I've felt like a boy? In order for this unitary identity to be asserted, in order for me to be a "responsible" subject, one who can be "identified," I have to exclude lots and lots of other possible modes of being, many of which I may, and probably do at one time or another, desire. Many of which, also, were the contents of my experience at one or another time prior to the putting on of this alien, unitary identity. The idea is that deep down, I desire an escape from this identity, an ability to play with multiple modes of being—because again, it's my pre-consciousness, primal, connected-with-the-whole experience that I, more than anything, want to return to. This desire, which is common to everyone, resists the identification or hailing that constitutes subjection, and that Althusser says reproduces working-class domination. This is why the image of a person, or group of people, who go only by goofy, beach-inspired nicknames is so alluring. The playful use of nicknames goes against the serious "integrity" and "authenticity" that bourgeois institutions promote in order to reproduce the working class as "responsible" subjects who "work by themselves", and instead taps into the powerful primal desires that oppose this subjection.

Surfer nicknames are "irresponsible"—you can't apply for a job with a name like that. You can't report your name to the police when you've been arrested with a name like that. In fact, during the fifties and sixties, when surfers were routinely being arrested for trespassing on Marine Corps property to surf (more on this later), an often-told tale in the surf culture literature recounts how the Marines and the police constantly complained that the surfers would never give their correct names, and, of course, never carried any identification. This irresponsibility is considered, within the ideological state apparatuses like the church and especially the school, to be, as Althusser says, "wicked." It's a refusal of interpellation that can't be tolerated by the part of bourgeois culture that acts on behalf of the bosses—but that the mass media couldn't stop broadcasting all over American culture.

Although Althusser says that "it is by the installation of the ISAs [institutions of ideological repression] in which this ideology is realized and realizes itself that it becomes the ruling ideology," he also adds that "this installation is not achieved all by itself; on the contrary, it is the stake in a very bitter and continuous class struggle . . ."[36] What he's laid out is one side of the class struggle, in which capital works to beat the natural resistance to subjection out of the working class. But there is, of course, another, antagonistic side alluded to in the word "struggle" itself. And Althusser actually begins the essay with a nod to the effectivity of working-class struggle within capitalism, in the realm of reproduction, when he says that the wage is the primary means of reproduction of the working class.

It is through the wage that, according to Marx, the worker is able to replenish his or her life force to come back to work the next day (and nourish the next generation of future workers). However,

> remember that this quantity of value (wages) necessary for the reproduction of labor power is determined not by the needs of a "biological" Guaranteed Minimum Wage alone, but by the needs of a historical minimum (Marx noted that English workers need beer while French proletarians need wine)—i.e. a historically variable minimum. I should also like to point out that this minimum is doubly historical in that it is not defined by the historical needs of the working class "recognized" by the capitalist class, but by the historical needs imposed by the proletarian class struggle (a double class struggle: against the lengthening of the working day and against the reduction of wages).[37]

So although Althusser's essay is all about the effectivity of capital in the realm of reproduction, he both begins and ends his piece pointing to the importance of working-class struggle within capital, and makes clear what this struggle looks like: for freedom in time, and against scarcity in material culture. For most of those who follow Althusser in seeing mass culture as ideology, such as Stuart Ewen and Fredric Jameson, any subversive desire or struggle is, like the rebellion of the child against the father in the Oedipus story, ultimately domesticated.

However, when we look at the early images of surfers, broadcast through the ideological channels of consumer culture, what we see is something not so easily domesticated: what Stanley Aronowitz calls the counterlogic of the working class (as against the logic of capital), the refusal to internalize subjection to the discipline of work. Typical of the press coverage, the "Humper!" article mentions the employment habits of these brave surfers. "They work, those who are not yet in military service, in the post offices, the stores, theatres, the fishing tackle and bait shops, and anywhere there are jobs not more than a half mile, by preference, from the surf. Such a [rough] sea becomes an automatic holiday for experts such as these."

The refusal of work is really the central theme present throughout the image of the surfer. More than anything, it's made up of a privileging of play over work. It's the image of a life constructed in the countercultural manner of making a leisure pursuit central and relegating paid employment to the margins of existence. Examples of this representation abound, even in the early articles: a 1929 piece in the *Review of Reviews* describes the surfer as "he speeds on in the grip of a living power, luckily catching wave after wave until he is swept joyously ashore . . ."[38] For the lucky, joyful surfer, paid employment never wins against good waves: "round Honolulu run the words 'big surf' and early in the afternoon young men desert the offices." Surfers are represented as against the subjection of a separate, fixed identity and the work discipline that it makes possible; for a playful, connected-to-the world pleasure. As we'll continue to see, this insistence on freedom and refusal of work is not only the most consistent theme that we encounter in examining the image of the surfer in popular culture; it's been the most enduring.

NOSTALGIA BOOKS AND NATURAL TIME

As we've seen, the myth of island pleasure and freedom was crafted into a surfer lifestyle of actual pleasure and freedom, or certainly more of these than most Americans were experiencing during the Depression years. Now images of *that* time form part of the founding mythology of surf culture today. The photos and memories that document that time make up a piece of surfing's Edenic founding mythology—in our memories, the Hawaiian paradise transplanted to southern California. This "origin" is part of what "surfing" and "surf culture" mean in the American imagination—especially now, when the market for nostalgic historical surfing material has never been larger. Since the early nineties, more and more books and documentaries have come out that focus on this early history of surf culture.

Besides the photos taken by Tom Blake, the most important archive from this era are the photographs taken by two other surfers: Don James and John Heath "Doc" Ball. Together, the work of these men provide a rich portrait of the seed that was planted by the Hawaiian beach boys and that eventually flowered into a full-on California surf counterculture during the 1950s.

Both James and Ball credit Blake as their inspiration for beginning to document the surf life that they were living. According to Don James, "When I saw Tom Blake's surfing photos in *National Geographic* that was it. We'd go to the library and pore over Blake's stuff . . ."[39] And James's photos are not just obscure documents, dusted off out of an attic somewhere—according to Craig Stecyk, "his images have become the icons by which the sport is identified, both within and outside of the culture. A claim can be made that he is the best known surfing photographer of all time . . ." He shot covers for *Vogue* and *Der Spiegel*, and contributed to *Time, The Saturday Evening Post, Honolulu,* and *Sports Illustrated*, as well as "national television, billboards, and advertising campaigns."[40]

Doc Ball, in a recent interview, said that "Tom Blake was one of my idols—he was a hero to me—the reason for all this was that he had a set of pictures, he photographed surfers surfing there at Waikiki Beach, printed in the Los Angeles Times—I just about flipped my lid—I put them under a glass tabletop and looked at them every day and thought—I gotta get some of this. Thomas, he was an inspiration to me, the way he lived and the way he took those pictures and everything . . ." Not only that, but these guys were both inspired by Duke Kahanamoku, just as Tom Blake was: according to the 1999 documentary *Doc Ball: Surfing's Legendary Lensman,* "like his good friend Tom Blake, one meeting with Duke (when Ball was a junior lifeguard in California) cemented his relationship to the ocean."[41] The primitive fantasy that came across in Blake's photos and ideas, in the character of Duke Kahanamoku, and in surfing's genesis story more generally, inspired both the creation and the further documentation of what became yet another in a long line of stories about the lost Eden that *past* surfers always seem to represent.

There's a deep longing that's unleashed with these images. One example is the collection of Don James' *Prewar Surfing Photographs* published in 2004.[42] In Matt Warshaw's introduction, he describes how the images in the book were discovered shortly after James' death in 1996. James was 16 at the time he took the pictures, just trying to document the life that he and his young friends were living. We can imagine that Warshaw speaks for several generations of surfers when he states that "I'm pretty well inoculated against surf nostalgia," but immediately follows by admitting that "I'm set into a light trance at the notion of a Southern California beachfront without the shrieking levels of ambient information—billboards and signs, bass-thumping car stereos, ad-covered trashcans and lifeguard towers. Just 200 people, give or take, were surfing in California in 1937, when the photos in this book were taken. Did James and his friends know how good they had it?"[43]

Although Matt Warshaw, like many surfer/writers, is highly critical of the commercialization of surfing and its image, he does point out, unwittingly, the way in which commercially disseminated images of surfing (like the ones in the James book—which was produced for profit on a market) tend to have an effect that may undermine the work discipline that capital demands.

> Linger on these pages for more than a few minutes, and it's just about impossible not to drift off and wonder what it was like to live and surf in southern California during the Roosevelt years; to hustle gas coupons and drive traffic-free down Highway One in a dingy Hudson roadster, stopping to poach avocados and oranges from roadside orchards; to casually pull lobsters and abalone from the rocky coves of Laguna Beach, and earn a few extra bucks by guiding Prohibition-busting rumrunners into the bay channels.[44]

Such thoughts can't help but compel a questioning—why can't life be more like that? When did things become so complicated?—that alienates the audience enough from contemporary life that they're able to imagine that it could be different. This is an important rupture—because it's a necessary (but of course not sufficient) condition for the emergence of something new.

Another collection of James's photos, published in 1996, is even more expressive of the easy beach lifestyle that always seems to accompany the activity of surfing. The sepia-toned shots depict a group of relaxed people enjoying themselves. They look tan and healthy, and seem to smile with a light behind their eyes. They are frequently laughing, and generally drinking beer. And although surfing is frequently described as a very solitary pursuit, these photos, like most surf photos, are almost always shots of people hanging out *together*. James is a skilled photographer, and is responsible for many of the innovations that made good surfing photography possible, so the pictures of surfing really give a feel for the speed and lightness, that ineffable feeling that surfing gives you, which surfers describe as the stoke.

"Doc" Ball's photos provide a third piece of the archive from that time. Ball's photos were similarly world-renowned: they were published in *Life, Parade, Panorama, the Encyclopedia Brittanica, National Geographic,* and the *London Daily Mirror*. According to Doc, he published his seminal 1946 collection, *California Surfrider*, because "the kids started demanding the photos that I took of them—so I figured I'd get all the negatives together and make a book."[45] Like the beach boys that came before them, surfers have always loved posing for the camera and watching themselves on film, which is why a major part of surf culture involves watching footage of other surfers, and it has been this way for a long time. For instance, Doc describes the founding of the legendary Palos Verdes Surfing Club as being primarily for the purpose of watching the moving films of surfing that Doc himself was taking. His 16mm film, also titled *California Surfrider*, contains some of the most compelling early moving footage of surfing's halcyon days. Taken together, all of these images, of Blake, Ball, and James, display the content of a very powerful fantasy of the genesis of American surfing—its lost paradise.

In this paradise, nobody works, boys can be girls and girls can be boys, there is complete freedom and utter abundance, and, above all, the purpose of life is to enjoy the moment. Consider James' 2004 collection. On first look, the thirty-seven photos in the book are all nearly the same. One boy surfing a wave. Two. Five. Maybe ten. In some ways, it seems repetitive and a little boring on the first look. But as you view the photos, something happens. Warshaw describes it thus: "the photos in this book are . . . slowed way down, into a kind of visual tree-time. They require a calmer, mellower gaze, and the further you drop into the page-viewing Zen, the richer James' prewar surfing world becomes."[46] There really is a certain mesmerizing, calming quality to perusing the photos of graceful surfers riding perfect waves on unspoiled sunny beaches. In this way, a commercially produced image of early surf culture gives us a certain access to what was so compelling about "the life." A countercultural moment is inspired by the photos: the clock time of industrial life (and the even more frenetic hyper time of post-industrial life) is erased and a different, more natural time-sense is encouraged. Looking at the photos inspires the same kind of inefficient experience of time that the surfers seemed to be living, and that E. P. Thompson cites as a major characteristic of what he calls a "bohemian revolt" against the dictates of capital.

ABUNDANCE AND ECOLOGY

This isn't surprising. These guys were, in many ways, an early seed of the counterculture. Everything that these early twentieth-century surfers embraced went counter to the spirit of hard work and competitive individualism that define bourgeois values. They made the beach, not the factory or the office, the center of their lives. They surfed all day, every day, and lived off the fat of the land, gleaning ripe fruit from picked-over orchards and pulling abalone and twenty-pound lobsters from the sea for nightly campfire dinners. They sold their time for money—on Hollywood films, running rum during Prohibition, and fishing for the local fancy restaurants—only when they needed cash for gasoline or beer.

In addition to the ubiquitous Hawaiian references—the thatched huts, the ukeleles—some other significant themes emerge from these representations of the early surf subculture. What's most apparent from even a casual perusal of these photos is the simple abundance that surrounded the subculture. This theme is related to the others, in that part of the embrace of the image of primitive simplicity and leisure is an acceptance of the idea of natural abundance. This contrast—to the artificial scarcity that capital needs to perpetuate in order to keep people working and striving—is particularly striking given that so many of these photographs were taken during the Great Depression. Scarcity was the order of the day. As far as most Americans understood, the *entire world* had been plunged into *massive crisis*. There simply *was not enough* for everyone. But for the surfers, things were different. According to Stecyk, "Don [James] recounted tales of catching reef fish and pulling huge abalone and twenty-pound lobsters from the sea that were then boiled over beach fires. He and his friends would raid orange groves for all the fruit they could eat."[47] The Great Depression was supposed to have quashed the irresponsible exuberance that characterized the Roaring Twenties. Americans, who'd spent the twenties buying the spectacular new consumer culture on credit, were now supposed to weather the crisis times of high unemployment with a newfound austerity. (In 2009, this sounds awfully familiar.) Seems that news, though, didn't make it out to the beach.

(It didn't really make it to the cities and farms, either—Americans at large were not so docile as capital might have hoped during the crisis. The unemployed took to the streets, effectively demanding transfer payments from the state, and the employed, who were supposed to be "grateful" for the alienating job that they did have, struck to create a newly militant labor movement and the organizations that reflected it. Crisis didn't make people desperate and docile. Capital was forced to admit that "on its own," it was unable to guarantee a rate of profit that would keep it from collapsing, and the Keynesian era was ushered in. Changes in the way that capital assures itself profitability are responses to its opponent—working class resistance, to alienating work and to austerity. I'm arguing here that when we look at all this working-class resistance during the Depression, we might want to expand our view to include the Southern California coast. Not only for reasons of historical accuracy, but also because the image of these surfers is one that is *alive* in American culture today in a way that, for better or worse, the sit-down strikes and mass demonstrations for unemployment insurance simply are not.)

When the surfers did need money, generally for gasoline to drive to other remote beaches, the "locals who knew both the lay of the land and the nuances of the sea always found lucrative employment functioning as guides, facilitators, and transporters in the underground economy"[48] of the illegal import trade. During the 1920s, this had meant running booze from Canadian boats to movie stars hanging out at the coast, and from that time forward "enterprising surf fishermen filled orders for copious amounts of lobster, crab, and fish for top restaurants, studio parties, and society dinners." Also, many of the guys were lifeguards during the summer, when, according to Stecyk, "there was no lifeguarding profession to speak of . . ."[49]

And of course, there were always the movies. Stecyk again: "golden boys seldom went hungry in this land of illusion, where looking good was a form of currency in itself."[50] Surfing actors like Duke, Buster Crabbe, Peter Lawford, and Johnny Weismuller hooked up their buddies with day jobs on films, with which, according to Don James, "you could pocket a hundred bucks a day."[51] Here was continued the revered surfer tradition, begun by Hawaii beach boys and continued today by pro surfers, of making money for being what you are primarily—a surfer. Paid work is always secondary to "the life." (Here is where the term "surf bum" originated. According to Doc Ball, "we sort of developed a whole new language—that was why people called us 'surf bums' and everything—they couldn't understand our language, I guess . . ."[52])

The most prized entity among these surfers couldn't be bought anyway. Waves were in abundance on the Southern California coast, and the energy to ride them came easy, from peaches and avocados plucked out of roadside orchards, and from the abundant fruit of the sea, boiled over beach fires at night. Several of the photos show happy surfers holding giant lobsters fully half their size, or depict scores of young people, women and men, gathered happily around a campfire, feasting on seafood as boys play ukeleles and the group sings. These photos are, it goes without saying, in stark contrast to the more familiar Depression-era images of dirty, haggard faces and breadlines.

Doc Ball had this to say about how surfers were affected by the Depression:

> well, as far as surf was concerned, not really. Of course, we had a little trouble getting gasoline, but then it was 7-cents a gallon in those days . . . it [the Depression] kept us kinda limited in certain ways, but we had surfin' to take care of everything. Long as there's waves, why, you didn't have to pay for those. All we had to do was buy the gas to get there.[53]

It's important not to confuse the abundance of truly having everything that you need with the scaled-back asceticism associated with exhortations to the austerity of "the simple life." The surfers participated in a primitive abundance in the particular sense in which Marshall Sahlins discusses *The Original Affluent Society*.[54] Debunking commonly-held notions about the life of scarcity lived by hunting and gathering societies, Sahlins argues that these simple societies had more abundance than our own, since people had everything that they needed. They didn't collect surplus items, food or otherwise, because "things" weighed them down from roaming around, but even more important, they consumed everything in the moment because they assumed abundance rather than scarcity. That is, the hunter-gatherers knew that there would always be more, so they just enjoyed whatever they had. In contrast, in our society—purportedly with so "much"—the ideology of scarcity is perpetuated at every turn. Whether the discourse is about energy, jobs, the environment, or the potential availability of public goods, contemporary capitalism encourages the same mentality: there's not enough.

In this way too, the commercial side of capitalism appeals to a desire in people that contests the work ethic. It's the expectation of future scarcity that drives the idea that one needs to delay gratification now, and work instead. Advertisers and purveyors of pop culture exhort people to have fun now and forget about work. Buy it on credit now—you'll have money later. Enjoy now, there's plenty of everything to go around. The belief in scarcity as the essential characteristic of life on earth is one of the key pillars of the culture that supports capitalism's exploitation of alienated labor. It's an unnatural and historically new belief, and one that is constantly undermined by capitalism's commercial promoters, as they disseminate images of timeless plenty such as the surfer.

The setting of all these images on the beach is key to the sense of plenty that they evoke. And besides representing an abundance that feeds the refusal of alienated labor, the image of the beach and its natural abundance has an ecological component as well. Since the inception of "the beach" in American life, just before the turn of the last century, it's been constructed as a space that's totally "other" to the routine alienation of the civilized world. It's where we all indulge our inner primitive—the sand in our bare feet, the sun and salt water on our bare skin. If America's newly industrial cities were the spaces of work, the (urbanizing) beach was explicitly coded as a space of play, and specifically of play with a benevolent natural world. Days on the beach are long and languorous, and what makes the hours on the beach so pleasurable—the sun, the sand, and the waves—are endlessly renewed, without human toil. The images that we see coming from early twentieth-century California evoke this free, joyful, relaxed connection with nature. This type of ecological connection is in stark contrast to the environmentalism based on neo-Puritan asceticism, one that encourages feelings of guilt in humans for taking up scarce energy and resources. The ecological spirit of the surfer image is not ascetic in any way—the connection with nature is not portrayed as a back to the land, "simple life"-style toiling. Here ecological connection, represented by the surfer on the wave and the "gang" on the sand, is all about the freedom and unalienated joy of this connection. Again, the fact that this image has been so inspirational is key to its political significance, here in terms of its (actual and potential) benefit to the environmental movement. (And surfers have, as we'll see, been quite active in ecological struggles, often consciously using the symbols associated with surfing to benefit the cause.) Nature, in this image, is not a stingy enemy that needs to be tamed and then used more efficiently—this notion, in fact, is the root of the ecological catastrophe that the contemporary world is facing. It's also part of the instrumental attitude to the lifeworld that constitutes the most alienating aspect of modern capitalism.

That this alienation is contested by one of American culture's most popular images tells us that in their deepest fantasies, people desire this unalienated connection to nature. This accords with the tenets of psychoanalysis, through which we know that people never stop wanting to return to the "oceanic" state of connection between ego and outside world. For any environmentalism that actually wants to win, the image of the joy and abundance of ecological living is an important one. And the idea that in order for humans to live in a harmonious balance with nature, commercial culture doesn't actually have to be dismantled—that there may actually be tendencies within in that can serve as allies to the environmental movement at its best—makes the possibility of a revolutionary win for the ecological perspective seem much less farfetched.

LIBIDO, LIBERATION, MEMORY

A third theme that greets the peruser of these early surfing photographs is also a profoundly countercultural one: surfing life as a collective, connected life, in contrast to the competitive individualism and alienation that was increasingly coming to define the industrialized, modern spaces of American life. Even the many shots of surfers riding waves more often than not depict several surfers riding a wave together. Men and women surf together, sing together, eat together, road-trip in beat-up, surfboard-laden cars together, camp on the beach together, and, more than anything else, are seen laughing together. Just as we saw in the journalistic representations of that time, the surfer life is depicted as one of collective frolic, play, and pleasure.

And once again, we see the representations of this pleasure as involving the pleasures of gender-bending on the part of the surfers. Like the Hawaiian beach boys revered by these surfers, the men in the photographs are not constricted by a dominating or austere masculinity. They are strong, powerful, and secure enough to frequently act downright feminine. In fact, several of the pictures are nothing if not homoerotic. Although most just represent a more often than not homosocial world of men enjoying the company of other men, drinking beer, playing music, eating, laughing, and, above all, surfing, several take the gender-bending of surf culture a bit further. One especially striking photo looks onto three naked surfers posing like pinups, lying next to one another on the sand. Looking back on the photo, Don James commented in 1996 that "this . . . bathing beauties parody has caused three decades of surfing magazine editors to recoil in disgust . . ." and goes on to identify one of the "beauties" as Bill Bridgeman, who later appeared on the cover of Time magazine in his role as a world-famous WWII fighter pilot.[55]

Another photo shows two surfers dancing gracefully atop a beached surfboard; they both face the camera, and the man in the rear has his hands on the hips of the foregrounded man. Both have their legs and feet in a dainty sort of curtsy.[56] Another shows three smiling boys lying on the beach, two of whose half-naked bodies are entangled in a languid pose.[57] And in Doc Ball's film, we see two surfers, each on his own board, maneuver the boards close to one another and then ride the wave in together, holding hands.[58] Other examples of an utter lack of the insecure, defensive machismo associated with the male identity, are ubiquitous—especially in the surfers' decidedly un-masculine habit of constantly posing for the camera. Again, Waikiki beach boy culture is echoed in the feminized posing, the comfort and pleasure that the surfers take in being the one beheld, the object rather than the originator of the admiring gaze at the half-naked body. And the surfers are frequently seen posing on their boards, self-consciously enjoying surfing *and* being watched surfing. All of these feminine images are surrounded by more typically masculine images of giant "bone-crushing monster" waves being ridden by fearless, strong, powerful men. In the early photos, just like the Hawaiian lifesaving/waterman/beach boys, the masculine and the feminine flow into one another.

As in the Hawaiian images we've seen, this is true for the women in the photos as much as it is for the men. Women, although not nearly as heavily represented in the photos (or among the "beachcombers"), are represented according to both typically feminine and more masculine signifiers. One particularly telling photo depicts three ukelele players on the sand—two men and one woman. In the foreground of the photo, facing the musicians, another woman, this one in a bikini, dances a hula-like dance in front of them. Here the woman is free to play both the masculine—generator, beholder, subject—and feminine—dancing, beheld, objectified—roles.[59] And everybody looks like they're having a pretty good time with the relative freedom from compulsory gender identities that seems to flow on the beach.

Another photo, this one taken by Doc Ball, is a perfectly lit glamour shot of a young woman in a bikini. Her hair is done, and she's posing like a Hollywood pinup. According to Doc, "she could have gotten a job in the movies with that picture."[60] A typical depiction of femaleness, until we realize that this woman is Mary Ann Hawkins, widely acknowledged to have been the best female surfer on the coast during those years, and just as strong and talented a surfer as the boys. The other photos of Hawkins show her in what was clearly her more usual stance—strong and joyful, riding a surfboard at 30 or 40 miles per hour, the men looking on admiringly. Other photos of men and women tandem surfing show the male and female as equals on the board. The women are free to play with the pleasure of the masculine and the feminine, just as the men are.

Overtly sexual pleasures rule on the beach as well as all the other libidinal freedom that we see. Many of the photos and the footage in Doc's film depict men and women in positions that would have been considered quite scandalous for the time—when, according to Cliff Tucker, the 1940 state surfing champion, "a *man* could still be arrested at Santa Monica Beach for not wearing a top."[61] The shorts worn by the men look more like tight little panties than the board shorts of today, and several photos show men and women lying on the beach together, kissing. There are also several shots—similar to ones from Waikiki beach—of a man and woman together on a board, paddling out on their stomachs together with the woman in front and the man's smiling face right between her spread legs.[62]

All the associations triggered by the image of the surfer were as inspirational then as they are now. In an early nod to the power of the moving image of surfing to inspire new surfers to join the tribe, Ball said of the Palos Verdes Surfing Club that "when we got that club going, it began to attract college kids, and high school kids, and they'd come down to see what was going on, and pretty soon they were stoked . . ."[63] The images of these early surfers had commercial beach developers and tourism advertisers to disseminate them, as well as surfers themselves. The upshot was that, with the interruption of the war years (when all surfers were either drafted into the service or dodged the draft, and the beaches themselves were locked down and militarized, but also when the new technologies that would revolutionize board design and make possible the mass production and mass use of surfboards were developed) a massive beach subculture grew that would take American popular culture by storm. So the images of this time provide a piece of the nostalgic tapestry that in many ways defines surfing's pop culture image. They also, through their dissemination in the popular culture of the time, inspired a whole generation of young people, for whom the economic and other conditions were ripe, to build a new beach counterculture out of these images of a lost Eden, the pleasures of which could be regained for the price of a surfboard and a tank of gas.

In participating (even as a consumer) in surf culture, one is accessing this Edenic history, which corresponds to the unconscious memory of peace and pleasure. This has proven to be a profoundly inspirational memory. The dynamic of a founding mythology of a primitive lost paradise being deployed to create a counterculture organized around a very primal pleasure is central to surf culture and to American counterculture more generally. But within surfing especially, it's huge. And when the audience pores over the photographs of Blake, James, and Ball, or consumes advertisements, movies, or television shows that invoke this mythical past, we participate in this dynamic, pregnant with the possibility of the subversive. To explain the existence of this dynamic, and to delve into its meaning, we need to return to psychoanalysis to understand the way that anti-capitalist forces have the power of the unconscious on their side.

Images are not a static reproduction or reference to the real—the image chases after, attempts to represent and thus capture, the "real," which is really the unconscious memory of a truly authentic, *unmediated* experience of pleasure, an "oceanic" oneness with the world. After we enter Lacan's "mirror stage," the moment we come to the alienating, traumatic realization that we're *not* one with the world, we enter the world of language, which is predicated on this alienated identity, or subject—the "I" that founds every utterance. Language, and this includes all representations, including visual images, is a means that we use to try to get back to that original state, by creating a representation of reality. We actually can't stop doing this—representing the world—because it's the only way we can try to access unmediated experience, outside, perhaps, sex, dancing, surfing, deep, deep laughter—experiences in which you "lose yourself" and feel totally at home in the world. All representations promise a return to the "real"—to the unmediated immediacy of vital energy and connection. Some, like the image of surfing, are especially promising in this regard. And they tend to be the most inspiring, and thus the most subversive of the forces of further alienation. The womblike sound of the water, the dance between the surfer and the wave, the joy and connection of the act of surfing—it is nothing if not "oceanic," in every way.

Psychoanalysis explains *why* there is such a powerful link, in history and in essence, between this popular cultural myth of primitive, Edenic pleasure and abundance, and counterculture, especially of the surfing variety. What should be clear is the power of memory and desire (and this is the true content of primitivism) in founding counterculture. Again, the question of whether or not the myth is true is beside the point. We're looking at what it *produces*—which is action intended to get back to oceanic pleasure. This fundamental human dynamic whereby we'll pursue an image that chases after the "real" or the unmediated, prelinguistic gratification that we unconsciously remember is a crucial one for understanding the relationship between popular culture, memory, desire, commercialism, and the building of countercultural formations.

The history of surfing traces the outline of this relationship, especially in the way that its cultural images continue to be animated by its own primitive founding myths, and these images in turn are some of the cultural material out of which young people construct their own countercultural formations. And as we've seen again and again, the material is provided by hucksters who understand that tapping into unconscious desire moves people to act collectively, in this case, to collectively buy what they're selling—things the image of which alludes to the (generally eternally deferred) sating of these desires.

This is why the commercially disseminated image of surfing is so laden with an Edenic historical memory. Whether it's the ancient Hawaiians, surfing and feasting all day and praying to the ocean gods for good waves, the image of whom animated the cultural formation of the beach boys, or the beach boys, the lifestyle of whom was broadcast to mainland Californians who self-consciously imitated the image and made their own beach counterculture, or the surfers of 1950s Malibu who referenced the earlier San Onofre surfers and the natives in their lifestyles, or the advertisements, books, magazines, movies, and television shows of today, which reference all of these images to continually build a signifier that only becomes more compelling as it gets more and more sophisticated in referencing its own past—the waves keep rolling in.

There is an intimate relationship between memory and desire, one that produces action aimed at recouping the pleasure that's been lost with "reality" but the memory of which is never erased. The more this memory is pumped up, the more chance that it will burst through civilized repression and push for real pleasure *now*. Herbert Marcuse is eloquent on this point:

> [Memory's] truth value lies in the specific function of memory to preserve promises and potentialities which are betrayed and even outlawed by the mature, civilized individual, but which had once been fulfilled in his dim past and which are never entirely forgotten. The reality principle restrains the cognitive function of memory—its commitment to the past experience of happiness which spurns the desire for its conscious re-creation. The . . . liberation of memory explodes the rationality of the repressed individual. As cognition gives way to recognition, the forbidden images and impulses of childhood begin to tell the truth that reason denies. Regression assumes a progressive function. The rediscovered past yields critical standards which are tabooed by the present. Moreover, the restoration of memory is accompanied by the restoration of the cognitive content of phantasy. Psychoanalytic theory removes these mental faculties from the noncommittal sphere of daydreaming and fiction and recaptures their strict truths. The weight of these discoveries must eventually shatter the framework in which they were made and confined. The liberation of the past does not end in its reconciliation with the present. Against the self-imposed restraint of the discoverer, the orientation on the past tends toward an orientation on the future. The *recherché du temps perdu* becomes the vehicle of future liberation.[64]

He's talking about the explosive power of psychoanalysis here, but the point is applicable to the memories invoked in the founding mythology of surfing as well. Both beach culture at Waikiki and the mid-century youth surfing counterculture in many ways owe their existence to the (constructed and framed, by some combination of reality and desire, like all) memories of a seemingly Edenic mythical past. To the extent that these images are inspirational enough to compel whole groups of people to organize their lives around them, they come to really matter politically—the potentially explosive nature of subversive image becomes a truly oppositional culture. With the release of the 1959 film *Gidget*, the conditions were right. Surfing exploded into mass culture and has never retreated since. *Gidget* profiled the fifties incarnation of surf culture, when it had moved its central location from San Onofre to Malibu, where a new group of rebels emulated Hawaiian life and embraced the gender-bending, the refusal of work, and the easy living on the beach that had characterized all the other incarnations of surf culture.

DORA AND THE FIFTIES

Images of 1950s Malibu form another, even more widely recognized, moment of the image of the lost surfer paradise, the Edenic memories of surfing. Tom Adler, a surfer and art director whose T. Adler books out of Santa Barbara put out the Don James collections, also published *Dora Lives*[65] (in addition to four other nostalgia surf photo books he's put out since 1997). When the book came out in 2005, surf conglomerate Quiksilver promoted it along with its own merchandise. Through this work, readers get a sense of the fifties subculture through one of its most colorful and prominent characters. In addition, we can see just what it is that consumers are buying when they consume images of mid-century surfing in Malibu's lost paradise. Without question, Dora has emerged as *the* historical figure that links surf culture with the rest of the counterculture.

The book's photos give a strong sense of the fifties Malibu image personified by Dora. One shows Miki in San Onofre in 1950, sitting on the hood of an old car, surfboard between his legs, staring out at the ocean with an intense, engaged look. In classic beat attire with a beach twist, he wears Wayfarers and a black beret with his bare feet and board shorts.[66] Another shows Dora in his wayfarers, flip-flops, and a black trench coat, rocking a mischievous, happy grin as he stares in the direction of the sea.[67] The book also features the now-classic group shots. One, taken in Malibu in 1951, shows a group of relaxed, tan young men and women, standing with their boards against the grass shack, barefoot, all staring intently in the direction of the ocean. There is a striking feeling of egalitarianism of the photo. The dress—simple, casual, relaxed—is not all that different for the men and the women. There seems to be little gender separation in terms of space, demeanor or activity, which is pretty unusual for the early fifties.[68] Another, earlier shot, depicts about seventy-five (mostly) young men and women, sitting and standing around three men playing guitar and singing. Many of the men wear floppy hats, the woodies and the boards are visible in the background, boys leaning against them—it's the picture of collective leisure, with very few clothes.[69] And of course, there are lots of photos of "Da Cat" doing what he did best—surfing. It's been said that his style on the surfboard was the origin of the term "laid back." Dora's complete focus and relaxation is unmistakable—in fact, Dora is probably the most easily recognizable surfer in the photos and in the surf footage included in so many Hollywood movies of the time.

Adler's book begins with Dora's 2002 obituary in the *London Times*, which is also the text on the back cover of the coffee-table book.

> Surfing hedonist who became a hero to a generation of beach bums, before turning his back on the waves Mickey Dora was everything that a surfer ought to be: he was tanned, he was good-looking, and he was trouble. West Coast archetype and antihero, he became the incarnation

> of surfing for the postwar generation . . . he was above all the siren voice of a nonconformist surfing lifestyle, making a career out of never holding down a serious job and injecting the brash hedonism of the beach into the culture at large . . . With the publication of . . . Gidget . . . and the subsequent . . . Hollywood romances, Dora was consecrated as the profane evangelist of a youthful counterculture . . . [70]

The text of the obituary forms the book's introduction, and goes on to say that Dora was "haunted by a deep sense of paradise lost . . ." The book then chronicles Dora's life surfing, which has this sense as a major theme. First of all, his stepfather was San Onofre star Gard Chapin, famous for his surfing and for introducing surf legend Bob Simmons to the sport. Second, Dora was one of the originals at the idyllic grass shack at Malibu (immortalized in *Gidget*, the novel and film versions). He was devastated by the popular culture explosion of surfing that followed *Gidget* and the way in which it crowded up his precious waves. The commercialization of surf culture, in which he had actually participated (by surfing as a stunt double for several stars of the Hollywood movies, including doubling Moondoggie in *Gidget*), warranted his undying venom.

And worse. Dora was among a group that made it loud and clear to the commercializers that they weren't welcome in Malibu. According to Craig Stecyk, in 1956, surfers dropped human excrement into the air-conditioning ducts of two black Cadillac limos which had pulled up at the Pit. Their riders, which included the director of *Gidget* and its star, Sandra Dee, had come to scout locations, find extras and stand-ins, and "soak up atmosphere." They got more than they bargained for, as the cars, "containing moguls and stars, travel about 300 yards, and stop abruptly while the cast and crew fall out of the cars and gag. Sandra Dee was reportedly observed vomiting on the center island of the Coast Highway."[71] Stecyk told this story with a wink and a smile in 1976—"Tubesteak figures if they hadn't needed air-conditioning, it never would of [sic] happened"—and it's retold the same way in the Dora book and in nearly every other surfing history book. The story is repeated as a badge of pride for surfers.

This is a recurring theme in the surf nostalgia material—the separation between "real," "authentic" surf culture and surfers, of which Dora is clearly canonized as one, and the phony surf image and its followers. It's a harder distinction to make in reality, though—even in the case of Miki Dora himself, who advertised his status as icon of authenticity through the very commercial media that he constantly railed on. As much as he hated the commercialization and all the new surfers it was bringing to the beach ("I hate to share my time with working slobs"[72]), he was actually very much part of the outlaw marketing that has always defined surfing's image. For instance, Miki did agree to a fellow surfer's idea to shape him a signature board that would be manufactured by Greg Noll's outfit, the biggest shop at the time. In Drew Kampion's words "Da Cat, a limited-edition surfboard, [was introduced with] a level of hype, satire, verbal abuse previously unseen in surf magazine advertising . . . by this time, Miki'd been interviewed by all the surf magazines and was universally referred to as "surfing's angry young man" or the "Black Knight."[73] One ad shows Dora leaning up against two boards in the shape of a cross, arms out in a crucifixion pose. Behind him is the graffiti "Da Cat"—playing off Miki's well-known idea that "assholes" are all out to get him and the reality that there is always Dora-related graffiti at the Malibu wall.[74] Dora criticized image and commerce even as he self-consciously created one of surfing's most iconic and commercial images.

Although surfing contests have always been a big part of surf culture, from ancient Hawaii to the widely-publicized Palos Verdes in 1928, to the contests in the sixties and seventies, featured on ABC's *Wide World of Sports*, to today's massive world pro tour, televised on 24-hour cable TV and promising millions in contest money, surf contests were included high on Miki's enemies list. In a sixties interview with *Surfer* magazine, he railed that

> the advent of "professionalism" to the sport will be the final blow. Professionalism will be completely destructive of any control an individual has over the sport at present. These few Wall Street flesh merchants desire to unify surfing only to extract the wealth. Under this "professional" regime, the wave rider will be forced into being totally subservient to the few in control in order to survive. The organizers will call the shots, collect the profits, while the wave rider does all the labor and receives little . . . the completion of such a partnership [between surfing and "the decadent big business interests"] will serve only to accelerate the art's demise. A surfer should think carefully before selling his being to these "people," since he's signing his own death warrant as a personal entity.[75]

Dora was one of the most eloquent exponents of the theory of co-optation—that there is something free and wild, and "they" just come and try to make it produce money, and in doing this, they ruin it. His resistance was legendary, and the source of some of surfing's funniest anecdotes:

> I know every one of the chubby flaccid pretenders. I did everything I could to screw them over and sabotage their methods . . . the challenge to the educated was to turn down the Tinsel Town lucre. A livelihood could be made of renting yourself out to these charlatans. I pressed the pass line and got by, or so I thought. Once I was sick as a dog from a rancorous case of dysentery I'd picked up in Mexico. On camera they're filming this sad-sack party scene with some Philly cheesesteak crooner up in the spotlight, and I'm in the background,

> puking. The director calls out, "hey, dark kid in the back, I like what you're doing. That's a marvelous look. Save it for the next scene." I knew I was kaput then.[76]

But he kept doing the movies, in the words of Kampion, taking their money with one hand and giving them the finger with the other. Dora approached contests with a similar attitude: during one, after surfing a wave perfectly, Dora walks off the beach, giving the audience, and the television cameras, the surfer's "brown eye"—that is, pulling down his pants and mooning them. The attention gave him the airtime to broadcast just what he thought about what was happening to surfing, which was that his old Malibu paradise was being ruined. And to the extent that more and more people were crowding up the waves, he was right. But the commercial broadcasting of the surf image wasn't killing either surfing or its subversiveness—just its exclusiveness.

The paradise that Miki felt had been lost was one that he'd seen as strictly outlaw territory, not to be trespassed on by the squares. Co-author (with Craig Stecyk and Miki Dora himself) Drew Kampion writes that Miki "fought to keep the sands free and unfettered . . . endeavoring to keep the coast wild, to maintain and even cultivate its manifest outlaw badland designation."[77] Dora and the boys were outlaws in the eyes of the Law, too: At the end of one summer, chronicled loosely in *Gidget*, Tubesteak set his shack on fire at the first annual luau. "The following summer, it was the cops that tore down the shack. Apparently, the city fathers were concerned that the trend at Malibu wasn't entirely wholesome; after all, it was a public beach."[78]

Without question, his outlaw orientation was explicitly emulated by other surfers: Miki tells the story of being caught by Marines trespassing at Camp Pendleton, the wave-blessed but officially off-limits military base. When asked for his name, Miki tells them and the Marine yells, "that's the twentieth Miki Dora we've caught this week! What, are all you guys named Dora?" The newly surf-obsessed media was making a star of outlaw Miki Dora. And, according to Kampion: "Miki was uniquely groomed for the celebrity; like no other surfer, he was there to optimize the situation. He was in position, and being in position, as every surfer knows, is the most important part of surfing."[79]

More than anything, it was the classic "surf bum" image, the refusal of paid labor and the insistence on living—surfing—in the moment, that characterizes the image of Dora on the beach. Tracey had gotten "square" jobs in town for himself and Dora in 1956, from which they were both promptly fired. Tracey just decided to build a shack and live on the beach, and according to Kampion, "Malibu was one big party, orchestrated by Tracey, and it ran all summer long . . ." He goes on to say that "For Miki, riding a wave was the ultimate metaphor as well as the ultimate reality, the center of gravity of his very existence. It was an utterly transitory act, yet it was the thing that mattered most to him. Because it was absolutely in the present. It was Now, and Now required nothing but his undivided attention and a Zen spontaneity."[80] Miki would have agreed. He once said that "Waves are the ultimate illusion. They come out of nowhere, instantaneously materialize and just as quickly they break and vanish. Chasing after such fleeting mirages is a complete waste of time. That is what I choose to do with my life." [81]

The wildness of the surfer life was not unconnected to the spontaneity and wildness of youth in other concurrent "scenes," and Dora's experience reflected this. According to Stecyk, "Dora would be a pathfinder in a new field of relationship that would connect the beat generation with the beach generation."[82] In popular culture as well as in the lives of counterculture participants, beats and surfers were strongly linked, just as surfers and hippies were in some places one and the same as the sixties progressed into the late sixties and seventies. Stecyk asserts that "Dora was a fixture at counterculture rites," attending poetry readings in Venice with Chet Baker backing up the poets, betting ponies with Charles Bukowski, seeing Johnny Otis play in Watts, and hanging out with Bill Graham, the Grateful Dead, Jim Morrison, Exene Cervenka and John Doe.[83]

And he took acid, which according to Stecyk he was introduced to by "the good doctors at UCLA Neuropsychiatric Institute, who liked to dose surfers to test their hand-eye coordination and balance while in altered states . . . Dr. Timothy Leary had Miki on stage as a performer during his Freak Out at the Santa Monica Civic Auditorium."[84]

In a 1967 *Surfer* magazine interview, Miki, famously sour and sarcastic about nearly everything in the culture, sounded a note of optimism when discussing the cultural changes going on at that time: "I can't help feeling that there's something happening and things are not going to stay the same. New philosophies are taking hold. There is a great deal of change accruing in certain segments of the sport, and I hope you want the same things I want, freedom to live and ride nature's waves, without the oppressive hang-up of the mad insane complex that runs the world and this sick, sick war . . . These are incredible times."[85]

The image of Miki Dora and Malibu in the fifties is an especially prominent one in contemporary popular culture, getting nostalgic play even outside the surf/coffee-table book market (this will most likely continue, as Leonardo diCaprio has already bought the film rights to Dora's story). For instance, in August of 2006, a cover story entitled "Malibu's Lost Boys" appeared in *Vanity Fair* magazine, visible from every newsstand in America.[86] The article outlines the late fifties Malibu scene through the words of several men and women who'd been there. The "dashing, lawless" Miki Dora is a major presence in this recounting of "an underground culture of big waves and wild times . . ." As in other depictions, Miki is represented as having one guiding principle to his life and his values: freedom. One friend remembers of Miki's stealing and scamming that "he did it all for a simple reason: freedom. Every guy on that beach wanted to do nothing but surf all day, but only Miki had found a way to do it."

Freedom from work—from *any* obligation—wasn't the only freedom highlighted in the article. Miki's ambiguous sexuality is hinted at in a few profiles, but, just as in the case of Tom Blake, the lack of a female partner in life is papered over with accounts of serial girlfriends. (Easier to do with Miki, who had many—Tom Blake was supposedly so "discreet" that nobody knew who he was with at any time. Hmmm.) Miki was also far more "out" with his mysterious sexuality—in a July 1989 "interview" in *Surfer* magazine, for which he was paid ten thousand dollars, the highest sum in the magazine's history, Miki answered the question "are you a homosexual?" by asking, "isn't everybody in this screwed-up country?"[87] It's important to note that the interview was a series of questions and answers written by Dora himself and sent to *Surfer*'s offices.

The Dora biography has some low-key references to Dora's ambiguity in this respect—a Hollywood actor's assertion that Dora tried to kiss him on the dance floor at a party is recounted and then heavily qualified—but the *Vanity Fair* piece is more direct. Pointing to Dora's "provocatively unplaceable sexuality," the author, Sheila Weller, says that

> in that homophobic time and place, Miki was at once extremely macho and undeniably effeminate. Many surfers thought he was not interested in women—a result of his total focus on waves—or struggling with suppressed gayness. "His body language was feminine: his wrist action, his long fingers, the way he put his hands on his hips—it was a little bit fey," says a woman who had a two-year relationship with him in the mid-60s, and who asks to be identified by her first name only. Speaking for the first time at length about Miki, she describes him as having been so sexually ineffectual and disinterested as to be a 'eunuch."[88]

Although surfers have been quite ambivalent about the homoeroticism that's sometimes associated with their image, Miki's undefined sexuality didn't keep the boys on the beach from idolizing and emulating him. Perhaps because his combination of macho and effeminate was part of what made his surfing so compelling—at once graceful and aggressive, his style is described in the article as "elegant," with a "balletic, feline grace" that "earned him the name Da Cat." Steve Pezman is quoted as saying that Miki "wasn't into survival surf—he was into the dance."[89] So Miki's homosexual, or at least effeminate, side, isn't just a piece of gossip. It's an important piece of the outlaw image of surfing, of which the persona of Miki Dora, effeminacy and all, has always represented.

The two are not unrelated. Queer *is* outlaw. It's outside of the regime of compulsory heterosexuality—the repression that posits that sexuality is primarily for reproduction and that gender identity is a fixed, stable substance, rooted in biology. In this regime, the body is to be primarily an instrument of labor—its function of giving and receiving pleasure is to be marginal. So playing with gender identity and difference has no place in this regime—it's all business. The fact that Miki's sexuality was considered a perversion of this regime and yet he was hero to all the Malibu boys, says a lot about the content of the subculture. And of the image that was broadcast commercially, and continues to be.

This image, as we've seen, contains many elements that can be understood as "queer" in this way. Surfing is always referred to as a dance, a sort of libidinal connection with the ocean. It's also frequently said to be "better than sex." It's not that surfers are generally gay—there are probably as many homosexual surfers as there are homosexual anybody elses—but that the image of their libidinal life is queer in that much of their sexual energy is channeled into getting pleasure from a nontraditional object, the ocean. Also, the ocean, usually referred to as a she, puts the surfer in a feminized position, in which the ocean is the powerful agent and the surfer survives and thrives to the extent that he or she doesn't try to dominate, but instead to connect with, the driving ocean. The image of the surfer—moving with the wave, never still, never riding the same wave twice, impossible to "pin down" or even to *name* properly, sexually ambiguous, in a connected, Zen relationship to the ocean—is an image that subverts the fixed identity required for the subjection to the capitalist system that Althusser lays out. And—again—it is super alluring. Why? It speaks to pre-subject desire, for multiplicity of experience, for the moment, against the fixed identity that is self-same throughout time, that orders experience rather than dancing with the chaos of it.

The *Vanity Fair* article's main focus, besides the human-interest angle of the teens from bad families who found refuge and pleasure in the waves and the community that formed around them, is the abundance that surrounded the surfers. The large, boldface text in the article comes from an interview with Tubesteak, in which he says "With 18-cent cheeseburgers, cheap gasoline, and $3-an-hour jobs at Safeway loading fruit from four to seven AM, you *could* be a surf bum."[90] This focus echoes that of many profiles of surfing "before the fall," when a postwar economic abundance made all kinds of cultural exploration and freedom possible. (*Riding Giants*, 2003's mega-hit documentary, for instance, makes the same case about Hawaii—that in the postwar decades, surfers were able to live off the fat of a fat economy, and so the subculture flowered in jungle cottages and big waves.) And it *is* crucial to understand the economic conditions for the possibility of cultural freedom—the fact that if people are stressed out about where their next meal (or their kids' college education, or their rent or mortgage payment . . .) is going to come from, they are not exactly candidates for getting wild. The counterculture in all its incarnations flowered in the fifties and sixties because a new generation of Americans were raised on affluence, and took things like the next meal utterly for granted. It's precisely this dynamic that capital recognized and put an end to with a new era of austerity for the working class. The hope of the capitalist class is that with austerity comes desperation, and desperation breeds good subjects. To some extent, this is true.

However, it's important not to miss the reciprocal dynamic, which I'm arguing is actually more important. For two reasons: one, if the above is the only dynamic that really counts, then all the cards are in capital's hands and we, the working class, can only have fun and be free when they allow it. Which, being avid students of the behavior of the working class, they obviously will never do again. And two, it's not historically accurate. The beach culture at Malibu was the flowering of a seed that was planted during the Depression—the most austere times of all—and was a *refusal* of austerity and desperation, not an affirmation of it. And the postwar affluence was an effect of a high wages-in-exchange-for-high productivity deal that capital had to make with the American working class because in response to Depression austerity, American workers had organized like crazy and created the whole framework for unions and collective bargaining. A deal, which, by the way, the working class broke in the sixties by taking the money and running—continuing upward pressure on wages while refusing to be good, productive workers—and going surfing instead, among other activities.

In any case, the key point in terms of understanding the relationship between cultural and economic history is that an analysis that posits capital as the independent variable and the working class as purely a dependent variable, only reacting to what capital does, allows no understanding of the way that regular folks can drive the course of economic history. Analytically, no class struggle in, no class struggle out. The Malibu of the 1950s, and the counterculture more generally, came into being as a result of what Antonio Negri would call the self-activity of the working class, and the way that capital responded to it. There is certainly a logic of capital, whereby every piece of space and time and body is disciplined and put to work. However, the class struggle is a *two-way* struggle, and what Stanley Aronowitz calls the counterlogic of the working class pushes for freedom, abundance, and pleasure—what people naturally desire. What our examination of the image and its relationship to the subculture of surfing can add to this insight is an understanding of the importance of libidinally inspirational images to the strength of the working-class side of this struggle.

MORE NOSTALGIA

The fascination with images of surf culture only continues to grow, and to be more profitable for its purveyors. In 2006, Taschen put out a giant book of photos by surfer and noted photographer LeRoy Grannis[91]—with an introductory price tag of $400. The young Grannis had been heavily influenced by his good friend Doc Ball to take pictures, and much later when Grannis was middle-aged and looking for a good hobby, he got his old camera out. The photos in this collection reflect his work in California and Hawaii during the 1960s and 1970s, and include many of surfing's most iconic images of Technicolor innocence. The sixties photos chronicle the flowering of the earlier seed culture into a full-fledged cultural phenomenon. Miki Dora may not have been enjoying himself anymore, but the rest of the surf-stoked kids certainly were. Along with the photos of surfers styling waves in crowded seas, we see beaches lined with hundreds of surfboards and parking lots filled with VW campers and woody wagons piled high with boards. Grannis also shot ads for sportswear companies such as Jantzen, Hang Ten, and Laguna swimwear, and what's striking about the ads is how similar the images are to the candid beach shots in the rest of the book. With the exception of being posed, the kids basically look the same as they normally did—fresh-faced, tan, happy, half-naked—a testament to how alluring the surfers seemed to the advertisers, without changing a thing.

In the Hawaii photos, the rides are faster and more thrilling, and the surfers look a bit more wild—living in Hawaii meant there was no chance you were a weekend surfer; you were totally committed to the life. But overall, the same themes come through in all the photos: for one, women were just as heavily represented among the kids on the beach (if not always in the water) as were men. Otherwise, the photos, sun-soaked and saturated in primary colors, evoke the texture of the era—beaches crowded with bikini-clad girls and shirtless, bleach-blond boys, hundreds of surfboards laying on the beach, smiling, tanned faces in big groups, enjoying watching and enjoying being watched, enjoying their collective leisure.

Another T.Adler publication, *Surf Contest*,[92] celebrates the photography of 1960s shooter Ron Church. Included in this collection are Church's photos from two Huntington Beach surf contests, one in 1963 and one in 1964. Several photos are especially striking: in one, a jacket-and-tie-clad sportscaster and his cameraman are waist-high in the surf, equipment and all, interviewing a laughing surfer girl—champion surfer Joyce Hoffman, it turns out—coming out of the water, board under her arm. The cameraman's face isn't visible, but the newscaster looks to be laughing hysterically, all worries about his clothing and belongings thrown to the wind in the presence of the free and easy surfers.[93] Another photo stands out because it's so familiar—a swarthy, long-haired Hawaiian guy smiles while playing ukelele and singing a song to a pretty blond in a bikini on the sand with him.[94] In the rest of the pictures of these contests, really tribal rituals of communion, what's most striking is how young and un-jaded everyone looks, and the sheer numbers of young bodies.

Brad Barrett puts it this way in the book's introduction: the "images perfectly portrayed the childlike innocence of surf life at the dawn of this new decade."[95] This childlike innocence—also known as "having fun"—was not to last for long. Perhaps the most striking image is one of a police officer, surrounded by the shirtless and bikini-clad teenagers—rows and rows and rows and rows of them, as we see in many other shots. They are quiet and well-behaved, but there is something that just feels explosive in seeing all these young people, all together, feeling their collective numbers for perhaps the first time. This may, of course, just be the hindsight of knowing what these kids went on to do, but the Huntington Beach police officer seems to sense the potentially incendiary combination of large numbers of young people and the freedom of the beach. His hat is over his heart, and he stares out to sea with a look of benevolent concern in his squinting eyes.[96]

Perhaps he sensed some of the changes that this alchemy would produce. In the Grannis book, the later sixties photos are different in that the kids seem more relaxed, more comfortable with themselves and with one another. A few years on the beach will do that to a person. And definitely less clean-cut than they'd been earlier in the decade. By the end of the sixties, surf culture was self-consciously part of the counterculture and youth politics. According to Barilotti, "psychedelic drugs raged through the surf culture like a wildfire . . . surfing became introverted and underground as former Jantzen-wearing hotdoggers morphed into bearded Zen-spouting mystics. Contests were no longer cool; nobody cared who came in first. Suddenly, surfing wasn't about tricks and trophies, but about balancing one's karmic flow within "crystalline cathedrals of molten glass," in the words of a *Surfer* magazine reader. As early as 1966, Rick Griffin was slipping sly drug references into his cartoons for *Surfer* . . ." Drew Kampion was the editor of Surfer magazine from 1968 to 1972, and is quoted in the book's introduction as repeating the countercultural phrase, "you were either on the bus or you were off the bus . . . you got it or you didn't. You believed in gravity or you believed in space. You were rigid or you flowed, and there was a whole lot of flowin' going on." Barilotti goes on to say of Kampion's "new, radicalized regime," that "*Surfer* became a vector of the burgeoning counterculture, celebrating peace, free love, tuberides, and every surfer's right to drop out and get really, really stoned. Kampion . . . was also openly critical of the escalation of the Vietnam War . . ."[97]

Surfing's countercultural turn, taken along with the rest of the young generation, is documented a bit in the Grannis images, although he's clearly got more of an eye for the "simple" and the "innocent." It's in yet another T. Adler imprint, *Surfing Photographs from the Seventies Taken by Jeff Divine*,[98] that the long hair and psychedelia of that decade's surf culture comes to take its place as a piece of surfing's nostalgic tapestry. The book's introduction, written by Scott Hulet, begins with Jeff Divine "coming clean" and enumerating all the countercultural paraphernalia that defined his lifestyle, such as "long hair. And pendletons. Mexican wedding shirts, bell bottoms, wallabies, tuna, wheat bread, and sprouts in the fridge. Santana, the Dead . . . I had a beaded curtain through which you entered my den . . ."

The links with the counterculture were political as well, according to Divine: "we were surfers, but we looked like hippies to the Korean War vet cops who rousted us almost daily at the beach. 'Where's your ID? What are you doing here?' They got even nastier on those days when Herbert Marcuse or Angela Davis were making anti-war, anti-Nixon, anti-police speeches up the hill at UCSD. With a draft lottery number on your head and the left-oriented teachers at college always talking about the war and how screwed up our society was, it was a strange time to say the least." Hulet, the voice of the introduction, goes on to say that "while the straight world's aura was perceived as reactionary, martial, and square, the surf vibe read mellow, open-minded and inclusive. A surfer had a chance to save the day with pure, simple optimism." Divine again: "It was all about the karma you had and going with the flow. We really believed that when the surf was on that's what it was all about: good vibes actually caused good waves to happen." He also says that "paradise revealed, no parental control, a lot of seemingly retired twenty-somethings, tropical lighting and a three-mile wave field that was any surf photographer's dream" constituted the scene.[99]

The cover of the book says it all. It's a close-up shot of Hawaiian surfer Buttons Kaluhiokalani, who with his brown skin, puffy afro, and confident smile could easily be a "black is beautiful" poster boy. He's paddling out to the ocean, looking back over his shoulder to give a peace sign to the folks on the beach. It's a great picture, and the fact that it's on the cover is really significant. For one thing, we've come full circle—the iconic image of surfing is again the primitive-looking, free-living, peace-love-and-aloha brown man. There's not a clean-cut male in sight. Everyone is a stoned-looking hippie longhair. The surfing style is very Zen, leaning gracefully into the wave, kicking back, very graceful—what Scott Hulet calls "body English . . . the brief arch, the hand foiling the chin life . . . all of those Mardi Gras mummers flourishes that referenced dance over sport."[100]

The book's first photograph is a two-pager, showing a perfectly curling wave breaking under a full rainbow, the back of a lone surfer and his dog looking out, digging it.[101] Another shot shows a surfer fast on the lip of a wave, but the processing of the photo is stylized impressionistically.[102] The major difference between these photos and some of the ones from earlier eras are stylistic—the surfers have long hair, beards, and moustaches, and the shortboards that "revolutionized" surfing in the late sixties have totally replaced the longboards of yore. Airbrushed, mystical psychedelia was definitely the fashion in board design. As the photos take the viewer through the late sixties and well into the seventies, it becomes apparent that surf culture held onto the trappings of the hippie life long after most Americans had moved on and taken up disco. This is because, as I hope I've shown, surf culture and counterculture are linked in affinity and in cultural connections, both of which endure to this day.

Taken together, all the books reframe the surfer image as a transhistorical phenomenon. When we look at them as a piece, we see an image of freedom, abundance, collective fun, laid-back pleasure, leisure, liberated sexuality—the surfer moves through every decade, transforming his image into what looked like freedom at the time, or what our memory of free living from that time is. The fifties, sixties, seventies—the look changes but the message doesn't. The surfer signifies the same thing, always, and it's these themes that are invoked in every surf nostalgia book, whatever the era's particularities. So although the images are animated by a sense of lost paradise, by an appeal to memory, it's not memory itself—the past as somehow inevitably better—that's being appealed to with nostalgic surfing images. It's the memory of something particular—pleasure. That's why the images have proven so inspirational, and have always had a privileged place in the American imagination.

4 Riders on the Storm
Surfers and the Sixties

> Surf culture is a bit like a Trojan horse. Its outward form—its energy and essential eroticism (what better natural metaphor for sex?)—makes it appealing and charismatic. Everyone wants a piece of it: it's cool to be associated with it; it's got the sizzle that makes the sell. But something else, something very ancient and esoteric, comes along with it, and when that gets loose in the culture at large—well, anything can happen. Things change. That old Polynesian seed starts to work its way into the rigid northern cultural soul and—*bam!*—people are stoked![1]
>
> —Drew Kampion, *Stoked: A History of Surf Culture*

SURFING AND THE "HAPPINESS EXPLOSION"

In 1968, Tom Wolfe immortalized the Southern California teenage surf scene while linking it to what he saw as essential in sixties culture. *The Pump House Gang*,[2] named after its first and most famous essay on surf culture in La Jolla, California, was a depiction of the many "statuspheres" that, for Wolfe, were transforming the face of American culture. According to the author, people today were ignoring the old "utopianisms" whereby the culture of the "happy worker" would be determined by the (essentially dull, socialist) communitarians who envisioned the future, and were instead creating their own little paradises. The masses were not only rejecting these old utopian standards, but *all* standards derived from the "community," period. "What an intriguing thought," Wolfe writes in the book's introduction, "for a man to take his new riches and free time and his machines and *split* from *communitas* and start his own league. He will still have status competition—but he invents the rules . . . all sorts of outlaws and outcasts, by necessity or by choice" have done this before, but "the intriguing thing today . . . is that so many Americans and Englishmen of middle and lower incomes are now doing the same thing. Not out of 'rebellion' or 'alienation'—they just want to be happy winners for a change."[3]

This is what the sixties were all about, according to Wolfe, and young surfers, who had "started their own league," epitomized these "happy winners." This is not surprising, given the fact that surfing entered the sixties already having had a long tradition of forming just this kind of affirmative culture around it. When the cultural conditions converged—the civil rights movement, the mass entrance into college, the baby boom, commercial culture, all the elements contributing to the spirit of the age—and combined with postwar mass prosperity, the alternative world that surfers created became possible on a larger scale than ever before:

> It's a magic economy—yes!—all up and down the coast from Los Angeles to Baja California kids can go to one of these beach towns and live the complete surfing life. They take off from home and get to the beach, and if they need a place to stay, well, somebody rents a garage for twenty bucks a month and everybody moves in, girls and boys . . . Cash—it's practically in the air." And besides, "What's the big orgy about money? It's warm, nobody even wears shoes, nobody is starving."[4]

Under these conditions of freedom, the kids surf and hang out at the beach, escaping the "hubby-mommy household with everybody getting neurotic hang-ups with each other," and "creat[ing] an autonomous world of their own." Rejecting the blandishments (and hang-ups) of the square world, they construct a lifestyle with its own set of values and (of course) a language that no outsiders can understand. The only thing accorded any respect or seriousness in their world of parties and pranks is the mystical, "mysterioso" "Oh Mighty Hulking Pacific Ocean." The only adults they look up to are guys like Bruce Brown, John Severson, Phil Edwards, and Hobie Alter, thirty-something surfer/entrepreneurs who are exempt from the criticism accorded other adults because they never "haired out" and gave up *the life*. These guys are rich, work as little as possible (frequently barefoot), and will never "get sucked into the ticky-tacky life with some insurance salesmen sitting forward in your stuffed chair on your wall-to-wall telling you that life is like a football game and you sit there and take that stuff. The hell with that!"[5]

It's important that in Wolfe's reading, the kids, like their Depression-era forebears, not only reject work but also reject the square world's insistence on *crisis*. Nothing is a crisis in the Pump House world—not even the riots in Watts. Wolfe tells a story in which one night, late, after a party which had gotten

> *very Dionysian* . . . everybody was stoned out of their hulking gourds and . . . everybody decided to go see the riots. These were the riots in Watts. The Los Angeles Times and the San Diego Union were all saying, WATTS NO-MAN'S LAND and STAY WAY FROM WATTS YOU GET YO' SEF KILLED, but naturally nobody believed that. Watts was a blast, and the Pump House gang was immune to the trembling gourd panic rattles of the L.A. Times black pan-thuhs [squares]. Immune!

What the surfers found was that

> the Negro kids didn't say kill Whitey or Geed'um or any of that. They just said, Come on, man, it's a party and it's free. After they had been in there for about three hours talking to Negroes and watching drunks collapse in the liquor stores, some cop with a helmet on came roaring up and said, "Get the hell out of here, you kids, we cannot and will not provide protection."[6]

Although the cops wrongly assumed that the kids were on their side, Wolfe argues that the surfers weren't actively rebelling against straight society either. They weren't angry. Straight "hair-outs" (cowards), because they didn't understand "the life", were the objects of the kids' mocking pity, not their rage. Wolfe wants to point out how different this was from traditional Other-centered forms of rebellion in which the primary focus is the opponent. Wolfe is right to distinguish the kids from angry rebels, but his idea that they were innocuous in the eyes of the straight world, wasn't really true.

The surfers may not have been targeting the straight world, but they became its targets. This is not so surprising, given their hedonistic, anti-work, "nobody owns the beach" anti-private property sensibilities. From the straight perspective, the kids had to be brought into line with the rules and standards of a society that expected them to get serious and be responsible (that is, to work and settle into a mortgage and a nuclear family, the things they disdained most). What is surprising is how many adults who might be expected to be sympathetic to the kids' lived critique of straight American society were instead partial to the crisis mentality that the Pump House Gang was rejecting.

In the book's introduction, Wolfe tells a story that, I think, clarifies some of the fundamental terms whereby the significance of cultural politics is evaluated. He prefaces it by contrasting the unbridled enjoyment that such massive numbers of people were experiencing in all their different scenes with the fact that "intellectuals and politicians currently exhibit a vast gummy nostalgia for the old restraints, the old limits, of the ancient ego-crusher: *calamity*. Historically, calamity has been the one serious concern of serious people . . ." Wolfe claims that "serious" intellectuals were relieved to "discover" poverty with Michael Harrington's 1963 *The Other America* and tend on principle only to care about things that are dour and depressing—everything else is considered "frivolous." "War, Poverty, Insurrection! Alienation! O Four Horsemen, you have not deserted us entirely. The game can go on.

> One night, in the middle of the period when I was writing these stories, I put on my electric-blue suit . . . and took part in a symposium at Princeton with Gunter Grass, Allen Ginsberg, and Gregory Markopoulos,

> who is an "underground" filmmaker, before 1200 students. The subject was "The Style of the Sixties" . . . the Horsemen charged on . . . very soon the entire discussion was centered on police repression, Gestapo tactics, the knock on the door, the Triumph of the Knout. I couldn't believe what was happening, but there it was.
>
> "What are you talking about?" I said. "We're in the middle of a . . . Happiness Explosion!" I might as well have said let's talk about the Fisher King. Happiness, said Saint-Just a century ago, is a new concept in Europe. Apparently it was new here, unheard-of almost. Ah, *philosophes*!—if we want to be *serious*, let us discuss the real apocalyptic future and things really scary . . . [7]

In celebrating "ego-expanding" happiness in the everyday lives of masses of Americans during the sixties, Wolfe—also, of course, the great chronicler of the Merry Pranksters in the Electric Kool-Aid Acid Test—found himself at odds with left intellectuals, who were dour as ever. (Not much has changed, for the most part—on the left, being *serious* equals talking about how bad things are.) But lefties certainly weren't the only ones thinking that American middle-class pleasures were debased. As we'll see, the editorial page of the Wall Street Journal was similarly opposed to the "utopian," "romantic" "frivolity" it saw emanating out from beatniks and hippies to the masses. And as surf culture grew along with mid-century youth culture, school and local police authorities—charged with maintaining law and order, private property, and the "discipline" of the work ethic—lined up squarely against the dangerous, outlaw "exuberance" that they saw thriving on the beaches. The traditional divide between "right" and "left" doesn't quite capture the difference that Wolfe is talking about here, a difference that is so pronounced when we look at the two diametrically opposed reactions that surfing in particular, and mid-century youth culture more generally, elicited in American life. Just as it happened in surfing's previous incarnations, popular culture broadcast subversive exuberance far and wide while those charged with enforcing discipline tried their best to extinguish it. In light of all this, perhaps a rethinking of political terms is in order—those *for* happiness explosions on one side, those *against* on the other.

An avid follower of the sixties counterculture in all its incarnations, Wolfe knew that surf culture was of a piece with all the rest of it. As we'll see, everyone else at the time was pretty clear on this as well: local authorities, all the press, national and local, and filmmakers, advertisers, and the other broadcasters of pop culture who were selling the image of the surfer in all its beat-hippie countercultural glory. Noted sociologist John Irwin also wrote about the free-living bohemianism of the surf scene and its inherent connection with the counterculture.[8] But since that time, the understanding of this connection has been lost. Now, the generally accepted narrative of mid-century bohemianism links the beats of the fifties with the hippies of the sixties through figures like Neil Cassady—a central character in both Kerouac's *On the Road* and on the Merry Prankster "Furthur" bus—and Allen Ginsburg, the beat poet who became an elder statesmen of the sixties counterculture. But in addition to an affinity of sensibility, there is a more concrete link, through the subculture of surfers. The fact is that surf culture, in California and in its reverberations nationwide, was a real connection between the two incarnations of mid-century youth culture. We might even say that beat went to the beach, got a tan, grew its hair, and turned hippie.

Surf culture remains more than a connection that passed into new sub- and countercultural incarnations, though. It's the one aspect of the bohemian explosion of the sixties that preceded it *and* that only continued to gain popularity after the others had faded out. Surf culture is the part of the sixties that's most alive in American popular culture. Surfing has turned out to be not only the most enduring countercultural form to come out of 1960s popular culture, it's also the one that always had the most powerful allure. Now as then, surfing is generally acknowledged to be a bohemian, anti-work, tribal subculture, but it remains one that everybody looks up to. Everyone wants to be a surfer—and this can't be said of the non-surfing hippie types of the sixties (or today). A recent *New York Times* article about the tony Hamptons makes this point: where in other wealthy beach towns, the rich vacationers often look down on the working class "townies" who serve them, in Southhampton and other hamlets, the surf instructors are idolized by even the wealthiest, most famous beachgoers, who want only to be cool enough to hang out at the surf shop.[9]

THE PROBLEM WITH EXUBERANCE

The surfer as outlaw was not always so well-loved by everyone, though. As surfing's "seed culture" of the thirties and forties grew into the heyday period of the fifties and especially the sixties, the popular press of the time paid more and more attention. And what was frequently portrayed was great concern on the part of parents, property owners, teachers, police, and community leaders that the new and growing crop of "surf bums" was an increasing threat to the law and order that they were enforcing. Almost no one at the time saw the surf subculture as a docile, all-American, conformist bunch of athletes. They were rebels, and to the defenders of all that was "straight," they had to be stopped. The Los Angeles area provides a characteristic case.

The early local newspaper coverage of the now-exploding post-*Gidget* scene definitely saw something "different" in the beach crowd. An *LA Times* columnist subheads his mid-sixties piece on surfers with the boldface: "these people live in world apart," and goes on to characterize surfers as "frenzied, dedicated addicts," "cultists," who are exhilarated by danger and who, most importantly, "won't work." In fact, "they feel sorry for YOU in that stuffy office."[10] A 1963 *LA Times* article claims that "surfers [are] spilled on a wave of ire" because "the perpetually indignant are turning their eyes to the happy-go-lucky-surfer" and that "the delinquent they hold in scorn spends his life on the beach, dyes his hair blond, never works and owns a surfboard."[11]

Local authority figures at the time were concerned about the links they saw between surfing and all the other aspects of the youth culture that was coming to be seen as such a threat. Once the surfing subculture began to grow beyond a harmless "lunatic fringe" on the beach, so did opposition to it.[12] Not surprisingly, this battle was covered most extensively by the *Los Angeles Times*. The *Times'* publisher, Otis Chandler, was a long-time surfer himself and a member of the San Onofre beach club, and thus extremely sympathetic to the surfers in their battles with local authorities. One strategy of the *Times* coverage was to refer to surfers' discipline problems as a thing of the past. As early as 1962, the *Times* was quoting a lifeguard and surfer as saying that "the bad name a few 'beach bums' gave it [surfing] a few years ago is disappearing . . ."[13]

This idea that surfers *used to be* "beach bums" continues through the newspaper coverage as a constant, even to this day. In fact, a 2006 *New York Times* article claims that "just over a half-century ago . . . surfers were legitimate counterculture types . . ." and that "concurrent with the arrival of the beats on the cultural landscape, surfing produced its own array of rebels, dropouts, and outlaws, albeit these radicals tended to have a tan."[14] According to this article, *Gidget* changed all that "when the commercial engines that drive the economy seized on this as another form of teenage rebellion they could commodify . . ." In this telling, post-1959 surf culture stopped being rebellious. But if this were really the case, mid-century surfers wouldn't have had to work so hard to improve their image with the authorities out to repress them.

But some did work quite hard to do just this. The strategy of a few surfers in this battle was to insist that they were innocent of the infractions they were being accused of, and to blame a small minority of beachgoers for the problems. The sympathetic *LA Times* gave voice to this idea over and over in its coverage, stating that the "behavior problems" associated with surfers are attributable to a "bad element" that constitutes a minority of the surfing community—a point of view put forth by the surfers in their quest to keep beaches and contests from being closed to them. This "bad element" was continually estimated to be "about 15%" of the surfers. According to one 1960 article, "probably the biggest opposition from officials is caused by a group of beatnik-type individuals, most of whom aren't true followers of the sport, but are just using it to get attention."[15]

The fact that these efforts bore little fruit didn't keep the *LA Times* from covering them extensively. In 1961, one article reported that "Surfers Join Club to Govern Selves: Members Pledge to Set Example of Good

School, Beach Behavior." This "club", "composed of both surfers and parents, formed to further the sport and to protect surfing areas from 'gremlin' activities as well as give surfers a better reputation. Every member joining the club must pledge to 'set a good example of behavior on the beach and in school' . . ." The article mentions that the surfers in this club are all 13–16 years old—that is, young enough that they still need their parents to drive them to the beach. This may be why they're willing to go along with parental rules around surfing. Or perhaps these kids were just that fabled 15%. "Surfers Out to Improve Their Image," another 1966 article claimed, stating that some surfers wanted to change the fact that "a teenager with long hair . . . no ambition and a penchant for getting in trouble is the usual image created by the word surfer." And in "Surfing: A Sport or a Public Nuisance?" the author points approvingly to the founding, in 1961 of the United States Surfing Association, "in an effort to improve the sport by having [otherwise "immature and irresponsible"] surfers recognize and assume their responsibilities."

Surfers may have claimed that only 15% of them were "beach bums" and "beatniks," but not everyone agreed. In a 1963 article covering a hearing on whether to ban surfing outright at Sunset Beach, many surfer witnesses invoked the 15% estimate, (out of an estimated 50,000 Los Angeles and Orange County surfers) but the author noted that "other speakers said the trouble-making element was more than 15% of those using the beaches. 'I'd say the bad guy-good guy ratio was about 60–40, with the good guys losing,' one witness said". Despite the protestations of the surfers, "witness after witness urged that some action be taken to eliminate problems created by the surfers."[16]

So what were these "problems"? The folks opposed to the surfers tended to invoke dramatic safety issues—"endangering women and children," for instance—but always, practically in the same breath, admitted that the problem was really "conduct." Surfers were repeatedly referred to by law enforcement officials and others as "parent-defying rowdies" and "beach bums." In 1959, the *Times* reported that Malibu "is set to impose stricter controls on surf riding in the wake of complaints from residents that surfers are endangering bathers and disregarding property rights . . . residents complained of teen-age surfers using private property as shortcuts to the beach and refusing to cooperate with residents when asked to do so." A captain in the sheriff's office "has been asked to intensify patrolling of all areas frequented by surfboard riders . . ." and the county supervisor was firm in saying that although the county has "no intention of discouraging surfing, which has become a popular sport . . . this does not mean that *youthful enthusiasm* will be permitted to ignore property rights . . ."[17] A 1966 article explained that "danger to swimmers was not the only reason for the restrictions . . . there had been problems of excessive noise, vandalism and various crimes attributed to surfers . . ."[18] In Sunset Beach, "property owners claimed the surfers caused damage to beachfront homes, used profane language, and blocked streets and driveways . . ."[19]

Property owners complained to police about the surfers throughout southern California. In 1962, wealthy Rincon residents "reversed the usual shoreline demand that freeways be routed inland," because, as one resident put it, "'we'd like to get rid of freeway noise at our doors but not at the price we'd have to pay. If the freeway is moved inland, it would make the present highway open to parking of cars and leave us at the mercy of surfers and beach bums . . . if the protection of the freeway's ban on parking is taken away from us, we'll be overrun with thousands of these beach bums . . . already, they are stealing anything left outside our homes and we are constantly calling the sheriff's office for deputies to protect us.'"[20] This theme, that both beachgoers and property owners need "protection" from the "exuberant" "rowdyism" of surfers, is one that's repeated over and over. In 1960, eighty-nine Newport Beach residents signed a petition "asking for additional police protection" on the beaches. The town followed the example of Santa Monica and restricted surfing to a small area of the beach, at designated early-morning hours. Later, Newport Beach began requiring licenses to surf there. One surfer at the 1963 Sunset Beach hearings understood that repressing surfing could have unintended consequences: "a ban would create an immense law enforcement problem and is certain to set off retaliations from the 'bad guy' element."[21] Only an estimated 10 to 15% of surfers did buy the $3 licenses (so perhaps the 15% "good guy" ratio was actually inverted), even though the police chief said "his officers would start arresting non-licensed surfers on July 1."[22]

In all of this coverage, the "problem" of the surfer is portrayed as one with the bohemianism and "exuberance"—read, lack of discipline—of youth more generally. In 1962, a Sunset Beach sheriff's deputy put it this way: "the fellows on the surfboards, of course, have no way of telling what time it is. Sometimes we have a problem shouting from the shore to the surfers to let them know their time is up."[23] But it wasn't just the eschewing of the rules of clock time that was the problem: criticizing the "'gremmies' with long shaggy hair," he insists that "it's perfectly possible to be a crack surfer without having hair that looks like it belongs on a sheepdog." Some municipalities got a little tougher on the longhairs: the *LA Times* reported in 1961 that a Hermosa Beach "Contest [was] to Bar Surf Bums." The mayor and the city council had decided that "no 'surf bums' will vie on paddleboards in the . . . contest" and that "to make sure the competition doesn't include 'beach bums' entrants will be allowed only from groups having adult sponsors and those which show they are 'self-policed.'"[24]

Another 1961 article, entitled "Surfers: Good Kids or Gangs of Rowdies? Parents, School Authorities Claim Sport Creating Discipline Problems," highlights the fact that all attempts to improve the image of surfers notwithstanding, they were still seen as serious discipline problems by school authorities and local police. Apparently, "school authorities are concerned because they say surfing is creating absentee and discipline problems."[25] As with the rest of America's youth, the refusal to discipline the hair with a haircut represented all the other discipline that the kids were refusing. In 1967, for instance, a 15-year-old boy was suspended from school because he "had surfer-style hair that was too long . . . and he refused to have it cut."[26] And these authorities understood the subtle difference between sport and subculture: according to the Hermosa Beach Chief of Police, "it's not that we object to surfing. We think it's a great sport, but when a boy adopts it as a way of life, that's when the trouble starts." More directly, "one south bay school administrator . . . sees defiance of authority . . . as the hallmark of the surfer . . ."[27]

The opposition between authority and the surfer-identified lack of discipline is instructive. Why is "exuberance"—a word many would code as positive—an opponent for discipline-enforcing authorities? What Marcuse calls the performance principle and what Marx calls the logic of capital insists that everything, all nature and all moments of human life, be made productive. In order for this to happen, the wildness of desire—changing from moment to moment, on a whim, irresponsible, something one can never "count" on, that is, calculate on the basis of—must be tamed. As any employee can tell you, the ability to work is founded primarily on the repression of desire. More generally, a relationship to the world—natural or human—that's libidinal, or inherently pleasurable in any way, is an obstacle to the efficient utilization of its material. So the school and police authorities who were so worried about the "exuberance" of the surf bums were not wrong to be concerned. Charged in their small way with enforcing the discipline—the repression of pleasure and spontaneity—that founds the whole capitalist system, they rightly saw the young surfers'exuberance as their opposition.

The surfers' refusal to respect private property—insisting on beach access no matter what—was another massive problem for straight-world authorities. Simply put, capitalism depends on the convention of private property. And within capitalism, private property and the repression of the performance principle—most simply, the imperative of work—are inextricably linked. Marx defines workers, or members of a class of "free" wage laborers, as those who are "free in the double sense"—free *of* anything else to sell on the market besides their power to work (and thus without land or other means of production) and free *to* sell their labor power (and thus not enslaved, but the true "owner" of their power to work). Thus the agreed-upon "reality" of private property is the basis of the whole capitalist system, and of its imperative to work. So too, the opposition to these are linked in the figure of the surfer, who doesn't just violate private property, but refuses to acknowledge it altogether. Who doesn't just refuse to work, but doesn't think much about work at all. And who doesn't just fight the repression that capital demands of the working class—the body as an instrument of labor rather than pleasure—but ignores it entirely, and exuberantly.

The word exuberance doesn't come up in the newspaper all that much. But when it comes to mid-century surfers, we see the word all the time. It refers to the joy that comes with a libidinal, rather than instrumental, relationship to nature and to the moments of life—and that is the polar opposite of the performance principle. This is the essence of the battle between authorities and surfers. If the ultimate "law" is the performance principle, the surfer is the outlaw. And to add insult to injury—the happy outlaw. Self-discipline depends on a certain alienation from self—you have to take yourself as an object, separate from yourself, in order for one part of yourself to discipline the other, to keep it under control. In that much of the sixties counterculture was contesting the alienation of modern life, the exuberance of surfers was intimately connected to the larger uprising in which discipline in all forms was refused, across American life. Most generally, it's this refusal of the discipline of the performance principle—work, the law of private property, rules of propriety more generally, etc.—that links surfers with the larger youth counterculture of which it was a part. Local authorities were not unaware of this. They reacted so strongly to surfers because they knew surfers were part of a larger trend that the authorities were deeply, deeply uncomfortable with.

In 1963, the *Los Angeles Times* reported that "the police had begun cracking down on the conduct of *unruly* youths in advance of the prolonged warm summer weather . . ." and that toward this end, "thirty-four teenagers were arrested recently on charges of inciting a riot and failure to disperse . . . when police broke up a beach crowd estimated in the hundreds . . . the incident resulted from the youngsters' practice of loitering . . ."[28] In 1965, beach property owners were agitating for a law outlawing loitering on beaches (one wonders what else there is to do on a beach but "loiter") and surfboarding in the water because, as the petitioners said, "gangs or groups of surfers or hangers-on of both sexes congregate at the entrances to the beachfront and on the beach level steps."[29]

In 1969, the *LA Times* continued the discourse about surfers' bad image being all in the past, painting surfers as "Bums No More" and pointing to a time "not too long ago" that "the word surfer evoked the image of a social outcast . . . a wild-haired guy with big feet, a bum in ripped shorts . . . an image as unsavory as that of a Hell's Angel." According to a lifeguard, "that fringe bunch is gone, now, thank goodness. They're probably the ones that have become pseudo hippies." A local Superior Court judge and surfer agreed: "those doltish groups that gave surfers a bad name are gone. Maybe they have all joined the Hell's Angels." The article quotes the Huntington Beach police chief as being relieved that the "undesirable hangers-on" are gone from the surfer community.[30] It seems that this was just wishful thinking, though. The police continued to work to discipline the behavior of surfers, and surfers continued to resist.

That same year, an *LA Times* headline shouted that "Huntington Beach Attracts Trouble"[31] from the teenage surfers and their "hangers-on." A riot began when local cops arrested a young kid on suspicion of being under the influence of drugs. A crowd of 3,000 spontaneously destroyed the police substation on the beach and fought with police, who sprayed tear gas to disperse the crowd. According to the director of harbors, beaches, and parks for the county, this wasn't an isolated incident. "Serious fights or riots have broken out on the beach in 1950, 1954, 1957, 1964, and 1967, all requiring scores of policemen to quell them." In the fifties, it was "beach bums" drinking and loitering that gained cops' attention; as the sixties progressed, it was the drugs. The one constant is the resistance that the beachgoers put up, and the fact that police were often forced to "draw back . . . and let it die out by itself . . ." In fact, by this time the police themselves were genuinely intimidated by the sheer masses of defiant young beachgoers: "we try to have a plainclothesman make the arrest quietly. The main thing is not to get something developing . . . it is this assembling of a crowd that provides fuel for trouble . . ."

Attempting to explain why Huntington Beach seemed to have more of its share of youths clashing with the police trying to arrest them, the article's author states first and foremost that "Huntington's surf is considered by surfers as among the best in the state," and that the U.S. Surfboard Championships are held there every year. Easy access to the beach is also cited as a factor. But when a Huntington Beach police captain is asked to give an explanation, he attributes the problem squarely to what he calls "a narcotics, anarchist subculture." In describing the subculture, he's explicit in making the links between surfing and the rest of the inscrutable, undisciplined youth culture. Young surfers come to live in town because of the "dilapidated" housing stock. "A couple of kids rent it, and 20 live there. There are business establishments there catering to this crowd and condoning it—psychedelic shops that sell narcotics equipment, and teen clubs. They let these runaway kids sleep there . . . they hate us because we enforce narcotics laws as much as possible. In the minds of most youth, this is unjust."

The article mentions "a long-haired, bearded youth" involved in starting the melee, as well as the "longhair types" who got involved. But the links with the counterculture and even the New Left are even more pronounced than that: the article profiles one Gilbert Covell, a local entrepreneur whom the police saw as a bad element in town because he operated a beach nightclub that the police claim is used "as a haven for runaways and narcotics users [that] offers them asylum from the police." According to the police chief, "he's the type who is part of our overall problem here. They encourage these kids, and it means trouble for us . . ." This statement could stand in for the whole relationship between the repressive apparatus, the counterculture, and the commercial promoters who "encouraged" it. Covell was allegedly harassed by police for years and arrested in the 1969 melee on charges of trying to incite youths on his parking lot to riot. Covell painted police as "anti-youth" and seemed to be part not only of surf culture and the youth counterculture, but the New Left as well. According to the article, "he has spoken at a meeting sponsored by the Students for a Democratic Society at Orange Coast College. He said he may sublease his building to SDS or some other activist organization if police make it impossible for him to operate. Maybe they would like to tackle somebody with a national civil rights organization. I'm just one individual . . ."

The police didn't take such threats lightly: they seemed to sense the connections that Covell represented. The chief asserted that "when we had hassles on the beach before, they died out right away, but there are some disturbing things about this one. They had a riot the same day in Venice. Maybe, just maybe, they were related. We saw guys with big, professional movie cameras and sound equipment a few minutes after the rock throwing started. We heard they were from the *LA Free Press* (an underground newspaper). Why were they there so soon after it started?"

The article ends by enumerating the steps that cops were taking in response to the threat—a second helicopter patrolling the beach, more tear gas on hand—but the last line adds: "And perhaps the most telling—there are no immediate plans to replace the glass on the beach substation." In a similar vein, most of the attempts to restrict surfers that had been mounted during the sixties were eventually abandoned as useless. As the sixties progressed, surf culture came to define the beach. It was so popular that it became impossible to repress. For instance, by 1967, a Newport Beach official is quoted as saying that "licensing simply isn't a realistic approach to controlling the anti-social activities . . . of beach attendants—and that's what these licensing laws really are aimed at."[32] Although "lifeguards and city officials [in Newport beach] like the measure which they say gives them better control over some of the more *exuberant* surfers who have been inclined to overstep the bounds of good behavior,"[33] the chief lifeguard is quoted as admitting that "registration per se won't stop rowdyism, but the kind of kid who will comply with the ordinance will be generally sold on law and order." In a turnaround, "this kind of kid" was estimated to be about 15% of surfers. And for good reason. It would be impossible to keep to "designated" hours if you were a surfer—the waves don't obey the clock or the law, and neither do surfers. Besides, once you get out on the water, you're pretty hard to catch. This resulted in increasing "disobedience" among surfers, and an ongoing game of cat-and-mouse with the police. Increasingly, the mice were winning.

In any case, by 1967 Newport Beach had lifted restrictions and licensing fees on surfers and by 1969, the *Times* reported that "the views of surfers will be strongly considered in a study on establishing small craft harbors from Santa Monica to the Ventura County line . . ."[34] By the early 1970s, surfers and their sympathizers had reached such a critical mass that they were able to be a major force in the California anti-beach development movement that resulted in the California Coastal Commission and an end, in 1973, to unregulated commercial development and destruction of coastal areas.[35] Organizations like Save Our Surf and the Surfrider Foundation grew out of these struggles and both Surfrider's membership list and list of victories has continued to grow ever since. Most recently, in February of 2008, the Commission voted overwhelmingly to shoot down an $875 million road plan that would have split the beach at the Trestles and ruined the wave. Surfers were the major force in the fight.[36]

The surfer victory that made all this possible, emboldening the surfers to fight for clean and open beaches, was over the Trestles, a fabulous wave that happened to break on the property of the Marine Corp's Camp Pendleton. In 1951, Marines erected a gate that blocked access to Trestles. Surfers' response was militant—members of the San Onofre Surf Club set fire to signs announcing the restrictions and to the railroad trestles that gave the beach its name. As the surfing subculture grew during the 1950s and exploded during the 1960s, the pitched battles between surfers and marines on the beach became more and more protracted. Surfers continually defied the Marines' authority to control access to the ocean and illegally surfed the waves every day. The Marines responded by using warships to nudge surfers back onto the beach where they were arrested and their boards were confiscated. Described as a "war" by many surfers involved at the time, the conflict raged on for years.

This war, and its significance, was highlighted prominently in the pages of *Surfer* magazine, widely referred to as the surfers' "Bible" since it began publication in 1960. In 1967, its editor, surfer and journalist Drew Kampion, wrote in its pages:

> The issue at stake is an absurd one: surfers do not wish to give up the privilege of floating in the Pacific Ocean adjacent to Camp Pendleton. The Marine Corps, because someone once said "it is your ocean," has to maintain that ocean. This maintenance consists of ejecting surfers . . . You can be a boat owner and boat through it, dragging a line, killing fish, spreading an aluminum minefield of beer cans. You can be an oil tanker driver and dump gobs of tar all over it. You can be an oil company and spill your waste into it. You can be a sewage plant and pump your feces into it. But you can't be a surfer and float on it.
>
> Obviously, there appears to be something happening here. It seems that surfing, a totally nondepletive, nondestructive sport, has been more or less singled out by the Jars. Perhaps it's because the thought of free bodies in a free ocean participating in a nondestructive, free activity is an excessive tax on the Marine mentality . . . It is all they have been trained to distrust. You don't salivate at the thought of freedom and brotherhood, or you get your hand slapped. Salivating is a pre-kill phenomenon . . . It is important that the surfers uphold their right to surf in these, and all, waters. It is important that surfers maintain themselves aloof from the storm-troop tactics of our brothers in khaki. It is

important that everybody gets behind this Trestles thing and makes his voice heard to someone. Someone besides a fellow surfer.[37]

The surfers ultimately emerged victorious in this battle when Nixon gave in and declared Trestles a public beach in 1973. The image of the surfer battling for the right to "float on water" with angry, jack-booted Marines was replaced with the image of victorious surfers enjoying their right to surf the Trestles, no longer even noticing the resentful Marines a few miles up the beach. The picture of barefooted freedom fighting the picture of uniformed repression was followed by the picture of freedom triumphant. An alluring set of images, indeed.

And when it was all over, Otis Chandler, and the surfers he spoke for, still wasn't satisfied. Shortly after the transfer, an *LA Times* editorial entitled "Pendleton Beach—a Good Start" exhorted its readers that "the fight must resume for public access to the remaining 10½ miles of the Camp Pendleton beachfront . . ."[38]

The exhortation to political action in defense of the free space of the beach became more and more explicit in the pages of *Surfer* magazine, especially after 1968. The image of the surfer became an image of a natural environmentalist. Activist-minded editors like Drew Kampion and Steve Pezman encouraged magazine readers to get organized and fight. In 1970, one of Pezman's first acts as editor was to establish a new magazine department, OMO (Our Mother Ocean), which dealt exclusively with environmental issues.

The identification of surfing and environmental activism has become increasingly prominent over the years, with a few notable exceptions to the rule. [39] Pierce Julius Flynn, former head of the Surfrider Foundation and Ph.D. in Semiotics, has written what is probably the most sophisticated intellectual treatment of the phenomenology and tribal subculture of surfing, "*Waves of Semiosis*."[40] In an interview that precedes the piece, Flynn describes the natural relationship between surfing and taking care of the ocean: " . . . the essential idea behind the Surfrider Foundation and what provides for its real greatness . . . [is] sharing the positive force that you have been given by the waves. Living aloha . . . That basic activity of 'returning the favor' is tremendously rewarding . . . 'pure experience' or surf stoke . . . creates charitable passion." Significantly, Flynn now heads Surfdog Inc., in which he uses his understanding of surfing, semiotics, and the power of popular culture to parlay surfing's commercial success into funds for environmental activism and to "help compose the direction of modern popular culture . . ." with the ever-powerful image of surfing.[41]

The surfers haven't just identified as environmentalists, though. Their political activity and predispositions demonstrate that they actually identify as sea creatures. In surf documentaries from the *Endless Summer* to 2002's *Step Into Liquid*, at least one early scene will highlight the effortless surfing performed by seals and dolphins, generally credited as much more natural surfers than humans could ever be. This identification with sea inhabitants that comes with the surfing lifestyle colors both the surfer image and the politics that have emerged out of the culture. Only the most recent of many surfer direct actions in defense of ocean creatures happened in February of 2008, when fifteen surfers on boards risked their lives by illegally floating next to a giant Australian dredging ship working to deepen a channel in Melbourne. One of the leaders told ABC news, "If we're at risk then dolphins and seals could easily be sucked into that ship."[42] A few months earlier, television actress Hayden Panettiere and a handful of other surfers got major press coverage when they paddled out on surfboards to block a Japanese whaling ship that kills thousands of whales and dolphins every year. And these are only two of the more recent direct actions. The point is that the image of the surfer has always been one of a natural environmentalist; since the sixties, this link has been more and more explicit and active.

The politics, like the image, resonate. In fall 2004, surfer Donna Frye—third-year City Council member, former surf shop owner, and wife of famed surfboard shaper Skip Frye—initiated a third party write-in candidacy for mayor of San Diego, just five weeks before the election. A founder of Surfers Tired of Pollution (STOP) and active in the Surfrider Foundation, Frye has always been a part of the surf community's heavy involvement with local environmentalism. And her identity as a member of San Diego's surfing community was central to her campaign.

Her clean-water platform and focus on straight-talking, grassroots democracy fired the imaginations of city residents, who wrote in enough votes for Frye to give her a victory in the three-way election. After heated controversy over the legitimacy of a write-in candidate, the Superior Court of San Diego ultimately invalidated thousands of the ballots of Frye's supporters because they hadn't filled in the bubble next to where they'd written her name. Still, Frye's campaign and her true victory were unprecedented. In Frye's words: "In five short weeks, we accomplished what no one believed possible. We defied logic and conventional wisdom. We defeated Mr. Status and Mr. Quo . . . To you, my friends, I say, our time shall come."[43]

RIDERS ON THE STORM: SURFERS AND THE COUNTERCULTURE

So much for the image of the surfer as the clean-cut all American square. Since the development of a lightweight board fueled the surf culture in the 1950s and then *Gidget* exploded it into the sixties, the surfer's image—a beach bum without ambition or respect for authority or property—followed that of youth counterculture more generally. Called "beatniks" in the fifties and "youthful hippies," "salt-water loafers" and even "beachniks" in the sixties, and "beach bums" or "surf bums" from the time they entered the mass imagination, it should be obvious by now that, contra Kirse Granat May and others, surfers were by no means considered "a safe alternative" to the other youth cultures of the day. Authority figures, cultural conservatives, and "officials" saw the counterculture types in a negative light, whereas young Americans loved and emulated them to the tune of millions of dollars in surfboards, music, old woody wagons and later VW buses, and fashion. If contemporary authors have a hard time seeing the links between surf culture and beat-hippie counterculture; mid-century magazine coverage—and its readers—just assumed it.

For instance, a 1968 *LA Times* article claimed in its headline that "Surfing Helps Youth Express Individuality" and went on to gush about surfers in language that is now generally associated with the counterculture. "Through involvement with the surf each person comes to experience the development of his own self in relation to the world around him . . . as he rides the wave, he is aware of a sense of freedom which comes from mastering the forces of life. He takes the wave and he and nature are united." The article's author is clear about surf culture being of a piece with the larger youth culture:

> and this is what youth desires—a freedom to learn for themselves through personal experience. It is this element of personal involvement united with freedom that has become the hallmark of our American youth . . . this insistence on personal involvement, leading to a form of "situational ethics" is, to a large extent, what is at the root of today's youth rebellion. No law, no man, no value system is granted "tenure" by the young. Each experience is new and perhaps different . . . in order to morally participate in this activistic form of societal life, youth must be free from the restrictions of the past and free for a life that is personally styled and developed. In a sense, this explains the popularity of surfing. The surfer is free . . . in his freedom, the surfer is what he makes himself to be . . . [44]

This hippie ethos is equally apparent in the national press treatment of surfers as well. Not bound by the imperative to cover local conflicts, publications like *Life, Time, Newsweek*, etc. were free to focus on the themes of surf culture that were clearly resonating with the public at large, if movie ticket, surfboard, and clothing sales were any indication. Focusing on the themes that made surfing attractive to the masses, frequently featuring them on the cover, helped these national magazines fly off the shelves. (In fact, many of the feature articles on surfing doubled as promotions for surf fashions and the corporations, like Jantzen and Catalina, that were supplying them.)

In the national coverage, the surfer is explicitly invoked as an instance and a symbol of the larger countercultural revolt of the young. For instance, a 1966 *Time* magazine article about the middle-age of life refers to "the revolt of the teen-aged" by pointing to "those tiny secessionist principalities of disdainful young that span the U.S. from the La Jolla, California surfing set to the hobohemians of Greenwich Village . . ."[45] In 1966, *Time* reported on a riot on LA's Sunset Strip with some background on the young countercultural "takeover" of the strip and the resulting police crackdown with this description: "teeny boppers and overaged juveniles, surfers and Hell's Angels, high school dropouts and stay-ins alike, pile in by the thousands to writhe to the electronic thunder of the Byrds, the Jefferson Airplane and the New Generation . . . the Strip became the perfect place for flaunting rebellion . . . experimenting with pot and acid and free sex . . ."[46]

In a 1965 article about the long hairstyles that "once were seen only atop Los Angeles and Greenwich Village beatniks" but now "have spread to the entire teen and post-teen population," *Time* magazine reports that "most of the longhairs can be parted into two groups—the 'greasers' and the 'surfers.'"[47] A 1966 *Time* article about surfers on beaches all over the country features the unique language—young people "have established such a free and easy way of life that they have had to invent a new language to describe it"—and the "sun, sand, suds, and sex" that constitutes this "free and easy" life. By day, there is surfing and volleyball, and "at night, it continues with beer drinking and frenzied frugging to ear-shattering rock bands in the local clubs . . . when the bars close, it's really time to swing, with all-night parties in motels and rooming houses . . . the conclusion is frequently sexual . . ."[48]

In all the coverage, young surfers are regularly called "surf bums," "beach bums," and "beachniks." In one of the first pieces of national magazine coverage, a 1950 *Life* magazine piece entitled "Life Revisits the Ski Bums (And Finds That Now They Are Beach Bums)," the author "looked up" the ski bums he'd profiled in the winter "and found them still leading a bum's life" in San Onofre. Although the beach provides "a less glamorous" form of "free-loading" than the expensive hotels of Sun Valley, the lifestyle is the same. "On the beach the bums spend every minute they can surfboarding, sunning, guzzling beer, making friends with the people who come down to be weekend beach bums. By taking jobs nearby as packers, lifeguards, bartenders, they earn just enough to fill their cups and stomachs and the gas tanks of the trucks in which they live and sleep." The article is filled with photos: of surfers in the water and hanging around San O's thatched hut, of shirtless men in straw hats pouring beer out of the back of the woody wagon they call home and flirting with bikini-clad women, of preparations for a beach feast, of people acting goofy and generally having a great time. [49]

And not much had changed by 1965, when *Life* again profiled this crowd in an article entitled "Aspen's Awful Problem: Surfers on Skis." The surf bum crowd had migrated back to the mountains for the winter and the locals were none too happy about it, apparently. In a familiar depiction, the author says of the "bums" that "They live on odd jobs and have earned the name 'skiniks' because of their beatnik attitude and long hair." Apparently, "the new invasion makes well-heeled Aspen very unhappy. It's not just the way the skiniks look—'they can grow their hair as long as they want provided they obey the law,' says Aspen's chief magistrate." But apparently, they don't—drug use and wild partying in overcrowded, rental houses was the norm, and a ski-shop owner claims that "these bums will steal you blind." The article included photographs of crowded, wild parties where everyone is dancing and laughing, and of kids riding surfboards down the slopes. And again, work is just what the young people do to be able to live. Paid labor is marginal to "real life"—having collective fun.[50]

In fact, it's this feature of surf culture that, more than any other, links it with counterculture more generally. Ocean waves, according to a 1963 *Sports Illustrated* article, have resisted all efforts at harnessing them—"the waves remain useless and wild." The same can be said of the surfer. The article, which like many, profiles strong female surfers, also describes the life of California surfer (now Dr.) Ricky Grigg, "the personification of this strange affliction, an established master of surfing" who now lives in Hawaii, working on his thesis in oceanography and supporting his wife. Although his work is more compelling and autonomous than that of most people, for him, surfing still comes first. All day long, he listens to the wave reports from outlying buoys and checks his favorite surf spots. If the surf comes up, all work is forgotten until it dies down again. The surfer tends always to be profiled this way—surfing first, work somewhere far down the list.[51]

Time Magazine's 1966 profile of Bruce Brown, auteur of the instant classic "Endless Summer," describes him as a "blond, 28-year-old Californian who probably qualifies as the world's foremost exponent of pleasure before business . . ." The article describes his subjects as "beachniks" living "the idle life"—Brown has just "made his pleasures pay" into a "fun-filled six-figure bracket."[52] This is characteristic of every profile of surfers, including the surfer/businessmen like John Severson, filmmaker, artist, and publisher of *Surfer* Magazine. In 1966's "Riding the Crest of Surfing's Wave," *Life* profiles Severson as being someone whose "success stems from his abhorrence of the frantic pace at which so many other people pursue their notion of success. 'There is no point waiting until I am 65 to have some fun,' he once told himself, and set about building a career out of what he had enjoyed doing most as a teen-ager." His workday consists of "a casual three hours a day," after which "he hurries back to what he regards as most important—his family, surfing, and his hobbies." As important as the magazine is, the waves still come first: "We could be in the middle of putting out the magazine but if someone said the surf is up, this place would be deserted in five minutes." The article's last line is his response to a question about his plans for the future: "Whatever happens I know I won't be punching a time clock." This interview takes place under a photo of Severson—"smiling, suntanned, and boyish, Severson shows the beneficent results of the good California beach life that he espouses." *Life* is clearly approving of what, despite Severson's anti-drug statements, is an attitude at odds with the imperatives of the work ethic.

Severson also espouses the surfer ethic of refusing to take life too seriously. "I just hate business. I try not to get emotionally involved with it. To some people everything is a crisis and it can be one if you want it to be. You have to be able to laugh. Very few things are really worth getting upset over."[53] Once again we see the image of the surfer as one who refuses the mindset of crisis and scarcity that I have argued undercuts the leverage of the working class with respect to capital. Another 1966 *Life* Magazine article asks, "Is J. J. Really King of the Surf?" and reports on the myth created by America's top surfers about "J. J. Moon," the fake persona of one of their buddies, supposedly "the greatest" surfer around. Miki Dora wrote an article in a surf magazine rating Moon as second only to Dora himself; when Malibu great Mickey Munoz was being interviewed prior to a major Hawaii surf competition, he said "the guy I really fear the most is the fabulous J. J. Moon." As a result of this whole put-on, "Moon" prequalified for the finals of the competition just on word of mouth alone, and became famous (and financially successful) himself. The article is almost incredulous in depicting surfers as using the commercial media and corporate sponsorship at their disposal in a playful way. "Moon" himself is, too: "It's insane. We're putting everybody on. Oh, baby, it's *beautiful*!"[54]

This putting-on of the public is characteristic of the mid-century surfer image (and another link with the counterculture a la the Merry Pranksters). One never knew, for instance, whether Miki Dora was telling the truth about anything—most of the stories he told the media were fabrications. The refusal to take things seriously was used by sixties surfers to shock, as well: *Time* reported in 1966 on the huge fad that surfers adapted from Hell's Angels and then spread around the country—the wearing of the German Iron Cross. According to one fifteen-year-old surfer, "It really upsets your parents. That's why everyone buys them." Parental disapproval and the shock and upset of local authorities didn't change the fact that "spread across the country by chain and variety stores, the crosses are now being made of copper, wood, enamel, and silver plate, and are being sold by such quality stores as Manhattan's Bergdorf Goodman and B. Altman." The nation's largest manufacturer of the crosses called them "the hottest single novelty item in years."[55] The commercial and media power of surf culture functioned to transform the meaning of things ordinarily taken seriously—work, business, competition, even WWII Germany—into put-ons. Also, like the singular language that is the subject of many profiles of its own, these moments are always in-jokes that make the subculture impossible to "pin down," to understand, by anyone on the outside. But still, the magazines tried—they were feeding a mass desire to participate in what was young and wild and fun.

The Saturday Evening Post first covered surfers in 1958, in an admiring article entitled "They Ride the Wild Water." The article features the grace and fearlessness of the surf "addicts" and breathlessly describes their activity in terms like, "now the riders are in the wave and riding wild and free."[56] By 1962, the magazine was calling them "a young, clannish bunch, with group eccentricities such as baggy bathing trunks and a private lingo" who say things like "surfing is our life . . . all the in-between days are bare existence." Residents of coastal towns are "less rhapsodic. Surfers, they say, are roughnecks who drink and go on rampages . . ."[57] In 1966, the magazine used the surf subculture as one of its three examples of the new dynamic whereby Californians "seek their own tribe—a group of soulmates who dress alike, talk alike, and make the same scene." The other two examples of "way-out people" typifying subcultures are motorcyle gangs and "free souls, or freaks." The three groups are treated as very similar in their total dedication to the leisure pursuits around which their groups are organized and in their stark difference from the mainstream.[58] By 1967, the *Post* was reprinting an extensive excerpt from surfer Phil Edwards' memoir, in which quotes like, "if it's one of those grim, zilch days, I can always go to work" are printed in large boldface and the author writes eloquently about the difference between the stoke that the surfer enjoys and the sad lives of those he famously calls "the legions of the unjazzed."[59]

In 1961, *Life* magazine featured "The Mad Happy Surfers," showing photographs of smiling young kids and captioning them with madcap stories about the "addicts" who made up a "cult" with its "own vocabulary."[60] In 1963, *Readers Digest* profiled surfers, focusing on a psychiatrist who "gave up his California practice and became a full-time 'surfing bum'" as typical of those on whom "surfing exerts a kind of hypnotic fascination bordering on the fanatical."[61] By later in the decade, the obsession with surfing was routinely referred to with the metaphor of drug use, another link with the counterculture. A 1964 *Time* magazine article begins, "Riding a board through the surf is like going on hashish. The addicts . . . listen to apostles, who preach: 'when the surf is good, you've got to go and get it. Work is secondary.'" (The addicts, of course, also "have their own fashions" and "speak their own lingo").[62] The truth is, though, work doesn't even come in second—it's drugs, sex, and parties that take up most of the surfers' time out of the water. In 1962, *Time* profiled the International Surfing Championships in the giant waves of Makaha. The first competitor interviewed "came primarily for the nightlong pre-meet beach parties. 'Surfing to me means more parties and good times. A lot of us learned to do the twist the night before the meet. We drink, we have a big party, and tomorrow we surf. The water revives you.'"[63]

In 1967, *The Ladies' Home Journal* did an in-depth examination of the California surf culture through a profile of one Skip Wright, a 23-year-old "beach bum," for whom "surf is a way of life." According to the author, Skip is "warm, appealing, energetic in a diffused and disorganized way, a cautious adventurer, tentative hedonist, passive rebel. But he is also a dropout who managed to keep out of the draft, a kicks seeker, disciple of the new hip culture, inarticulate non-activist protester against the American way of life

. . . vain, naïve, misinformed, without ambition . . . and, most alarming of all: contagious." He's a good surfer ("*Surfer* magazine ranks him the 181st best surfer in the world") and makes money sanding surfboards for Gordon-Smith, because "not many jobs permit a man to come in at 11 because the morning tide was too beautiful to abandon or take off at 2 in the afternoon because the sea is super surfs-up." His Ocean Beach apartment is filled with primitive-looking knick-knacks from the Orient and Africa, Marvel comics "featuring 'the psychedelic adventures of The Fantastic Four' with its hero, The Silver Surfer," with "shrines" to his idols, Bob Dylan and the Beatles, and with friends like "Moto" and "Sqwacky," who "has a very good philosophy of life . . . yeh, he thinks the world owes him a living."[64]

By 1971, *Sports Illustrated* was describing the Smirnoff Pro-Am, surfing's biggest contest, on Sunset Beach in Hawaii, in terms appropriate for describing a be-in. "An extraordinary aura of peace lay over the scene . . . [of] surfers, hippies, and locals . . ." a scene that looked "at first glance like a Far Far West convention of the Woodstock Nation." Surface followed substance here, in that the hippie vibe permeated the essence of the event: "Imagine a world championship event in which neither the time nor the place are decided until the morning of the first day, and in which the only consideration is the test offered the competitors." And why do the young men (of which only one "was the only really short-haired surfer in a field of 42 professionals") compete? The event's champion put it this way: "now I can stay a while and surf some more. I do not have to get a job so soon."[65] And by 1975, the magazine was calling one surfer's idea that "you can't just surf and lie around," that "you need a job," a "heresy" among "Hawaii's North Shore surfing colony, whose members think surfing is the only way of life—at least as long as welfare and food stamps exist."[66]

Other pieces highlighted the more explicitly political links between surfers and the mass uprisings of the 1960s. *Time* magazine proclaimed incredulously in the last line of one article about the calcium deposits that surfers develop (many said purposely) on their knees and that makes it "impossible for a surfer to wear high-cut G.I. shoes," that "the beachniks are beating the draft!"[67] In 1970, *Time* reported on a riot on the UC Santa Barbara Campus. The "surfing, suntanned students" "rose up for three days of insane violence" over the firing of a popular faculty member and then "the reasons to riot became diffused—Viet Nam, pollution, the Establishment . . . the Chicago Seven Verdict." They were called "cowardly little bums" by Ronald Reagan, who sent in 400 National Guardsmen to the campus who ultimately "restored peace."[68]

THE PHENOMENOLOGY OF WAVES: THE EXISTENTIAL THRILL

From the start, the surfer has been profiled as one who looks danger in the face and effectively conquers fear. Big-wave surfers, especially, have always been covered with great admiration. Surfers tend to be quoted as brushing off the danger with an existentialist comment. This characteristic of the surfer image—which defines it to this day—is yet another countercultural trait. In Norman Mailer's formulation, the defining characteristic of "hip" is a complete absorption in the present that results from living with danger—with an insecurity that makes delayed gratification impossible. For Mailer, black culture has always had this characteristic because white violence so often lurks around the next corner, and now bohemian whites are developing this existentialism as a result of the globally dangerous conditions of the twentieth century—mass death in world wars and the possibility of nuclear annihilation of the entire globe with the push of a button. Big-wave surfers, as represented in American culture, cultivate this existential quality, living entirely in the moment partly as a result of the danger that constantly confronts them as part and parcel of their life's activity. This characteristic is highlighted in the image of the surfer almost from the moment it enters the American imagination. And it continues to define this image, in many ways, even in present-day popular films like *Riding Giants* and *Step Into Liquid* in which the big-wave surfers being glorified echo the same existential themes that their predecessors in the earlier twentieth century had.

The surfers' treating the possibility of death as inconsequential has a rare power. The fact is, the Man has nothing on you if you're not afraid to die. Capitalist elites depend on fear and the desire to be protected to provide support for imperialist adventures and the domestic repression that comes with them—then as now. In mid-century America, it was fear of the USSR and the bomb; today it's fear of the terrorists. Either way, an audacious refusal of fear, an ability to live fully in the face of danger, is a radical position.

The fearless acceptance of the possibility of death that grounds an existential relationship to the moment is prominent in surfer-generated images as well. One of the "mythical" stories that surfers tell involves a legend of islanders seeing that their villages were about to be wiped away by a tidal wave—and instead of despairing, surfing the tidal wave as their last, greatest act.[69] (In fact, stories of surfers surfing the 2004 tsunami in Thailand made their way all around the internet.) And more recent images, even of surfing smaller waves, convey the same relationship to danger and the moment. In Daniel Duane's words: "the great white . . . serves reasonably well as an embodiment of one's relationship to fate: you know they're out there, you even know they're more likely to be at one place than another, and, yet, the odds are on your side. You either quit surfing (unthinkable), or accept a sentiment commonly shared in the water: "Yeah, I figure if a shark's going to eat me, he's going to eat me.'"[70]

It's not inconsequential when a legendary tube-rider like Gerry Lopez talks about riding giant, perilous waves and says that he looks out and thinks, "well, I guess today's a good day to die." Or Jeff Clark, who says in *Riding Giants* that in order to surf giant waves, you have to commit totally, against all self-preservation, and say "if I eat it, I eat it, but I'm going."[71] And just go. Accepting the possibility of death is portrayed as not only brave, but also as the road to full, total, connected pleasure.

The surfer dismisses the danger involved in surfing because of the intense thrill that surfing provides. *Life* Magazine's 1963 profile of big-wave surfers, "Riding the Wild Waves" is subtitled: "elite surfers' *peril and ecstasy* in Hawaii." Photos of legendary surfers like Greg Noll, Ricky Grigg, Jose Angel, Buzzy Trent, and Fred Van Dyke riding 20-foot waves and frequently wiping out in them are accompanied by statements attempting to describe "the sheer breathless joy," of surfing, "the fierce exultation of the moment." And living in the moment is only possible when it's the priority of one's life. Van Dyke is the surfer extensively interviewed for the piece. He talks about his fear, and the (traditionally feminine-associated) desire to show off and perform for an audience as part of life for big-wave surfers. He also says that "by the time I went to college . . . I'd already decided that leisure time was more important to me than making money . . ." He became a teacher to have the maximum of leisure time but "I still get carried away when I hear the big surf is running. If I'm teaching, I find it hard to concentrate . . ." The article's last words are Van Dyke's: "your worries vanish . . . when you drop down the face of a perfect wave, you're sure you know why you're here. You're free."[72]

The sentiments of big-wave riders as popularly portrayed haven't changed much since then. In the oft-repeated words of Mark Foo, one of the world's top big-wave surfers until he died riding one: "If you want the ultimate thrill, you've got to be willing to pay the ultimate price." Another surfer, profiled in *Sports Illustrated* in the late seventies, says of riding inside the breaking wave that "part of the ecstasy of getting tubed is knowing you're so close to wiping out. The more you hang in there on the brink of disaster, the more elated you feel about it."[73] This insight, that big-wave surfers take the biggest risks, so they get the best, most joyful rides, is a constant characteristic of the surfer image. The intense awareness of the moment that the imminent presence of death produces is portrayed as the source of the greatest pleasure, and this existentialism links surfing with bohemianism of every stripe in the American imagination.

A related connection between this existential attitude of surfers and the bohemian refusal of work that is the most prominent feature of their pop culture image is the utterly different relation to time and the moment that characterizes the phenomenology of surfing perhaps above all else. A 1969 *Sports Illustrated* article lays it out clearly. Profiling the Smirnoff International Pro-Am, the biggest surfing contest of that year, the article focuses on the difficulties involved with the contest—first, because "no two waves are the same," "truly objective scoring is nearly impossible in surfing," and second, the legions of "freedom fighters," or townies, were refusing to leave the water and claiming that "surfing is a free man's art." Still, troubles aside, the real reason surf contests exist is to use the image of surfing to improve the image of the corporate sponsors by association. *Sports Illustrated* documented this image through Champion Corky Carroll "out on the waves . . . lives in the present, which is how he likes it. Recently he got tired of knowing what time it was, so he threw his watch away. 'I looked at it one day,' he said, 'and didn't know why.'"[74] In 1971, *Sports Illustrated* put it simply, titling its article on surfing, "The Closest Thing to Being Born."[75]

This existential relationship to time and the moment continues to characterize the pop culture image of surfing. Daniel Duane's *Caught Inside: A Surfer's Year on the California Coast*, describes one surf session this way:

> the moment was all the more precious for the knowledge that tomorrow, perhaps even in an hour, it would pass . . . I thought how, with the peeling wave as an ideal of perfection, the surfer's object of passion becomes the very essence of ephemerality—not a thing to be owned or a goal to be attained but rather a fleeting state to inhabit . . . Unlike so many other passions: while one might, I suppose, wish for a bloom to remain in blossom, for a ripening grape to hang always on the vine . . . the understandably hopeless hope that we might freeze our world's better moments—the wave's plenitude is rather in the peeling of the petal, the very motion of the falling fruit."[76] He goes on: "one often hears surfing compared to sex . . . in the unself-conscious participation in a pattern of energy, in a constant physical response to a changing medium—at its best, emptying your mind of past and future . . . each wave washes away all that has come before.[77]

Pro surfer Midget Farrelly put it this way in his book, *The Surfing Life*: "You go into oblivion. Suddenly all your life is there in this long, stretched-out wave. You're removed from the past, everything on your mind becomes immaterial, everything turns to jelly, and you feel completely removed from the world around you. Nothing matters but you and the board and the wave and this instant in time."[78] The most famous formulation of the relationship between surfing and time is probably pro surfer Shaun Tomson's statement that "Time expands in the tube."[79]

Surfers portray a life activity that produces a time consciousness focused on every instant, rather than on life as a narrative structure in which past and future distract from the present. This is why delayed gratification and the security it produces tend to be outside the consciousness of the surfer, at least in his and her cultural representation. Duane is eloquent on this point: "A surf session is a small occurrence outside the linear march of time; sure, you can catch your last wave, but rather than a natural conclusion to a well-lived tale, it will simply be the point at which the circle was snipped. No conflict, no crisis and resolution, no difficult goal obtained or struggle between teams or even with oneself."[80] What we understand as consciousness involves putting the "I" into a comprehensible narrative structure, but as we've seen, the image of surfing conveys a pre-consciousness, connected, or oceanic reality as opposed to the rational separation of I and Other that grounds the ability to tell a story. Interestingly, though, as we've seen, the attempts to put the ephemeral nature of surfing into a narrative structure have been part of the image of surfing from the start. Like the unconscious which its image mirrors, surfing produces reams of narrative—people are always grasping, attempting to put language to it. Duane says,

> I thought again about throwing language all over a scene, wondered if the emotional mystery of one's response to place doesn't lie in the inchoate play of *possible* words, of felt meanings and poetries, of the sublime, the romantic, the picturesque, Zen; even, perhaps, something new. And perhaps that twinge of disappointment one always feels at the words chosen—and thus also at the glorious scene—comes from the dream that in that instant of indecision and all-decision before your mind clarified its response to beauty, you just might have held within you language finally saturated with all the earth's meaning.[81]

What the experience of surfing encourages, and the image of surfing conveys, is a relationship to time that's impossible to quantify. Marx begins the first chapter of *Capital* by explaining the difference between seeing nature and the moments of a human life in a quantitative way, and experiencing them qualitatively. For capital, the key process is what Marx calls "abstraction," or the stripping away of all that is particular and concrete about an object or a particular kind of human labor. Unlike human beings, capital has no interest in things or activities in themselves. All commodities, and especially the commodity of human labor-power, must be "reduced" to what is common to all of them (which is human labor "in the abstract," or just a mathematical slice of the average labor of society), so that essential calculations can be made. The important point here is that in order for capital to produce profit, the qualitative essence of objects and the actual activity of people has to be understood in the abstract, so that it can be quantified for the purpose of rational, reliable calculation. (This is one of many places that Marx's analysis of capitalism links up with that of Weber: the latter posits calculability as *the* major characteristic that distinguishes the rationality of modern capitalism from all other economic forms.)

The difference between the qualitative and the quantitative underlies the whole class struggle as described in *Capital*: the working class always sees its own activity, and the objects of its needs and desires, in qualitative terms, in opposition to the abstraction and quantification that characterize the calculations of capital. For instance, from my own perspective, the qualitative difference between a beer and a bomb is paramount. They couldn't be more different. For capital, each of those commodities is primarily a repository of so much quantitative value—in terms of what matters for capital, they are the same, products manufactured to be sold on the market for profit.

Similarly with labor, or the way human beings spend the moments of their lives—for capital, the concrete uniqueness of each moment in a human life is inconsequential. "Hours of labor time"—only in that way does activity actually matter. Human labor time is something to be quantified, "in the abstract," for the purpose of producing and calculating profit. The image of the surfer, on the other hand, conveys a fully-qualitative appreciation of the spontaneous uniqueness of each moment—one can simply never surf the same wave twice. In yet another way, we see that the figure of the surfer is just no use to capital's production side.

THE CLEAN-CUT SURFER?

Throughout the national coverage of surfers (as well as the local coverage we've already treated), the theme that their "beach bum" image was a thing of the "past" is a constant (and continues to this day). As early as 1963, *Time* Magazine, in a profile entitled "Surf's Up!" claims that "after [*Gidget*] came the surf bums, the peroxided boys and girls who first gave surfing a bad name—and not only because of their outlandish hairdos. Throbbing to guitars at midnight twist parties, they were fond of nudity and occasional ransacking of beach homes. But slowly the genuine challenge of the sport attracted a better ilk, and bit by bit an entire subculture emerged."[82] In 1964, a *Sports Illustrated* article claimed that "the gremmie of yesteryear—a long-haired, unwashed, blue-jeaned rowdy—is vanishing from the scene, and today's hot-dogger is a clean-cut type . . ."[83] The year before, *Newsweek* had claimed that the "bad element"—"the long-locked, peroxide-blond boys and bikini-clad shorebound girls who adore Dick Dale's surfing music and for whom the real kicks take place on the sand, not the surf"—may be "abandoning the surfboards." According to John Severson, publisher of *Surfer* magazine and one who (for a time, anyway) seemed to favor the clean-cut surfer image, "the music really has nothing to do with surfing—but it gave us a bad name—and a bad element." The article claims that at a recent surfing championship, the kids were strumming folk music like Joan Baez on the guitars rather than surf music.[84] However, this reflected the changing tastes of youth and the development of rock and roll more than some kind of new docility—which it would be quite silly to claim that Joan Baez represented, anyway.

In 1966, *Newsweek* claimed that "five or six years ago, the World Surfing Championships would have been about as welcome in a U.S. city as the Pot-Smoking Olympics . . ." because "surfers seemed to swing in an irresponsible little world of their own, complete with an arcane language no reputable citizen would recognize . . ." and that "outraged officials in several towns along the Atlantic and Pacific coasts went so far as to rule their coasts off-limits, muttering indelicacies about those scroungy sons of the beach in their fraying sweatshirts and baggies."[85] The article claimed that surfing had cleaned up its act, as did a 1967 *Newsweek* article, "Surf's Up: The Wet-Set Revolution." The article begins by saying that surfing's great popularity has "rehabilitated" its image but goes on to feature the following facts: mainland surfers coming to Hawaii "provide a conduit for marijuana, pep pills, and LSD"; some of surfing's "problem children" are emigrating to Hawaii and others are "defecting" to the "motorcycle and hippie cults." All this, supposedly, is contributing to the new, more marketable image of the clean-cut surfer. Most of the article, however, constructs a somewhat different image: "Significantly, perhaps, their [surfers'] explanations [of surfing's "siren song"] struck chords almost in tune with the rhapsodies of the hallucinogenic cult." One surfer is quoted as saying "your mind is blown out." Another says: "when you leave the land and go to the ocean you become one with the ocean because everything on the land leaves your mind . . . I would lose track of time, find an inner space, and find myself in myself." Ricky Grigg adds that surfing "offers complete disassociation from society" and that in surfing, "there is no authority . . ."[86] In 1967, everybody knew that this was not clean-cut square talk. Far from it.

Other evidence that this was largely wishful thinking comes from articles in the journals read by recreation professionals, like *Parks and Recreation* and *Recreation*. Articles in both these magazines during the sixties featured ways that authorities might deal with "the lack of understanding and complete disregard for local beach rules among this crowd," with a 1965 article mentioning that none of the measures taken by beach communities so far had been successful: "the conduct of surfers had not improved."[87] In another article, "Explorers in the Surf: An Invasion of 'Hot Curl' Guys Menaces a Staid Beachfront Community," the author mentions the attempt to "channel the exuberance of the surfers into proper and less offensive behavior patterns."[88] The exuberance was currently expressing itself in heavy drinking, loud voices, bleached long hair, and the habit of public nudity encouraged by surfers changing in plain sight of everyone.

A 1965 profile on surfers in *Sports Illustrated* highlights the female surfing champion, Joyce Hoffman, supposedly a model of the clean, competitive surfer as athlete. In this piece like so many others, the countercultural nature of surf culture overtakes the article. Readers might already have been familiar with Hoffman from her endorsement of Triumph convertibles in print ads highlighting her surfboard and the "Booming surf. Roaring engine. A pretty girl's smile. Triumph Spitfire."[89] Hoffman is not a "beach bum" but she's not your typical young girl, either. Most of the article focuses on her intensely competitive nature, and how unusual it is for a girl to be this way. According to her father, pro surfer Walter Hoffman, "my daughter's real weird. She wants to win. The other girls couldn't care less." But apparently, the other boys couldn't, either—according to Joyce, "I'm the only surfer I know of that trains. Surfers aren't athletes yet. So far the sport's not that competitive, not that precise. You don't have to be in shape.

You can stay up late, smoke, drink, and still pull through. Most surfers couldn't make it in any other sport." Once again the image of the surfer upends traditional gender roles—the article focuses on the masculine competitiveness of this blond, gorgeous young girl, and then quotes her father as saying that for the most part, "surfing's not masculine . . . most big-wave riders are latent homosexuals."[90]

But for all Joyce's difference from other surfers, she does share one thing in common with them: her disdain for work. "I can't imagine what I'd do if I didn't surf . . . I sure wouldn't work. I have a phobia against work." In this article, surfing represents female power, male submissiveness to the giant wave (which, like the ocean, is always referred to with the feminine pronoun), and, more than anything, freedom. "According to Dr. Harvey Powelson, the chief psychiatrist at the University of California at Berkeley, members of the middle class have taken over surfing . . . because they saw in it an expression of a freedom that they felt that had been deprived of . . ." In fact, the article goes on to explain that Dr. Powelson and Erving Goffman, also at Berkeley, had proposed a participant observation study of the surfing subculture "but it was not approved by the university administration."

The characterization of surfers as clean-cut, all-American, nonthreatening types may not have been accurate, but it did exist for a reason: some within the mid-century surfing community wanted very badly to expunge the "beach bum" image from surfing. There seem to be two reasons for this fact: one, as surfers got more and more grief from the forces trying to repress them, some surfers concluded that the best defense was to assure everybody they were "cleaning house" internally, and therefore didn't need outside regulation to deal with the "hooligans." The other reason was a similarly opportunistic one: those inside the subculture who had aspired to "legitimize" surfing as a sport, with competitions and Olympics and television coverage, etc.—saw, rightly or wrongly, that the only way to make this happen was to "clean up" surfing's image. Their accounts of how much trouble they had with the hippie types make them some of the most important sources on just how countercultural surf culture and its image had, by the 1960s, become.

To find evidence that surfing in the sixties was part-and-parcel of the counterculture, we need look no further than surfer and politician Fred Hemmings, who's spent much of his professional career battling surfing's ubiquitous and lasting countercultural tendencies. A world champion surfer, a haole from Hawaii, and later a state legislator, Hemmings was among the crowd who thought surfing could take its rightful place among "legitimate" sports if only the "bad element" was eliminated from surfing. He founded the International Professional Surfing Association to promote the legitimate, competitive aspect of surfing in the face of a negative reaction to "objective" judging and competition on the part of many surfers. These anti-competitive forces insisted on the impossibility of quantifying surfing in competitive "points" and were known as "soul surfers." That soul surfing was becoming the mainstream of surf culture is clear from how serious a threat Hemmings saw them as being to the sport: he came out and said that soul surfers would ruin surfing.

In 1969, Hemmings wrote an article in *Surfer* magazine that the editors entitled "Professionalism is White." In the article, he attempts to convince the surfing community that "Surfing needs professionalism! The most important job a professional organization would do is to qualify surfing as a legitimate sport . . . Some claim riding waves is an art, others say it is a cult or way of life . . ."[91] Hemmings rejects these characterizations in favor of surfing as (drug-free) sport. In another article he wrote in *International Surfing Magazine* in1970,

> the surfing superstar must be a positive influence not only for the surfing community but more importantly for everyone who comes into contact with the sport. The surfing super stars have a heavy debt and responsibility to the wonderful sport of surfing. With them they carry the representation of the great surfing life. The surfing elite must feel an obligation to their fellow surfers to present the best on behalf of our sport. The gift of surfing has brought the super stars much. They in turn must represent the sport with as much dignity and honor as possible.[92]

Hemmings did a surfboard ad in 1969 depicting him on a wave next to the giant words: "Surfing is Reality." Reprinted in his 1996 book, he captions the ad by saying: "By 1969 the hallucinogenic acid trippers were ragging me because I was too regular—no trips for me. I had a surfboard ad run that stated my feelings about surfing. Notice my red, white, and blue all-American board—there was a message there, too. I did get a six-pack of crappola for the ad from the hard-core space pilots. Such is life."[93] The drug abuse rampant in surfing, and in American society at large, was a preoccupation of his. According to him,

> my long-standing opposition to drugs sometimes put me at odds with the surfing underground. When I was elected to the Hawaii legislature, I cut back on my surfing activities. In the meantime, I was proud to be honored as an Association of Surfing Professionals 'life' member. In that capacity and feeling that the sport of surfing should make a strong statement against drugs, I called on ASP to institute a drug testing program as was being done in pro football and the Olympics . . . a prominent surfer from years gone by took out a newspaper advertisement denouncing my initiative and ridiculing me . . . I cannot think of anyone who has benefited from a drug habit, though there are a few surfing punks who have made big bucks from selling drugs, often at the expense of young surfers and Hawaiian kids on the North Shore . . . To their credit, the Association of Surfing Professionals ended up taking a

> stand in favor of drug testing. It sent a strong message out that surfing would join other responsible sports in fighting drug abuse.[94]

Well, message or no message, there is still no drug testing in pro surfing. And even Hemmings, the anti-"dope" crusader, is far more measured about drugs than most social conservatives. He admits in 1996 that "my daughters . . . recently read the close-to-30 years old editorial and laughed. They explained to their naïve father (that's me) that "dope" most often refers to marijuana. I certainly don't consider marijuana the plague that hard drugs are . . ."

Hemmings was nevertheless fighting desperately to get surfers to represent themselves in a more "square" way. Most surfers didn't share his desire. If surfing were inherently clean-cut, responsible, and legitimate, he wouldn't have had to work so hard to try to make it so, to "improve the image" of the surfer. Hemmings knew that besides surfers themselves, another powerful force was arrayed against him: "the character and personality of surfing has been influenced (tainted) by what I call the 'bad boy sell.' Down through the years, a few surfers and commercial interests have used anti-establishment-in-your-face marketing to sell their products. The 'bad boy sell,' which highlights punk imagery, has impacted surfing . . ."[95]

Far more representative of surf culture was Australian Nat Young, like Hemmings a world champion, book author, and future legislator:

> To call it a sport—that's really limiting. There aren't any lines to cross, no goal posts, no time period. Christ, we were pacifists, we wouldn't go to war, we have this history of being anti-sportsmen, and we should be proud of that. We should adhere to that. It's our heritage.

And Young's characterization of the late sixties and seventies in surfing goes like this:

> Soul surfing became the fashion. The longhaired, back-to-nature surf stars of the time were heavily involved in meditation, astrology, health foods, the self, the striving for physical perfection . . . and drugs. Taking psychedelic drugs and smoking marijuana became the norm. Surfers began dropping out and experimenting with communal living . . . Smoking pot was a sign of the times; it was the "look inward" era of flower power, mysticism, the Maharishi and the popularization of Eastern cults, which affected everyone from the Beatles and the Rolling stones to surfers.[96]

Young put it most simply when he wrote: "by simply surfing we are supporting the revolution."[97]

Counterposing the words of Young with those of Hemmings functions as a validity check on the point we're making about the "clean-cut" surfer—it was more a crusade than a cultural reality. If both opponents of the counterculture and its fans saw surfing as part and parcel of it, for better or worse, it's probably a characterization with some validity. More important for our argument, the image of the surfer as wild and free won out over that of the clean-cut square in the American imagination. The commercial forces that were using the "bad boy sell" had more success than those using the clean sell to develop a legitimate sport. Surfing remains without much legitimacy as a "real" sport *and* retains a countercultural image in mass culture.[98] If we see the market as a translator of mass taste, it seems that Americans were more turned on by the image of the hippie surfer dude than by that of the competitive square. In the battle to define the content of surfing's pop culture image, the free-and-easy beach bum continued to define the image of the surfer, because it continued to constitute its appeal.

Adding to the hippie image, two major figures of the American counterculture identified surfing as one with their projects of liberation through drugs and music. According to Nat Young, Jimi Hendrix got to know many surfers during his trips to Hawaii, and apparently, "Jimi considered surfers to be a chosen race on earth."[99] Hendrix appears as himself in the psychedelic 1972 surf film, *Rainbow Bridge,* in which Jimi's character visits the planetary meditation cult of the same name on Maui.[100] The film is full of stoned, hippie philosophizing, including by Jimi himself, as well as by the stashing of large amounts of hash inside surfboards (a strategy actually used by The Brotherhood, a notorious band of surfing drug smugglers). Mike Hynson, interviewed later about the film, recounts how in California theatres, surfers watching the film lit up their hash pipes in tandem with the hippies on the screen.[101] The film's climax comes with Jimi's concert for the commune members on the slopes of the volcano, Pali Gap.

Timothy Leary used to give his lectures with the image of a surfer behind him, illustrating visually what he wanted audiences to see. In a late 1960s *Surfer* magazine interview, Leary said of surfing:

> Well, we're all attempting to find words and metaphors for processes that are . . . hard to describe in words. One of the best ways of describing what we're doing is to define our roles as 'evolutionary surfers.' Everything is made of waves. At the level of electrons and neutrons, it's part of a wave theory. Historical waves, cultural waves . . . One of the great lessons you learn in the ocean is that while you are totally insignificant to the total mass, you can survive in it by being part of it. Surfing gives you very elemental illustrations of broader truths by serving as a microcosm that we can grasp. I've been doing a lot of lecturing, and I've picked out as my symbol, surf. Behind me, I want to have a film of a surfer right at that point moving along constantly right at the edge of the tube. That position is the metaphor of life to me, the highly conscious life . . . what the evolutionary meaning of it is, you see, I think surfers are truly advanced people. That on any planet like ours,

> when you get a culture that gets into surfing, it's a sign of maturity on the part of that species . . . [102]

Whether cop or reformer, those who wanted to discipline the surfers had the problem that precisely what they abhorred about surf culture was being broadcast far and wide to the tune of millions of dollars—complete with the themes of not working, doing drugs, loafing at the beach, the homosexual/gender-bending images, refusal of the discipline of scarcity, and sex. The story of the representation of the surfer is the story of how pop culture picks up on subversive activity, broadcasts it and inspires people to act in its image. This was true of the hippie counterculture, which grew in large part due to the organizing work that popular culture did for it. Radio and television broadcast hippie activities and music far and wide—so that a young person in middle America knew just where to go to meet up with like-minded young people just from hearing song lyrics such as "If you're going to San Francisco, be sure to wear some flowers in your hair . . ."[103] And it was true of the surf subculture as well, in which the content of this subversiveness is a laid-back, anti-work subculture—just the kind that the Calvinists were not willing to tolerate in Hawaii and that I argue capitalists still have to contend with as cultural opposition. With every popular culture amplification of the image of the surfer, more and more Americans took to the water and blew off work.

There is no question that despite the concerns of parents, teachers, cops, and bosses, commercial forces worked to spread surfing around the country. In one of countless advertising examples, Clairol, which during the sixties was heavily marketing a peroxide dye for males called "Sudden Summer," underwrote a giant Arizona wave pool, complete with thatched huts all around it and, in echoes of turn of the century Redondo Beach, surfing demonstrations by famous pros, to the tune of two million dollars.[104] But it was through music and film, more than anything, that the surfer image was disseminated through American culture, inspiring people to join the party—on the waves and off.

Surf music was part and parcel of the rock and roll explosion that defined and bonded the young boomer generation in the sound of liberation. It was another major connection between the youth culture that became counterculture and the surf scene that fed into it. The most comprehensive treatment of surf music to date is Brian Chidester and Dominic Priore's *Pop Surf Culture: Music, Film and Fashion from the Bohemian Surf Era.*[105] Their work demonstrates with exhaustive detail both that surf music's relegation to a footnote in the history of rock and roll is a devastating omission, and that it's impossible to understand the flowering of the counterculture—in music, art, fashion, film, and lifestyle—without having a sense of the centrality of California surf culture to it.

Surfer Dick Dale was named "king of the surf guitar" as a result of playing his guitar to sound like the building intensity of an ocean wave and entertaining young Southern Californians in big dancehalls, who invented the "surfer's stomp" as they listened to Dale's stylings. In 1963, *Newsweek* profiled Dale and described the music this way: "the surf music sound Dale strives for is 'a heavy staccato sound on the low-key guitar strings, with a heavy throbbing beat—like thunder, or waves breaking over you. This is played full volume and piped through an eerily reverberating echo chamber. The resultant keening, droning morass of sound drives teen-agers into such dance steps as the stomp and the frugue . . ." When asked about the wild reaction of his surfer audiences when they first began hearing his music, he recalls that "It seemed to bring out the primitiveness of the surfers." Capitol records saw potential profit there; *Newsweek* reported that "Capitol records is currently spending $50,000 on a national promotion tour" for Dale's new record, *Surfer's Choice*.[106]

Dale's success inspired legions of other surf bands, some of the most successful of which were the Surfaris, know for their still-famous "Wipeout," the Trashmen's "Surfin' Bird," the Chantays, and literally hundreds of others. Although the British invasion supplanted surf music after 1964 as the country's most popular form of rock and roll, its evocation of life on the beach and surfing a wave made its way deep into the American imagination. And in addition to spawning a new and wildly popular form of surf music, less musically and more lyrically evocative of beach life—the Beach Boys, Jan and Dean—the original surf music made its way into the very British invasion and then psychedelic rock that displaced it.

Keith Moon, legendary drummer of The Who, had originally been into the surfing scene, the style of which English mods had adopted as their own. He'd actually played in a surf music band called the Beachcombers. As lead singer of The Who Roger Daltrey tells the story, of when he first saw Moon, "he had dyed his hair blond to look like a 'beach boy'." And during the Who's heyday, according to guitarist Pete Townshend, Moon was heavy into the Beach Boys and their "girly backup vocals"—which Townshend didn't like. But he loved Moon's drumming, some of the very fastest and most intense in all of rock and roll, and definitely influenced by, if not one with, the thunderous drumming of early surf music. Townsend called Moon "a genius," showing his preference for the original surf music over what purists dismissively call Beach Boys-style "surf songs."[107]

Jimi Hendrix, probably the guitarist most identified with psychedelic, sixties rock and roll, was a fan of Dick Dale's. In fact, according to historian Ben Marcus, at the end of his 1967 record, after a psychedelic guitar jam, Jimi whispers, "and you'll never hear surf music again . . ." The comment was Jimi's dedication of the record to Dick Dale, who had cancer at the time and who, that day, had been falsely rumored to have been dying. Jimi heard the rumor, and whispered his sad statement into the mike.[108]

The heavy-reverb surf guitar sound made its way into other psychedelic acid rock as well (including the very LA sound of The Doors). The guitar solos in early sixties surf music share a sound with psychedelic rock as it developed and was best exemplified by Jerry Garcia's tripped-out guitar solos for the Grateful Dead, the San Francisco band most associated with the hippie scene. It was all part-and-parcel of the development of rock and roll: Hawaiian slack-key guitar was incorporated into country music via crying pedal-steel guitars, and then rock and roll developed as a hybrid of blues and country music. Surf music was an integral part of it from the beginning.

ENDLESS SUMMER: THE SURFER ON FILM

Many of the surf music bands were advertised in trailers for *Beach Party* movies and featured in the films themselves. And more than anything, it's in the image of the surfer on film that we see its truly countercultural nature—in terms of its essential characteristics as well as the reality of connections between surf culture and the other manifestations of mid-century American youth culture. Surfing has always been particularly well-suited to filmic representations—from early twentieth-century Hawaiian shorts to Doc Ball's 1930s footage through the 1950s, when the surf movie really developed as an art form. Filmmakers like Bud Browne, , John Severson, Bruce Brown and others followed the lead of Tom Blake and Doc Ball in innovating new ways to shoot surfers. The films they shot, of their friends surfing particularly good waves in both California and Hawaii, became cult favorites in the surf crowd. The filmmakers schlepped their reels up and down the California coast, printing flyers and showing up in high school and civic auditoriums, narrating the footage live and playing rock and roll as films were being shown. These rowdy, sold-out film showings became rituals bonding the surfing tribe, and followed in the long surfer tradition of getting together when the surf wasn't up to watch waves being surfed. (This tradition has been carried forward ever since, its more recent incarnation being in the living rooms of surfers where groups gather around video players to watch some of the countless surf videos available today. They keep on coming out, every month. It's still a huge market.)

Numbering nearly a thousand, these early movies are some of America's first "indie" films. The auteurs tended to see their work as a labor of love, an art form from which they barely made enough money to begin the next film. Still, as noncommercial as these films were, some were still advertised with the sponsorship of interested companies—usually surfboard makers who raffled off a few boards, but also, in several cases, Pan Am Airlines, which advertised one film with a giveaway of a free round trip flight to Hawaii. Qantas airlines helped produce another, as did Renault, working to tap the nomadic nature of the surf tribe. One film was "presented by Foremost Instant Breakfast." Most of the films are lost to us now, having never been transferred from film, but a look at some of the promotional posters that were ubiquitous in beach towns during the sixties tells us something about the changing contours of the subculture.[109]

Through the fifties and early sixties, the posters, like the films, highlighted the pure image of the surfer on the wave. As the sixties progressed, the poster images, and the films, followed the subculture in its increasingly psychedelic turn. Two essentially countercultural characteristics are most prominent: an ecological sensibility based on the joy of connecting with nature, and the freedom from work and repression that largely accompanies a life organized around surfing. The first is so clearly portrayed in the "dance" between the wave and the surfer captured by the camera in all these films—including those that are made today—that the ecological perspective barely needs articulating in words. It's immanent in the image, always.

Greg Macgillivray and Jim Freeman's 1967 cult hit is advertised with the text: "Surfers live differently than other people. They live a unique, carefree life. To a surfer only two things are important: the sun and the surf. This free and easy attitude is depicted in the new, color film "Free and Easy" . . ."[110] As the sixties progressed, the graphics on the posters became more and more psychedelic and began regularly to include badges of membership in the surf counterculture—VW buses, woody wagons, girls in bikinis and bearded beat-looking guys in Wayfarers. And as the poster art got trippier, the text became more and more evocative of the lifestyle. Consider 1968's *Nomads*: "The nomad doesn't work, seldom eats, but always surfs . . . a penetrating new look into the world of surfing." Or *The Golden Breed*, that same year: "To the man of The Golden Breed, sex is a beautiful wave!"[111] In 1969 *The Natural Art* stated, under a picture that fully evokes an LSD trip, "The Natural Art is a colorful surfing film fantasy . . . The Natural Art is an organic 90 minutes of positive vibrations . . . The Natural Art is heavy. The Natural Art is light. The Natural Art is whatever you want it to be. The Natural Art is ready if you are. At your local magic theater soon."[112] *The Cosmic Children*, from 1970, advertises itself thus: The cosmic children are the space age, spaced out, radical, dynamic surfers of today."[113] The footage making up the trippy *Innermost Limits of Pure Fun* is promoted with a poster comprised mostly of polka-dotted mushrooms. The films became more and more psychedelic as surf culture and the larger youth culture did. Several of the most famous, like John Severson's 1970 *Pacific Vibrations* (called by Entertainment Today magazine "Like Woodstock on a Wave") and MacGillivray and Freeman's 1972 *Five Summer Stories* were promoted with totally psychedelic posters created by Rick Griffin. (It seems by this point that Severson's opposition to the use and promotion of drugs by and for surfers had faded away.)

Griffin's artwork is one of the unmistakable signs of the San Francisco psychedelic rock and roll counterculture. The famous concert posters for the Grateful Dead, Jimi Hendrix, Big Brother and the Holding Company, Jefferson Airplane, and anybody else who was anybody in the scene, are his tripped-out creations. Griffin also designed the original magazine logo for *Rolling Stone*. But before he was a countercultural icon, he was a surf artist. He drew the famous "Murph the Surf" cartoon for *Surfer* magazine, and was, according to Sam George, "*Surfer's* dominant artistic force throughout the sixties."[114] Much of the art in *Surfer* magazine during that time was a true marriage of surf and psychedelia.

During the seventies, some of the surf footage movies were advertised with language reminiscent of that describing hard-core pornography. The poster for the 1975 film *Tales from the Tube* reads "FEATURING the hottest wave riders in the hottest tubes, NON-STOP ACTION that will put you at the edge of your seat "going for it." TALES FROM THE TUBE puts you inside the best waves in the world! Crystal clear blue super stokers in Living Color. DON'T MISS IT!"[115] *Super Session*, a surf and skateboarding film from 1975, advertises itself as "*the* new film people are talking about because every ride is HOT, the music is HOT, the SUPERSTARS are HOT, the skateboarding is THE BEST, and the photography is SUPERB!"[116] Surfing has always been portrayed as being a lot like sex—in the pleasure, the connection, the absorption in the moment, the loss of conscious self and flow into something transcendent. But it wasn't only surfers—who know this metaphor from experience—who responded to the libidinal nature of the images. Certainly it's surfers who constitute the largest and most constant audience for film footage of surfing. But the general public has made hits of the surf footage films just as they made hits of the feature film treatments of the surf lifestyle.

The Endless Summer was far and away the most successful of these early inside-the-subculture films. Bruce Brown was convinced that the footage of two surfers on a world journey to chase never-ending summer and find the perfect wave, complete with the kind of droll narration generally heard in auditoriums, could be a commercial hit. The studios didn't believe him, even though *Gidget* had already spawned sequels by the time it came out. Brown was determined to prove them wrong, so he rented a theatre himself in Wichita, Kansas—the place least likely to love a surf movie—and the film played to sold-out crowds for its entire two-week run. Brown booked the Kipps Bay Theater in New York City and the same thing happened. The film also gained critical adulation: *The New Yorker* called it "Brilliant . . . A perfect movie . . . A great movie . . ."[117] and spoke to how inspiring surfing footage is to non-surfers, mentioning that the surfing footage is the most compelling part of the film. A 1966 *Life* magazine review echoed the same sentiment: "for a moment you can understand the exhilaration of slipping down a glassy wall of water, the challenge of a 30-foot heaving monster, the terrifying wipe-outs under tons of churning water and lethal boards—and the beautiful peace of sitting offshore in the sunset waiting for the last ride of the day."

According to the reviewer, far more compelling than the (nonexistent) plot or the characters is the "breathtaking" surf footage, which makes you really feel it.[118] The author understands what critic Thad Ziolkowski misses in his well-put but wrongheaded comment that surf footage has the same effect on non-surfers as does hard-core pornography to a toddler.[119] What feeds the constant stream of surf footage videos as well as pop culture images of surfers in the water, riding waves, is the compelling, and inspiring, nature of the footage. It makes you want to try it, because it connects with something very deep in the human psyche—the oceanic. The moving image evokes the phenomenology of surfing quite well. The unusual combination of feeling totally free while being locked in a connected dance with something unfathomably larger than the self—the transcendent freedom of surfing is like nothing else, and watching the surfer on the wave gives the viewer a palpable sense of it.

After the sold-out runs and the reviews, distributors came knocking and the rest is history—*Endless Summer* became one of the most successful and best-known films of all time. Why? The cover of the DVD says simply of the two surfers: "They live their dream." The movie portrays gliding over the water—reacting to, channeling, and above all enjoying the energy of the wave—and also, the lifestyle of the surfer comes across in all its free, goofy fun. Two California surfers, Mike Hynson and Robert August, don skinny ties, Wayfarers, pointy shoes and matching natty suits, comb their hair back, and carry their boards on a search to chase summer all around the world, from southern Africa up the eastern coast, on to Australia and then to the surfers' mecca, Hawaii. On the way, they find "the perfect wave" in Cape St. Francis, South Africa, and turn on native Nigerians, old and young alike, to the joy of surfing.[120]

In addition to the image of the surfers on wave after wave after wave, in fact, the relationship between the white American surfers and the African natives is one of the most striking features of the film. Although the irreverent tone of Brown's narration sounds politically incorrect to our more culturally sensitive ears, the attitude is one of playful ribbing for all the film's subjects, including the stars. The only things in the movie that earn the respect of either the surfers or the narrator are the waves. The surfers' relationship to the "primitives" in Africa goes deeper than silly jokes about fear of the natives coming to eat them, though. In a classic scene, we see the appreciation for surfing on the part of the natives, who gather on the beach to watch and cheer with thrilled astonishment, and who eventually make their own boards from planks and start surfing themselves. The pleasure of riding waves seems to transcend barriers of language and culture—in this way, the film projects a utopianism whereby people who are supposedly totally different, totally alien, connect through the pleasure of play.[121]

The iconic image on the film's poster—of silhouetted surfers with boards, looking out to the water against a fiery orange and pink horizon at sunset—is one of American culture's most recognized images. The fact that the surfers can't be identified is key. Surfing is probably the most democratic of all the images of "living the dream" in American culture—all you need is a board and a beach and you're a surfer. The movie poster says as much with the silhouette—this could be you. The last line of the film says it all: "with enough time and enough money, you could spend the rest of your life following the summer around the world."

The surfer-made films were so close to their audience—members of the subculture making films for the subculture about the subculture, and being (loudly and sometimes physically) reviewed on the spot—that in some ways they broadcast things about surf culture more authentically than other, more mass-directed media like Hollywood pictures. But as cultural analysts, we don't read Hollywood movies to determine the level of authenticity of the representations. We read them for something that is in many ways much more significant—as a projection of the dreams and desires that masses of Americans share, and pay good money to see indulged.

Siegfried Kracauer argues that because popular films must appeal to a mass audience, they constitute an attempt to "satisfy mass desires . . . The distorting influence of Hollywood mass entertainment should not be overrated. *The manipulator depends upon the inherent qualities of his material* . . ." Thus, popular films can be read as indicators of these desires—"those deep layers of collective mentality which extend more or less below the dimension of consciousness." Kracauer quotes Library of Congress film archivist, Barbara Deming, on why both major and minor (or in our case, both "A" and "B" films) are equally important for our purposes: "Even if one could figure out . . . which were the most popular films, it might turn out that in saving those at the top, one would be saving the same dream over and over again . . . and losing other dreams which did not happen to appear in the most popular individual pictures but did appear over and over again in a great number of cheaper, less popular pictures."[122] By either standard, the dream represented by the figure of the surfer is massive in the American imagination.

Ultimately it was not the surfers-filming-surfers genre that launched the Hollywood surf craze in the late fifties and through the sixties, although more and more of this type of film is produced these days. (Recent examples are 2003's *Step Into Liquid* and 2004's *Riding Giants*[123]—both films made up primarily of intense surfing footage in the old tradition, with some interviews and documentary analysis as well. Both films were produced in association with surf industry corporations, who understand the impact of this kind of film in terms of inspiring Americans to buy a surfboard and hit the waves.) The key moment came with a novel delineating a fifteen-year-old girl's sexual coming of age through the image of surfing. *Gidget*—the true story of a young girl who ingratiated herself with the "surf bums" of Malibu so she could learn to surf and hang out in the scene—was a nationwide bestseller. Published in 1957, it was really quite racy. It was also pop culture's most prominent example of the image of the surfer as strong female. Gidget's female teenage sexuality is not lost on *Time* magazine, for one, who calls her "the pelvic oracle of surfdom."[124]

(Although post-*Gidget* film images of women frequently tended to paint girls as beach-bound ornaments, this began to change starting with 1991's *Point Break*. Lori Petty's character is one of the gang, as competent a surfer as the rest of them. In a gender turnaround of the surf film trope in which the surfer male rescues the girl from drowning—most famously enacted in *Gidget*—Petty saves Keanu Reeves' protagonist in the early scenes of the film. He begs her to teach him to surf, and she only reluctantly agrees. Also, 2001's *Blue Crush* was a film all about female big-wave surfing. The macho football player who becomes surfer Kate Bosworth's boyfriend takes the (usually female) position of worried cheerleader back on the beach as the female champion rides the giant waves of Pipeline. In fact, as Krista Comer points out in her upcoming *Surfing the New World Order*, female—or "grrrl"—surfers figure more prominently in surf culture's twenty-first-century pop culture incarnation than ever before.)

In the novel, Gidget is a raunchy-talking, street-smart teenager, hormones coursing wildly through her body. She's a far cry from the film version, in which Sandra Dee plays her as a wide-eyed innocent surrounded by sexual debauchery, concerned that she's not feeling it herself and thinking maybe she should.[125] Sandra Dee plays Gidget as square as they come, but in the book, Gidget's no angel. Her first person narration dismisses the youth group her parents would like her to attend: "those wholesome squares . . . bore the living hell out of me with their crummy meetings."[126] She's just finished reading "*From Here to Eternity* for the sixth time (meaning the dirty passages)."[127] In fact, she refers later to the classic novels she can never get through, except for the sexy parts. She loves the surf bums' bawdy talk: "There was some dialogue that got pretty rough. I pretended not to listen but got hotter and hotter . . . I lapped up every word of that sexy talk, every single syllable of it . . ."[128] In the film, her father tells her to "turn down that infernal racket," but it's big band swing she's listening to, not the Fats Domino records that she listens to in the book.

In the novel, Gidget's parents appear only as concerned elder (immigrant) squares, fearful of the "sex mania" of Americans. Their only real role is to be lied to by Gidget. In the tamer film, on the other hand, they provide the benevolent paternalistic guidance (the father) and the warm, sweet appropriate gender socialization (the mother). Other characters are similarly transformed: Kahoona, the king of the surf bums, who lives in the thatched shack, is portrayed in the novel as taking great pleasure in his life of freedom, and also as being a pretty wise, philosophical cat. He lives off the fruit of the sea and the kindness of friends, and follows the sun wherever summer takes him. He's a surf bum by choice, and for pleasure. In the film, however, his lifestyle is seen as a symptom of an inability to connect with others and to "grow up," over which he's apparently very conflicted. Not so in the novel (or in the real life of Terry "Tubesteak" Tracey on whom his character is largely based)—in which he lives happily ever after as a well-loved legendary surfer.

There are many such differences between the novel and the film. In the novel, Gidget's sexuality and love of surfing are front and center, but in the film, they take a back seat to the domesticating morality tale that comes at the film's end (and that is nowhere to be found in the novel). The clearest example of this emerges when we compare the final scenes of each. In the *film*, the story's climactic end-of-summer luau at the shack ends up with a frightened Gidget pretending to desire the Kahoona in order to make her true love, Moondoggie (a.k.a. Jeff), jealous. Moondoggie chases them to the beach cottage, scene of the fake tryst, and punches Kahoona to save Gidget's honor. A big fight ensues, the police come, and Gidget winds up being taken to a police station, where her worried parents are waiting with open arms. She's learned her lesson.[129]

The *novel* ends with a very different scene. Unable to get home after the big luau, Gidget finds herself crashing in Kahoona's bed for the night (her parents are away for the weekend). Although she's been in love with Moondoggie all summer (who is conflicted about her age but is also in love with Gidget), when Kahoona comes into the shack, her desire fixes itself upon him. (The novel is far more about Gidget's desire, which can attach onto different objects, than it is about her love affair with Moondoggie.)

> My fingers began trembling, my pulse went rapidly. All kinds of thoughts raced through my head, some of them so startlingly romantic and biological that they surprised and shocked me. The next thought that rushed to my head was, what would happen if I invited him to lie down with me?

She does, and

> the most violent emotions were beating against me. And the surf pounding against the dunes was supplying the proper background music . . . It was shocking and overwhelming, feeling a man's body like that. At this moment I knew I had never lived at all. Maybe I had not even been born yet. All my fears and frustrations seemed to melt away in a sudden blaze.

A tender scene ensues in which Gidget and the "superannuated Huckleberry Finn" acknowledge their attraction but the older, wiser Kahoona tells her that for her first sexual experience, "the time must be really ripe."[130] Gidget cries coming-of-age tears, and the two sleep locked in a sweet embrace. When morning comes (and brings giant waves), Moondoggie finds Gidget having slept in Kahoona's bed and a fight breaks out between the two men. But in the book, this is no trauma for Gidget. The climactic scene ends with Gidget on a wave, not at the police station with her parents.

Suddenly, it hit me. I guess "like lightning" is too corny to write down, but Jeez, it fits to a T. It hit me that this wasn't a crummy movie I was watching. Two grown-up men had almost killed each other on account of little me—the gnomie, the shortie—the Gidget!

I noticed some blood trickling from Jeff's nose as he lay stymied and bleary-eyed against the wall of the hut, but instead of feeling compassion nothing but a pang of joy went through me. This was the pinnacle, this was the most. Surely nothing more wonderful would happen to me, ever.

Had I shouted they would certainly have thought I had gone crazy. So I did the next best thing to give vent to my soaring spirits. I lifted the board in my hands over my head and ran down to the water . . .

A few more strokes and I was beyond the surf line. I couldn't see the coast any more, so high rose the wall of waves before me. I whirled around and brought the board into position. There was no waiting. I shot toward the first set of forming waves and rose.

I stood it. I have to come in standing, I told myself. I gritted my teeth.

"Shoot it," I yelled.

I was lifted up sky high . . . and went down. But I stood it. One wave, another one.

"Ole!" I yelled. "Ole!"

Up I was—and down I went.

And still standing.

I was so jazzed up I didn't care whether I would break my neck or ever see Jeff again—or the great Kahoona.

I stood, high like on a mountain peak and dove down, but I stood it.

This victorious ending to the novel is not reproduced in the film. The movie's final scenes find Gidget having abandoned the alluring but ultimately scary debauchery of the Malibu crew for the warm domesticity of the family and the woman's role in it, exemplified, her mother tells her, by her grandmother's framed embroidery on the wall: "To be a real woman is to bring out the best in a man." As it happens, her father has wanted her to date a "respectable" boy, a son of a distinguished friend. When Gidget sees him, it turns out to be Moondoggie, a.k.a. Jeff, in a nice combination of romantic happy-ending and the patriarchal passing on of women between father and "approved" husband. Gidget and Moondoggie head to the beach to bid farewell to Kahoona and everything he represents, only to find him tearing down the beach shack and packing to leave and get a job. The camera lingers long on his new "Employee Pass," where we see for the first time his real name. Kahoona intimates that it's Gidget that got him "thinking" about his future, and when Moondoggie asks what he meant, Gidget says coyly: "oh, just something between my grandmother, my mother, and me." And instead of ending with Gidget independent and triumphant on the giant wave, in the film, Gidget's final victory is to win Jeff's fraternity pin now that he's decided to go back to college.

It's important to understand that the *novel*—the epilogue of which ends with Gidget minimizing the importance of the men and saying "but with the board and the sun and the waves it was for real. All things considered—maybe I was just a woman in love with a surfboard. It's as simple as that."[131] The novel was a huge hit with 1950s audiences. Hollywood saw the ability to make a profit from the great allure of these adventures of a young woman full of moxie and sexuality, and the surf bums of Malibu. The studios were operating under substantial restrictions, however. Foremost was the Hollywood Production Code, a code of self-censorship that the studios adopted in 1930 and strengthened four years later. As movies became more and more popular (and gained sound), outcry about their moral degeneracy grew louder too, especially from religious leaders (who've always feared the power of culture to tap into currents that are subversive of "good" behavior). The studios read the writing on the wall, and adopted the code to avoid the costs of redoing a movie after the state censors had gotten to it. They also hoped to avoid intensified government censorship, which the studios figured would be worse than self-censorship. The Hollywood Production Code, and the Production Code Administration that enforced it, upheld neo-Puritan moral standards about sexuality, domesticity, work, and the law.[132]

The Code remained in effect until 1968, when, under the competitive pressure of television and more racy foreign films—the showing of which the studios couldn't control ever since the 1948 anti-trust ruling that prohibited studios from owning theatres too—it was abandoned. It's important to understand that all pre-1968 films, and especially those produced during the late fifties and early sixties, before the code was relaxed, have to be read through its lens—studios tried to project the most alluring material they could without getting busted. So in *Gidget*, the female sexual desire—feared enemy of Puritan morals—is domesticated, especially through the maneuver of switching the reader/viewer's identification. In the film, the viewer is now to identify as an innocent among an explosion of sexuality and debauchery, rather than, as in the novel, one whose lust for life made her search out the libidinal pleasures of surfing and sex. This way, the perspective of "the film" could uphold the code's moral standards while subverting them with its subject matter.

(One subversive association from the history of surf culture did make it into the movie, although not via the novel. Moondoggie plays in the old tradition of the beach boy as gigolo, hired for the pleasure of the consuming female, when through a series of misunderstandings he winds up being hired by Gidget to be her escort to the luau.)

Nevertheless, the story is set in a sexually explosive space where beat culture met the uncivilized wildness of the beach and work is disdained as a primitive association—bare feet, bongo drums, dancing around bonfires—abounded. The filmmakers couldn't get away from the essential outlines of the story, no matter what kind of corny ending they slapped on it. The plot line may have worked, in the end, to pathologize the handsome surf bum and domesticate the "decent" kids who were tempted by him, but most of the movie is constituted by half-naked, young, tan bodies; surfing and dancing, using raunchy language and living in their own world on the beach. It's this—"the Malibu surf scene"—that made it into the movie and that accounts for its huge success, judging by how profoundly the movie's release transformed American surf culture. After *Gidget*, teens became surf-obsessed for years and the waves never went back to being uncrowded. It's fair to assume from the film that it wasn't the fraternity pin or the parents that inspired all the surfing—it was the evocation of life on the beach that did it. It was the beach-bum culture evoked in *Gidget* that sent masses of Americans out onto the waves, not the life of the domesticated square that presumably begins when the final credits end.

To evoke this life, several themes from the book *are* reproduced faithfully in the film—the total disdain for work, the raunchy language, and the centrality of the luau, constantly referred to as an "orgy." It's the open sexuality on the beach, the primitive associations, and the use of (great footage of) surfing to represent all of this, that the novel and the film have in common and that account for the popularity of each of them. In the film, Kahoona may be dethroned at the end, but in the meantime, he gets such fabulous lines as "gotta follow the sun," "I'm a surf bum—you know, ride the waves, sleep, eat—not a care in the world," and "when that Korean bit was over, I knew there was one thing I didn't want in life—chains." And he is portrayed with a dark, dangerous allure by the dashing Cliff Robertson. The "gang," known only by their nicknames, has the same attitude, including "Lord Byron—the beard means he digs existentialism," and Stinky, "the fastest parking lot attendant West of the Rockies." "When he works!" "Who works when the surf is good?" This echoes the extended discussion in the novel of the nonexistent work ethic of the Malibu gang, which Gidget describes early in the novel:

> Which brings me to the subject of explaining what makes a surf bum a surf bum . . . adhering to the adage 'Early to bed, early to work is strictly for those who've gone berserk.' To join the fraternity you have to swear on a stack of abalones never to do a day's honest work—at least not while the season is going.[133]

Gidget Goes Hawaiian[134] and *Gidget Goes to Rome* soon followed the original films' success. Neither hit had the cultural impact of the first, but the fact that the Gidget character was elaborated in the sequels—and in two network television shows and prime time specials, as well as sequels to the novel—shows what a compelling character the young girl had become in the American imagination. In *Gidget Goes Hawaiian*, her character has the outside, plot-driven accoutrements of innocence, but she's basically back to being a personification of female sexual coming of age. She shows off her athletic prowess, flirts and leads on all the boys, and when a jealous rival starts a "reputation"-ruining rumor about her being loose, shame isn't the first thing on her mind. Instead, the viewer is treated to the fantasies that this turn of events has unleashed in Gidget—first, she sees sailors on the beach and imagines herself an old-fashioned lamppost harlot in a red dress. Next, she's doing a striptease with large feathered fans, tossing out her underwear behind them. These are just her fantasies, though—in the film, the "real" Gidget remains pure, which satisfied the Production Code Administration, I suppose.

Beach Party movies follow the same trajectory—neatly tied up at the end, but unleashing all kinds of subversiveness between the credits. The filmmakers knew it wasn't the back-to-work-and-domesticity resolution that was selling tickets. According to William Asher, director of the *Beach Party* movies, "I didn't want to see any parents, I didn't want to see any schools. I wanted to see them at the moment when freedom arrives and I wanted to see them have a good time. I didn't want to see them doing anything but having a good time without any supervision and that's pretty much what these pictures were."[135] That's how they were advertised, too: *Beach Party* itself was promoted with a series of posters, some of surfing, some of dancing, all accompanied by the text: "It's what happens when 10,000 kids meet on 5,000 beach blankets!"

The film is full of sexual double-entendres and even the lily-pure Annette Funicello explains to Frankie why she refuses to be alone with him: "I don't trust myself when I'm alone with you, Frankie . . ."[136] The libido of the teenagers courses through the film as its life energy, animating the scenes of their dancing around the fire, surfing, and ultimately turning on the nerdy old academic voyeur too with all the "primitive sexuality."

The other primitive instinct, aggression, is represented by Eric Von Zipper and his crew (when Professor Sutwell sees them for the first time, he mutters "aggressive" into his tape recorder). The movie ends, as do many of the *Beach Party* movies to come, with a brawl between the surfers and the bikers, representing the "battle of the Titans" between sex and aggression that Freud, in *Civilization and its Discontents*, posits as the basis of all life, individual and social. In a sense, all the *Beach Party* films are enactments of the victory of libido over destrudo, of sex over aggression, of pleasure over pain (Von Zipper's gang never has any fun).

An interesting twist emerges in the third *Beach Party* movie, 1964's *Bikini Beach*. Youthful sexual desire is the film's constant motif, as is female sexual power. The opening shots find the camera squarely following a walking, bikini-clad female posterior, the sight of which throws boys off their surfboards, and causes car accidents and numerous other mishaps (this echoes a similar scene in *Beach Party* in which the sight of a girl in a bikini stretching causes all the boys to come totally unglued. The stretcher enjoys her power, announcing gleefully that it "does it every time.") Also, Candy, the incredibly fast "Perpetual Motion Dancer" who wears tight outfits on which her dancing keeps the rows and rows of fringe constantly standing on end, has, in the second movie, developed the power to throw men literally off their feet just by swinging her hips like a weapon anywhere near them. (In *Muscle Beach Party*, Candy's dancing to Little Stevie Wonder cracks the camera during the closing credits.) "That Candy, she's got the power," says one of the boys, and her power comes in handy in helping the surfers win the film's final brawl.

In the *Bikini Beach*[137] film, the sexuality of the surfer kids has a new enemy: one Henry Huntington Honeywagon III, a caricature of a Puritan WASP-y type, complete with old-fashioned buttoned-up suit, Rolls Royce, and constant pontificating about "old morals" and "the ways of our fathers." The film opens on a shot of a big open truck full of dancing, singing young people and surfboards—a mobile dance party. Peering out the curtained window of his car, disapprovingly, is Honeywagon, who we find out is the proprietor of a senior citizens' resort just up from Bikini Beach. He looks at the chimp in the car with him and says, "they're doing your dance."

Honeywagon's comparing of the surfers to the chimp is a new twist on the original movie: where the voyeuristic anthropologist saw the surfers admiringly as "primitive," the Puritan sees them disparagingly as "animal." When his chimp-surfing stunt is received with enthusiasm by the kids, Henry launches into a lecture. "The point is not whether or not the chimp is sharp. The point is that the intelligence of you young people has fallen to his level. I'm determined to prove that you young people are borderline cases leading to feeble-mindedness, with an abnormal preoccupation with sex." To this, the kids reply, "well, yeah," in unison, with both Frankie and Annette giving knowing, approving smiles.

Huntington goes on to say, "the only display of [your] knowledge [is] of a carnal nature," and that "your irresponsible behavior has become an eyesore . . ." In a refracted image of what was really going on in many beach communities, the next day's newspaper headline screamed "TODAY'S TEENAGERS TRUE SUBCULTURE" with a picture of the chimp surfing next to all the other surfers. Inside, Huntington's editorial (it turns out that he's also the paper's publisher) is entitled "Youth of Today Leaves No Hope for Tomorrow," and describes "scenes of wild perversion and abandonment" by "juvenile delinquents." Huntington is horrified by the bikinis and by the sight of "boys and girls sleeping side by side on the beach together—what kind of society would allow this?" He hates the music, too—"this music of today is straight out of the jungle. The savage music stimulates their post-adolescent desire for sex. They're really animals," he says later.

Huntington becomes friendly with a young, pretty teacher who approaches him angrily after reading the editorial. Vivian Clements is sympathetic to the surfers (and the drag racers, another teen subculture that AIP figured it could tap into as well) and tries to convince Henry that the kids are alright. He becomes more open to her point of view as he falls for her, and after he runs into Von Zipper, who tells him how much he admires the editorial and how "perverted" the surfers are—"they *are* bums," he says. "Look who's on your side," the schoolteacher smilingly condescends to Henry. He attempts to distance himself from this personification of aggression, but the film gets the terms right. The moralistic Puritan boss fears sex and finds a natural ally in aggression.

Huntington and Vivian get closer and closer until she finds out that Huntington really wants to expand his "Sea-Esta" resort for senior citizens onto the land "illegally called Bikini Beach." "I found out why you're opposing those kids," she yells accusingly. "For purely moral reasons," Huntington says, truthfully. "You mean purely commercial reasons," the schoolteacher says, not believing him. But Huntington's not lying—he is the personification of the authentically felt morality that buttresses the wealth of the Puritan type. According to the tenets of the Protestant work ethic, those who are successful have become rich as a result of God shining down on them. Riches are recognition of a life properly lived, of a person's being with God rather than with evil. Debauchery and poverty go together in this discourse (this is still the case—look at the continuing American discussion of the "morals" of the urban poor, for instance), and so do upstanding morals and financial success. Huntington isn't masking economic interests with an inauthentic morality. In his persona, they are one and the same.

The schoolteacher lays into him, scolding him that he's running "a vegetable farm," and that he may as well provide shovels for his customers to dig their own graves. (An earlier scene does find Sea-Esta running a tour bus to a local mausoleum.) "The beach is a place to live, not to die," she says angrily as she slams the thick door behind her.

Next, we see the newspaper headlines announcing all of Huntington's "retractions" and discussing his "turnaround." He's decided that the surfers are good kids, just out to have a little fun. When the teacher happily confronts him, he says suggestively that he wanted to show her that there was "something else" in him, presumably some sex. They plan to marry, and another newspaper headline announces the senior bus trip—this time to the drag races that have become part of the plot. The old folks are seen betting and yelling and having a wild time. Afterwards, they all head out to Big Drag's Pit Stop, a café full of the eccentric proprietor's abstract artwork (along with his bird, "freedom.") After the requisite vanquishing of Von Zipper and friends, who are angry that their "ally" against the surfers has been seduced away to the other side, the old folks and the young surfers all dance together joyously to Little Stevie Wonder's first film performance.

The requisite utopian ending is consummated with some soul music. In the *Beach Party* movies, as in the discourse of the counterculture, everybody can potentially be turned on. In the films, nobody is impervious to the lure of the pleasures of surfing and sex. And the perspective of the film, Production Code notwithstanding, is so squarely on the side of libido, so very overtly against the Puritan position, that it's shocking to realize how many analysts have understood these films to be animated by a conservative morality. These popular films—of which *Beach Blanket Bingo* and *Muscle Beach Party* are more of the same—are a perfect enactment of the reality we're describing. The commercial, popular culture side of capitalism is, quite self-consciously, against the Puritan, anti-sex, work-ethic centered side of it.

The Hawaiian surfing subculture had grown and developed after WWII just as the California scene had. In fact, during the fifties, the Californians who'd migrated to Hawaii did much to craft the shape of the culture—Hawaii was the mecca for surfers, and the surf bums of California made the trip to Hawaii whenever possible, bringing back news from the Hawaiian "authorities." The subculture came full circle back to its Hawaiian roots, and the pop culture representation has followed closely ever since. If surfing represented the youthful "California dream," then Hawaiian surfing was the dream within the dream—the fantasy held (and followed) by the objects of the American fantasy, the surfers themselves. The growth of the subculture in Hawaii is yet another good example of how the commercial broadcasting of surf images has an inspirational effect on people and winds up growing the subculture. In 1953, a photo from Hawaii, of three surfers racing down the face of a 30-foot wave at Makaha, found its way onto the front page of the *Santa Monica Evening Outlook*. California surfers, used to far smaller waves, were incredulous. A mass migration to Hawaii ensued, and this next generation of Californian migrants crafted many of the outlines of surf culture as we know it.

The surfers shacked up together in small cottages on the beach, dove for lobster, fish, and turtle and picked coconuts for food, and surfed all day, every day. "The whole thing was waiting for waves . . . we were always just trying to amuse ourselves and each other . . ." says Mickey Munoz. According to Randy Rarick, "this was the counterculture of its day . . . you were bucking the system and you went to Hawaii and you rode waves. They were the pioneers, not only of riding big waves, but of the culture of surfing. They're the ones that set the pace—this kind of free and easy lifestyle . . ."[138] The photographic images coming out of Hawaii during this time broadcast the hippie life surfers were living there—one of the decade's most iconic images artistically showed legendary shaper Dick Brewer and Zen master of the Pipeline Gerry Lopez in lotus position, eyes closed, meditating next to their surfboards.

The 1964 movie *Ride the Wild Surf*[139] was a cinematic attempt to capture life riding the big waves on the North Shore of Hawaii. Constituted primarily by great footage of big wave surfing set to classic sixties surf music, including music written by Jan and Dean and Brian Wilson, the film dramatically enacts the now-classic conflict between "responsibility" and the life of the "surf bum." Although it wouldn't be until the 1991 film *Point Break* and then *Blue Crush* that Hollywood would resurrect the female-surfer archetype that had been left behind by the *Beach Party* movies after

Gidget, Ride the Wild Surf did feature Barbara Eden as Augie, black belt in karate who kicks the boys' asses for fun and successfully gets "square" surfer Chase Colton to loosen up and get wild. Still, in a classic mid-century trope, Shelley Fabares' character, like Hollywood's Gidget and Annette, is the domesticating force in the life of Fabian's surf bum, Jody Wallis. Jody does agree to go back to school at the end of the film, after winning a surf contest at Waimea Bay, but again, in this film like in all the others, the taming of desire is fully secondary to its unleashing during the film. In fact, this movie is much more like the surfer-made films that surfers themselves were going to see at this time—everything besides the surf footage seems like an afterthought. This is especially true during those moments when, inexplicably, a Bruce Brown-type third-person narrator busts in and starts giving the play-by-play, as if we were watching *The Endless Summer.*

In the fabled summer of 1967, *Sports Illustrated* covered what it called "A Summer-in at Waikiki" in a cover story entitled "The Summer Surfers Invade Hawaii." The article's author couldn't find any domesticating forces at all among the "20,000 coeds, hippies, beachies, blasters, bleachies, and just plain beach bums strewn all along Waikiki beach having a delicious summit meeting of copper-toned tummies." Apparently, "Waikiki has become one of the youth cult's grand rites of summer . . . for those in their late teens or early 20s, Waikiki is the beginning, or the middle, in a series of dropout summers given over to beach reclining, ocean tiptoeing, booze cruising, picnicking, and romance seeking . . . a final prelude to all of the unimaginable miseries that the mainland holds: a steady job, a wife or husband or children." The article follows the young "surfers"—many of whom rarely surf—as they loll on the beach and organize giant parades and parties. Many are tripping on LSD and most are at least high on pot. There's a weekly underground newspaper reporting stories about new "head" shops and the "out-of-sight pads" that are opening all over, as well as the decreasing price of marijuana.

The article's author was able to find some "straights" to disparage the kids at Waikiki (and California) and their "scene"—"celebrated big-wave riders Fred Hemmings" and friends. According to Hemmings, riding giant waves is "real" surfing. "Everything else is for hot dogs, and I mean all of California, man. That scene on Waikiki is so far away from the sport of surfing, it's ridiculous. There's nobody down there but dreamers." Hemmings, reliably, credits the commercial entrepreneurs like Severson, Brown, and Hobie Alter for the existence of such a wild scene attached to surfing. "The Dana Point mafia is what's responsible for that zoo on Waikiki," he says.

The requisite domesticating ending was nowhere to be found in the *Sports Illustrated* subject. So the author, at times bemused, at others irritated, had to provide it himself. The article's last paragraph is smug: quoting Hemmings saying that "'those dreamers ought to go back to California and stop giving our sport a bad name,'" the author follows up by saying: "Someday they will, Fred. In another year or so they will, by necessity, discover a new kind of trip. It goes like this: you do this goofy thing that this straight cat tells you to do for about eight hours a day for about five or six days a week, and then this cat lays some bread on you. You spend it, and then you start in doing the same goofy thing again. Totally amazing. It's called work."[140] Just like in the movies, the going back to work is slapped on as a fiction at the end.

As I've attempted to demonstrate, within American popular culture, surf culture was represented as one with the larger youth cultural uprising that began in the fifties, gained momentum and mass exposure in the sixties, and by the seventies had come to infiltrate the social fabric as a whole. *Life* Magazine seemed to say as much when in December 1969, the magazine put out a whole issue entitled "The Sixties: Decade of Tumult and Change." Telling the story of the sixties with a series of iconic photos, the editors put, on the penultimate page, just before the picture of the earth taken from space, a photo of a lone surfer on a giant wave. Above the picture, the text: "The rewards of exuberant health and youth, timeless realities of any age, still lie in the curl of a wave."[141] The "timeless" pleasure of surfing—both representing and transcending the sixties. *Life* was prescient in this analysis.

The surfer brings the countercultural sensibility of the sixties into every film in which he or she appears. And since the early seventies, the figure of the surfer has been a constant trope in American film, those about surfing and those that feature surfer characters. Francis Ford Coppola's masterpiece *Apocalypse Now* contains one of the most prominent uses of the metaphor of surfing as typically American libidinal freedom, and as indelibly associated with the sixties.[142] Coppola co-wrote the screenplay with John Milius, who also wrote *Big Wednesday*, considered by many surfers to be one of the more "authentic" of Hollywood's portrayals of sixties surfing. This is partly due to the fact that Milius cast actors who could actually surf, and partly because Milius himself is a surfer from California.

Apocalypse Now lays bare the insanity at the heart of the "rational," "responsible" American "civilizing"—imperial—project. The Americans see the Vietnamese, and their land, as uncivilized and primitive, nothing more than objects of their own, ultimately if not immediately benign, imperialist action. But the film shows that the repression that founds this action—repression of native people and their land, and of the primitive libido that these represent—turns the world into the primitive's other face: the nightmarish hell of insane violence. Marcuse reads Freud to say that when primitive or unconscious libido is repressed, violence is unleashed because libido is the only force capable of neutralizing primitive aggression. *Apocalypse Now* is the visual and literary rendering of this theory, showing through image and metaphor the hellish violence that the "rational" repression of libido ultimately gives rise to.

One of the film's most evocative scenes is the surreal "Charlie Don't Surf" sequence, which, early in the film, introduces the viewer to the irrational sadism that underlay the war's purportedly "rational" project of defeating the Communist "threat." This sadism is represented in the figure of Robert Duvall's Captain Kilgore. Kilgore commands an airborne unit that wreaks horror and destruction upon Vietnamese villages from the air. When flying in, the planes blast Wagner to announce the terrifying destruction to come. Kilgore relishes every second of it.

When Kilgore meets Martin Sheen's Captain Willard, Willard has already begun his mission up the river to find the renegade Colonel Kurtz. The soldiers accompanying Willard on his journey represent the libidinal side of American life in contrast to the naked aggression that marks the war. Clean is the young black mechanic from the South Bronx; Chef is the saucier from New Orleans, who wants to go into the jungle and pick mangoes; and Lance is "a surfer from Southern California, who looked like he'd never fired a weapon in his life." These are typical American boys whose sensibilities were formed by the hedonistic cultural milieu at home, just as the darkness unleashed in Willard and in Kurtz has been forged by the violent hell of the war.

Kilgore is charged with providing air cover for the boat to enter the river. In some ways, the soldiers' time with Kilgore provides the surface image of the war, before the long journey up the river and down into the darkness that Coppola (and Conrad) see at the heart of "rational" man. Kilgore's got a cowboy swagger and, as Willard observes, "you just knew he wasn't going to get a scratch on him over here." When Kilgore finds out that one of Willard's men is Lance Johnson, he gets starstruck—"Lance Johnson, the surfer?" He's honored to meet him and introduces several of his boys as surfers. They get to talking during the "beach party"—complete with barbeque and guitar—that Kilgore throws with his men after their victory. While Willard suggests that they sneak silently into the river's mouth at dawn, Kilgore finds out that another entrance to the river is a great surf break. "But it's real hairy," protests one of his boys. "That's Charlie's point," the soldier says over and over. In one of Duvall's many immortal lines, he barks back, "Charlie don't surf!"

Kilgore destroys an entire peaceful village, and sacrifices several of his own men, so that he can force Lance and some of the other soldiers to surf the point. The scene is absurd: terrified young men attempt to surf as bombs drop in the water all around them. Kilgore rips his shirt off and says he'll surf too, but we never actually see this happen. What we see is a classic macho cowboy type destroying for his own pleasure. On the surface, this is the story of American imperialism—the ruthless destroy so that they can enjoy. The native "other" is nothing more than material for the sadistic enjoyment of the powerful. And in some ways, Kilgore does represent the American figure in the war. But our time with Kilgore begins and ends early in the film, *before* Willard takes us on the metaphorical journey up the river and down into the unconscious dynamics that drive the supposedly rational ordering of the world that the Vietnam war represents. But as we take the journey with Willard into the heart of darkness, we see that something more original, something even more "primitive" is at work in this war.

As the viewer journeys deeper and deeper into the heart of darkness, we see that the content of the primitive is indeed *split* between the libido and the destrudo. Dennis Hopper's photojournalist is a member of Kurtz's cult and the first American they see—he repeats "I'm an American!" over and over—at the end of their journey. Hopper's character preaches at one point that there's only love and hate, "no fractions," no gradations. The deeper we go into the war, the more we see the pure aggression that's unleashed with the repression—by violence—of primitive libido. Native children playing in a peaceful village are one representation of this primitive libido, or the connectedness that marks the premodern social bond and relationship to nature. Primitive destrudo, however, exists fully in the figure of Americans.

The river's journey is bookended by two colonels—Kilgore at the beginning and Kurtz at the end. If Kilgore enjoys violence as a means to gain power and pleasure, Kurtz has come to so embody violence—for him, pure will—that pleasure becomes impossible for him and ultimately he welcomes Willard's mission to "terminate his command." Kurtz is pure violence, the "heart" of the war, although the generals have "rationally" concluded that he has gone "insane." He's not insane as much as he is clear about the pure aggression—"without judgment"—at the heart of the imperial project. Instead of papering it over with phony "reasons," he embraces it as a vital act.

In an interview, Milius talks about his choice of the surf metaphor: "I wrote that scene [Charlie don't surf] because I saw Vietnam as a California war. World War II movies always had guys from the East Coast with accents, but Vietnam was a rock and roll war. A California war."[143] Captain Kilgore is usually associated with the metaphor of surfing in the film, but the first image of surfing actually comes in a context very different from the "Charlie Don't Surf" scene. The boat is riding through a "safe" area. The Rolling Stones' "I Can't Get No Satisfaction" comes on the radio and Clean, smoking a joint, turns it up, loud, and dances, as Lance surfs the boat's wake on waterskis and even the staid, serious Chief, the boat's captain, guns the engine and speeds down the river. Speed, surfing, pot, and rock and roll—for a moment, the men, and the viewer, are transported back to what we recognize as American life. Wagner it ain't.

Lance is actually the key surfer character in the film, not Kilgore. He represents pure libido (not fused with destrudo, as in the case of Kilgore's sadism). As the boat goes further and further into the "primitive" jungle, further and further from "civilization," he neither loses it, as Chef routinely does, nor gets killed, as Clean, and ultimately, Chef do. He is able to merge with the primitive, painting his face in jungle camouflage and ultimately feeling one with the natives in Kurtz's camp. Along the journey, Lance has several key actions: he nurtures a small puppy taken after the soldiers overreact and massacre an innocent boatload of Vietnamese, he holds the dead Chief in the water, kissing his head to give him a tender baptismal funeral sendoff, and he drops acid before encountering a major battle. Tripping on LSD, he is in some ways the only character who experiences the war just as the viewer does—in all the awesome, terrible beauty of the film. At Kurtz's camp, we see Lance dancing with the natives around a fire during a ritual, holding and playing with the native toddlers, and tenderly bathing the bull that is to be ritually slaughtered, just as Kurtz is slaughtered by Willard. Throughout the journey, Lance the surfer represents the libidinal, connected side of the primitive, or unconscious, that the film explores. When Willard takes his hand and guides Lance out of the camp, we see the two figures—one pure, violent will, the other messy, connected, yielding—walk out of "the horror, the horror" of Kurtz's world. Neither will be the same, but Lance is actually the more intact figure, spaced out as he is, whereas we know that Willard has taken Kurtz's advice to heart, to "make a friend of the horror." Libido makes it out of hell alive, presumably to surf another day.

As for surfers' reaction to what is probably the most intense film portrayal of surfing in all of cinema, popular graffiti from the seventies, reproduced in Kampion's *Stoked*, says it all: SURF NOW APOCALYPSE LATER. This would certainly be a sentiment shared by another one of the big screen's most famous surfers: Sean Penn's classic character Jeff Spicoli in *Fast Times at Ridgemont High*.[144] In Cameron Crowe's 1982 comedy about American high school life, Spicoli is a perpetually stoned surfer who says things like, "All I need is a cool buzz and some tasty waves and I'm fine." Spicoli epitomized the spaced-out, mellow southern California surfer-dude stereotype, and is the character that made *Fast Times* an enduring classic. He is characterized by two things: he's stoked, and he refuses the discipline of work that's represented by the rather sadistic history teacher, Mr. Hand, whose main lessons consist of encouraging the students to understand the difference between "my time" and "your time."

Spicoli refuses this basic objectification of time and continually shows up late or not at all for class. He contests Mr. Hand's employer-like characterization of class time as "my" (Hand's) time: "Mr. Hand, if I'm here and you're here, doesn't that make this our time?" The idea that the "owner" of someone's time has the right to determine how it's spent, and Spicoli's refusal to accept this system, is a representation of the struggle over time that happens in every workplace, every day, especially among young workers in what Donna Gaines has called "shit jobs."[145] Like the young black McDonald's workers that Robin Kelley profiles in "Shiftless of the World, Unite!" Spicoli resists the total colonization of the moments of his life by the authority figures who claim to own his (in-school) time and thus the right to dominate him. Constantly stoned, ordering pizza and making jokes in class, Spicoli fights to style his life according to his own desires, no matter what his time's conventional "owner" wants him to do.

In the end, Mr. Hand pays Spicoli a visit in his bedroom just before a graduation dance. "According to my calculations," he says, "you've wasted eight hours of my time this year . . . I want to settle accounts," says Mr. Hand, the veneer of rationality rather thin over his purely punitive intentions. He threatens Spicoli with failure and keeping him from graduation, and forces him to study with him for several hours (during which Spicoli's surfer wisdom displays surprising profundity). But, looking around the room, filled with pot smoke and posters of surfers on waves and naked girls, Hand gives a resigned, bemused look, decides that Spicoli is incorrigible, and agrees that Spicoli will indeed "squeak by" and "cruise history." Ultimately, Spicoli triumphs over Hand, is never forced into submission, and, in a graduation dance ending reminiscent of the Beach Party movies, performs on stage with the band as all the characters dance to the music.

5 The Malibu Surfer Problem

Play and the Cultural Politics of the Class Struggle

Since the American anti-work uprising of the sixties and early seventies was countered with the devastating neoliberal policies designed to shut it down, there has been comparatively little discussion of the imperative to work—what Marcuse called the "performance principle"—as the central problem confronting American life. And those who do take the alienation of work and overwork seriously as dire social problems tend to blame consumerism for its perpetuation. Ben Hunnicutt, the prominent (and probably sole) figure in contemporary American Leisure Studies, laments the concession of defeat by American labor in its historic, and very nearly successful, struggle to shorten the hours of labor. In both his analysis of the end of the national shorter hours movement and of the end of the six-hour day at Kellogg's Battle Creek,[1] Michigan plant, Hunnicutt blames the advent of consumerism and the "alienated" leisure that came with it as in large part responsible for ending these struggles. This, even though Hunnicutt quotes a nineteenth-century labor song at the start of *Work Without End:* "Whether you work by the piece or by the day, decreasing the hours increases the pay." Workers for a long time understood that less work meant more consuming ability—a win-win situation. Unfortunately, many authors like Hunnicutt who criticize our obsession with work see Americans' desire to purchase consumer goods as a friendly amendment to, rather than the other of, the work ethic.

This is also true of economist Juliet Shor, whose 1992 classic, *The Overworked American,* targets ever-increasing hours of work as the biggest and most invisible social problem that Americans face. Her analysis also places blame for overwork on our enslavement to consumer society, which traps us in an "insidious cycle of work and spend" from which it's impossible to escape. Her answer to the problem is that public policy makers and corporations need to offer workers the opportunity to choose more free time over higher wages as their share of the postwar "productivity dividend." Again, consumerism is analyzed as undergirding the ethos of productivity rather than the subterranean values of play that oppose it. Interestingly, Shor points to the necessity of a "culture of resistance" to long work hours if anything's ever going to change.[2] The question is: does a culture of resistance to work emerge out of an ascetic refusal to consume, a scaling back of material culture? Or is the historical lesson to be taken from the 1960s that a certain hedonism—and the consumerism that pumps up hedonistic values—tends instead to breed an antagonism to work and to the ethos of productivity in all its forms?

Several historians have looked back to the beginnings of consumer society and found evidence that the values promoted by consumerism did oppose those defined by the Protestant work ethic. In Kathy Peiss's *Cheap Amusements: Working Women and Leisure in Turn-of-the-Century New York*, the author traces the liberatory effects for women of new commercialized leisure forms like dance halls and movie houses. Although the traditional, patriarchal immigrant cultures that these young working women came from encouraged their docility, the new world of commercialized recreation "fostered a youth-oriented, mixed-sex world of pleasure, where female participation was profitable and encouraged." Peiss is clear about who was encouraging young working women's liberation from oppressive traditional roles: middle-class Protestant reformers "sought to repress or at least contain the heterosocial sexually expressive culture of these working women, but they met with limited success. In contrast, an emergent group of leisure entrepreneurs encouraged that culture, played with its forms, and ultimately popularized it for a broad audience."[3]

In her 1999 book, *Ladies of Labor, Girls of Adventure: Working Women, Popular Culture, and Labor Politics at the Turn of the Century*, Nan Enstad writes a friendly, but crucial corrective to Peiss's work. Enstad notes that Peiss and others have focused solely on this group of women outside of the workplace. One would never know that this same cohort of women—acting up and having such a wild time in the new dance halls, putting on style on the cheap from department stores—engaged in one of the biggest and most significant strike waves that this nation has ever seen. These young women were militant on the job, and their militance was shaped in many ways by their interaction with popular culture: movies, dime novels, fashion, etc. The women forged a "utopian language of entitlement" out of their participation in commercialized popular culture.

It's interesting to note that then as now, the workers' interest in fun and popular culture was not taken seriously by the left or by the unions that aimed to "lead" them. In fact, labor leaders "routinely chastised working women" for their preoccupation with fashion, dime novels, and movies, fearing that "such practices kept women from serious and practical concerns like labor organizing." The women were encouraged to "adopt a more serious demeanor and more sensible shoes." But "when working women went on strike, they utilized the subjectivities and languages they developed through pop culture practices to claim formal political status." Their militance in opposing long hours, low pay, sexual harassment, and disrespect on the job, was in no way watered down by their commercialized leisure pursuits or the commodities they loved to consume, as so many on the left and in the labor movement, then and now, would have us believe. In fact, it was pumped up by them.[4]

Stephen Norwood's history of young female telephone operators at the turn of the last century, *Labor's Flaming Youth*, is another important historical document of the transformative power of living to have a good time. The young women whose union struggles are the subject of the book struck for shorter hours and higher pay because they wanted both the leisure time and the disposable income that would allow them to enjoy the fruits of a new commercial capitalism. "New commercialized forms of recreation—dance halls, amusement parks, and movie theaters—encouraged young women's participation and profited from their vitality and desire for excitement . . . [while] the consumer culture that emerged in the early twentieth century encouraged women to . . . purchase from among a dazzling array of new commodities . . ."

The young telephone operators profiled by Norwood, who frequently struck their bosses during springtime, "walked the picket line in fur coats, high heels, and fashionable headgear," evidence for the fact that "the consumer culture could encourage unionization by heightening expectations about enjoying commodities, which could not be purchased with low wages." Not surprisingly, although the retail stores and commercial dance halls encouraged women's desires to have fun and be free, "the Bell companies denounced the new fashions in dress and attempted to persuade—or in earlier years even compel—its operators to wear more conservative styles." Norwood's story of solidaristic, celebratory union activity and its allies and opponents documents the way in which from its inception, consumer culture has encouraged and profited from the desire for freedom.[5] This desire opposes and threatens a very different agent of capital—the (necessarily neo-Puritan) boss.

Robin D. G. Kelley's work is foremost among those historians who take cultural politics seriously in just this way. *Race Rebels*,[6] his study of everyday insubordination among African-Americans, rejects "the tendency to dichotomize people's lives, to assume that clear-cut 'political' motivations exist separately from issues of economic well-being, safety, pleasure, cultural expression, sexuality, freedom of mobility, and other facets of everyday life. Politics is not separate from lived experience or the imaginary world of what is possible; to the contrary, politics is about these things. Politics comprises the many battles to roll back constraints and exercise some power, or create some space within, the institutions and social relationships that dominate our lives."[7]

Much of what runs through the essays that comprise the book is a focus on the politics of refusing work. In "Shiftless of the World, Unite!" Kelley recounts his own experiences working at McDonalds, where he and his young co-workers employed countless creative, below-the-radar strategies to take back time from the employer—to transform alienated labortime into free time and to transform their bodies from interchangeable instruments of labor to personally stylized instruments of pleasure. This has been a prominent feature of African-American strategies of negotiating exploitative, racist workplaces, says Kelley, and to deny its political significance is to miss the true extent of black working-class resistance.

I've made the case that what characterizes a countercultural orientation to the world is this kind of non-instrumental relationship to time and nature: one in which being-for-itself is privileged over the means-end logic of capitalist rationality. A countercultural orientation values experience for its own sake, and the calculating mentality involved in "using" time or nature for profit is only engaged in when absolutely necessary and even then, thoroughly disdained. If the essence of capitalist rationality is, as I've argued on the basis of Freud, Weber, and Marcuse, repression of instinct and especially of libido (a repression of the only power that, Marcuse argues, can hold back the terrible destrudo), the essence of counterculture is an embrace of libido and a rejection of repression. If the condition for repression of instinct is alienation from instinct, that is, the separation from natural self that grounds the possibility of taking it as an object and repressing it, then the essence of counterculture is the refusal, or the transcendence, of this alienation—a connection among people and between people and the natural world, and between each person and his or her libido. The image of the surfer, as I hope I've demonstrated, represents these connections in opposition to the dictates of the repressive capitalist performance principle as Marcuse lays it out.

By 1971, the perception of the surfer was so fully identified with carefree leisure and the refusal of work that among philosophers and economists, a discussion emerged that centered on what they called "The Malibu Surfer Problem." That year, political philosopher John Rawls wrote his epic *A Theory of Justice*,[8] which makes a case for a conception of justice as "fairness," a conception he claims can form an alternative to utilitarianism as the philosophical basis of liberal, constitutional democracies. In Rawls' theory, the most just distribution of wealth is the one that is most fair to the least advantaged member of society. In a capitalist society, which Rawls assumes, the condition of fairness would be a guaranteed annual income for all members of society, regardless of the person's talents or the work that the person performed. But this principle of fairness doesn't apply to lazy surfers, who would "unjustly" take their share without pulling their weight by contributing. According to a later Rawls essay, "those who surf all day off Malibu must find a way to support themselves and would not be entitled to public funds."[9] And in all the discussions around Rawls' theory that have, for decades now, riffed on this question, the "Malibu Surfer Problem" has continued to refer to the "issue" that if income were unconditionally guaranteed, some members of society would steadfastly refuse to work and "free ride" (no pun acknowledged, either) on the other members of society, who work productively and "earn" their share of the negative tax.

One of the more recent, notable contributions to the debate has come from Philippe Van Parijs, whose 1995 book *Real Freedom for All*[10] has on its dustjacket a surfer riding a wave. Van Parijs embraces Rawls' theory minus the ambivalence about the free surfers, touting a "real-libertarian" perspective whereby "welfare hippies and Malibu surfers" are due the same unconditional income as those who work. Under the condition of guaranteed income for all, workaholics are referred to as "crazies" and surfers as "lazies," and both types deserve the same right as everyone else, not to starve. In fact, Van Parijs entitles one of his earlier articles *Why Surfers Should be Fed: the Liberal Case for an Unconditional Basic Income.*[11]

In welfare discourse in Australia, this identification between the surfer and the refusal of work is even more pronounced. According to Alan Law in *Surfing the Safety Net: 'Dole Bludging', 'Surfies' and Governmentality in Australia,* the figure of the surfer was used by "administrators of income support in Australia in the 1970s" to represent "lazy subjects who were the antithesis of the ideal, productive citizen of liberal democratic states," and the "broader 'problem of idleness' that has faced liberal-democratic governments since the 19th century."[12] During the 1970s, administrators of state Unemployment Benefits were explicitly instructed to ensure that claimants were not "dole bludgers," a new term formed for the "surfies." A manual for the social workers warned them that "the need to ensure that a claimant is genuinely looking for work applies especially to: members of 'Hippie' colonies; members of the 'Surfie' element . . . unemployment benefit is not ordinarily to be granted to young single persons who come within the above categories . . ."[13] Around the globe, the surfer came to be identified with the "laziness" and "hedonism" that is the polar opposite of the ascetic Puritan work ethic.

All welfare schemes, including that of some basic guaranteed annual income, are grounded in the idea of fairness—that it's not fair if some people don't have enough to meet their basic needs. The fact that the Malibu surfer has become a universally acknowledged symbol of the "problem" with justice-promoting welfare schemes—much like the American Cadillac-driving "welfare queen"—is no accident. The surfer symbolizes precisely what gets in the way of even the most well-intentioned rational system of justice—the desire for freedom. Although it's frequently proposed that economic justice is the condition that makes freedom possible for more than a minority, it's worth rethinking this idea in light of the fact that Rawls' rational system of justice and fairness is so complex that it takes in almost everything—except there's no room for the Malibu surfer. What does this mean?

It brings up the essential *contradiction* between freedom and justice. In *Civilization and its Discontents*, Freud lays out this contradiction in world-historical terms. After defining civilization as a social order in which a group of people all agree to restrict their own instinctual freedom in exchange for the security guaranteed by the fact that everyone else, no matter how weak or strong, is similarly restricted, Freud states that

> the liberty of the individual is no gift of civilization. It was greatest before there was any civilization, though then, it is true, it had for the most part no value, since the individual was scarcely in a position to defend it. The development of civilization imposes restrictions on it, and justice demands that no one shall escape these restrictions. What makes itself felt in a human community as a desire for freedom may be their revolt against some existing injustice, and so may prove favourable to a further development of civilization . . . But it may also spring from the remains of their original personality, which is still untamed by civilization and may thus become the basis in them of hostility to civilization. The urge for freedom, therefore, is directed against particular forms and demands of civilization or against civilization altogether. . . . A good part of the struggles of mankind center round the single task of finding an expedient accommodation—that is, one that will bring happiness—between the claim of the individual and the cultural claims of the group; and one of the problems that touches the fate of humanity is whether such an accommodation can be reached by means of some particular form of civilization or *whether this conflict is irreconcilable* . . . [14]

Economic justice is about a fairer distribution of (essentially scarce) material goods. In order to have economic justice, a certain austerity has to be in place in the individuals and groups whose desire and capacity for getting more would have to be tamed in such a redistributive scheme. Pure capitalism is not just. It depends on inequality between the classes for its growth, and growth is its life. It can grow the pie, that is, create abundance, but those with the most raw power get the biggest slice. At least in the theory of laissez-faire capitalism (not a reality in practice of course, since states and, in the last instance, their militaries, guarantee unfair competitive advantages for the owners of capital over the working class), the freedom to get more reigns at the cost of social justice. Between freedom and justice, it's a zero-sum game. So does embracing the freedom—the hedonistic unwillingness to restrict the ability for pleasure without work—represented by the figure of the "Malibu surfer" mean abandoning good progressive politics?

Not at all. But it does mean thinking about improving the fortunes of workers in terms more aligned with the wildness of the market than with the regulation or taming implied by rational ideas of redistributive justice. In fact, embracing the unbounded freedom represented by the surfing beach bum is *precisely* the route to a more just *and* abundant distribution of wealth—through the movement for shorter hours. In *Labor's Time*,[15] Jonathan Cutler lays out the solidaristic rationale behind the labor movement demand for less work at the same pay. Under capitalism, labor-power is bought and sold as a commodity on the market. Its price is determined through the mechanism of supply and demand:[16] if there is an oversupply of labor relative to employer demand, the price of labor will fall. Conversely, if in the face of heavy employer demand, there isn't enough labor supplied to the market, wages will rise because workers will have the leverage to press for higher pay. If workers are a dime a dozen, they won't have much leverage. If workers are scarce, each one will have a much stronger negotiating position with an employer, who needs the worker more than the worker needs him.

The demand for labor has too often been seen as determined only by the fortunes of capital and the rate of capital investment. And when unions have attempted to regulate the supply of labor coming on the market, as did the old AFL and remaining craft unions (such as construction) today, they've tended to do it by excluding whole groups of people from the market on the basis of skill but (in the face of capital's response of technological deskilling) also on the basis of gender, race, ethnicity, or national origin. Either way, this strategy, while possibly successful in the short run, is unsustainable in the long run. A resentful group of workers is created which employers can easily use to undercut the union workers' demands. This is precisely what has happened as a result of a non-solidaristic labor movement strategy.

But, as Cutler points out, there does exist another strategy for controlling the amount of labor that workers supply to the market. This is the "shorter hours" strategy that was, for a long time, a major contender for labor's strategy and for public policy. Agitating for a 30-hour week at 40 hours' pay, as mid-century auto workers did, is an inherently solidaristic way to limit the supply of labor provided to employers, thus giving workers greater leverage to drive up wages and achieve other demands. And best of all, freedom from work is both the means *and* the end of this strategy. How do workers get to the point of having more free time and higher wages? Collectively working less, that's how.

Workers have organized, throughout labor movement history, to enshrine the shorter hours demand in union platforms and negotiated contracts. (We can thank them, "the folks who brought you the weekend," for the 40-hour week that everyone's so busy giving back.) But there is another, arguably more effective way to achieve the same goals, and that's where the cultural politics of the class struggle come in. To the extent that a culture encouraging leisure and freedom spreads, people tend to be inspired to work less. That is, the working class as a whole tends to supply less labor overall to the market, bending the supply and demand curve in their favor. So the less people collectively work, the more power *and* free time they gain.

In this sense, we see that freedom ought to be a labor movement question (and not the right-wing slogan masking policies of war and imperialism to which the concept has been largely reduced within American political discourse). Freedom simply cannot be achieved with complicated, rational structures of regulation, no matter how well-intentioned. The importance of the strategy of shorter hours in the labor movement, and the centrality of cultural questions about freedom and pleasure to the possibility of a resurgence of this movement, underscores the political importance of popular culture images of freedom that are inspirational of collective action. The surfer, it should be clear by now, is such an image.

We've seen that there is nothing culturally conservative about the commercial impulse of capitalism—in the instance of the figure of the surfer (as one example of countless others), the themes that are most subversive of the discipline of work are the ones that are highlighted most prominently. It's these themes that link surf culture with the larger mid-century counterculture that it was so seminal a part of. The explosion of surf culture and the counterculture were part of what Jock Young calls *The Hippie Solution*,[17] the idea that as work became more and more automated, it was both less possible and less culturally necessary for people to gain meaning and identity through work. In the context of technical possibility, repression loses its raison d'etre. The widespread realization of this fact was a structural dislocation, or problem, to which the counterculture provided a tentative solution. But not everyone was so thrilled about the mass acknowledgment of the possibility of leisure as were the hippies and the purveyors of commercial culture.[18]

Commercial capitalists may have embraced the profitable potential in counterculture. But if Thomas Frank is right and capitalists as a whole are in favor of counterculture, somebody should tell the folks at the *Wall Street Journal*. Its editorial page is not an impartial space, and does not attempt to be. The editorials are clearly partial to the interests, not of one or another firm or economic sector, but of capital—or, as they put it, "the business environment"—as a whole. My own close reading of the *Journal's* editorial mentions of bohemianism, counterculture, beat, hippie, and the work ethic between the years of 1955 and 1980[19] demonstrates that capitalists took the refusal of discipline that it saw among American mid-century masses very seriously as a major threat—and they continue to obsess about signs of counterculture even as so many of those on the left dismiss them as insignificant.

According to the *Journal*, what happens when the "utopian" and "romantic" fantasy of abundance and freedom without toil takes hold of the population? A perilous relaxation of neo-Puritan morality, that's what. The Puritans that Weber analyzed were similarly unopposed to wealth itself, but "the real moral objection is to relaxation in the security of possession, the enjoyment of wealth with the consequence of idleness and the temptations of the flesh . . . it is only because possession involves this danger of relaxation that it is objectionable at all . . ."[20] In 1965, the *Journal* was referring to this relaxation as "a crisis in values," and could only hope that "the comparative liberality of contemporary sexual mores, for example, could itself generate a new wave of Puritanism . . . a revitalization of religious belief . . . or new affirmations of the old."[21]

The major danger is "the apparent acceptance by many Americans of the idea that they don't need to work very hard; their apparent preference to get by with the least effort and indeed to demand progressively higher pay for progressively less work." The editors are horrified to behold in the sixties "shirking on a scale more widespread than ever before in this country," in and out of unions. This shirking is explicitly called "immoral." The attitude encouraged by "the union and statist philosophy of indolence"—Keynesianism—is to "remove from the individual many of the cares of dealing with life, and most particularly remove his sense of responsibility . . ." This problem is, above all, "a moral one," and the Journal recommends that "a little *moral indignation* ought to be directed at the salesmen of sloth that weaken our society."[22]

In this editorial, the salesmen were union leaders; in others, the culprits are writers, artists, musicians, intellectuals, and "the adult publicists who celebrate them [hippies], *usually for profit*." These particular profit-seekers are portrayed as being "dangerously naïve" in broadcasting the ideas of "liberated youth" as against the "ancient truths" about the necessity of "control and restraint." One editorial even mocks a popular song (sold and broadcast by commercial capitalists) to make its point: "specific guidelines and moral codes are outdated and repressive in this liberated age . . . so long as we all 'love one another right now,' all the age-old problems of morality will be solved."[23]

The "permissiveness" that's at large in the land is resulting in the worrisome fact that "the work ethic is being derided." This is the real problem with the new "situational ethics," or, "in the vulgar hippie phrase, doing your own thing."[24] In editorials that Max Weber would well have recognized, the *Journal* is extremely concerned about the hippie ethic that privileges spontaneity over rationality. Extolling "The Value of Inhibition" in 1969, an editorial discusses the fact that the "common complaint of varying dissident groups is the lack of spontaneity in modern life: the highly structured institutions of society . . . inhibit the individual's capacity to develop or express human passions and desires." In criticizing the "street people" who "trespassed" to create People's Park, the editors warn of "spur-of-the-moment behavior" that "to seek social solutions by substituting uninhibited action for rational thinking and planning is dangerous . . ."[25]

It's only "dangerous" to some. Weber lays out the terms of opposition in much the same way: "The Puritan, like every rational type of asceticism, tried to enable a man to maintain and act upon his constant motives, especially those which it taught him itself, against the emotions . . . the end of this asceticism was to be able to lead an alert, intelligent life, the most urgent task the *destruction of spontaneous, impulsive enjoyment*, the most important means was to bring *order* into the conduct of its adherents."[26]

It's important to remember that in its shrill, incessant raging against the "romanticism," "spontaneity," "slovenliness," and "utopianism" of the day, the *Journal* is not saying that the counterculture is "potentially" dangerous—if properly organized. Surfers have organized themselves into politically active groups and engaged in direct action, to defend the ocean from pollution and the beach from restricted access. The politics of surfing as an organized social movement could comprise a book of its own. And there is no doubt that the larger the surfing subculture becomes, the more inspired people are to get involved with surfer-associated political causes. In this way, commercial forces like advertising and pop culture do egg on subversive politics.

But it's the culture of surfing and its inspirational image—ecologically connected, gender-bending, anti-work and libidinal—that's much more important politically than even the largest and best organized group of surfers. Sadly, it's become fashionable these days to assert that when people get together and collectively slow down, privilege pleasure over work, and constitute time on their own terms, it doesn't matter. But perhaps the death of the impact of countercultural living has been, to quote Mark Twain, "greatly exaggerated." It is true that the working class hasn't been doing so hot over the past few decades. Since capital hit back after the sixties uprisings, it's been pretty tough going. But to look at this retaliation as evidence that the essential nature of capitalism has changed rather than as an instance of the class struggle that is its central dynamic would, I believe, be a mistake. In fact, signs of the transformative collective desire for life over labor are everywhere. To see them, those who would oppose the logic of capital must look at popular culture and the mass response to it with fresh eyes.

The image of the surfer is still everywhere in American popular culture. Consider HBO's 2007 show, *John From Cincinnati*.[27] The opening credits resemble one of the amateurish, grainy, sixties-era movies that were taken by surfer cinematographers like Bruce Brown, Bud Browne, and John Severson, and taken around to high schools and auditoriums in coastal areas, being narrated by the filmmakers. Pure footage of great surfing, impossible to tell if it was taken in the sixties, seventies, or today. Even the font used for the credits and the sweet, simple folk-pop song in the background evoke the memory of these early surf films. Also, the mystical character of "John" *is* the image of the surfer that we've seen on the beach at San Onofre during the forties and into the 1950s. His hair, his clothes, his simplicity—his only dialogue involves repeating back to the characters what they've already said, serving as a screen on which they project their own unconscious desires and are then able to see their own truth and presumably, heal—he is the image of the purity of surfing, back in the day. And with every episode, the characters find him more and more mesmerizing. (Audiences—not so much. The show was canceled after one season, but it's fair to assume that Milch's stilted, Mamet-like dialogue was an acquired taste.)

In other ways as well, the show dramatizes substantial themes in the historical image of surfing. For instance, the commercial sale of the image of surfing, and its relationship to "authentic" surfing, has been a major debate throughout the history of surfing (as has "selling out" to most other instances of American counterculture). This tension has been a theme of countless popular culture portrayals of surfing, especially the ones, like the 1987 film *North Shore*[28] that explicitly counterposed the figure of the "soul surfer" to the zoo of corporate sponsorship and international competition. And it comes up again in the HBO show. One scene is particularly rich.

The character of Linc, the conniving promoter who works for the big companies, is wooing a very eager Shaun, the surf phenom and preteen grandson (and charge) of Mitch Yost, patriarch of a famous surfing family. Shaun is Butchie's son, and Butchie's drug-addicted failures provide the object lesson in how commercialism can ruin something great. So Mitch, the old school longboard soul surfer, who's venomous toward the inauthentic whoring of commercial sponsorship and the impossible quantification of the sublime that characterizes surf competitions, is telling Linc to get lost. Linc is flattering young Shaun by saying, earnestly, that

> "a lot of people can paddle out there and get that rush—tap into something, bigger—but the ones who can give them a taste of it just by watching? That's something different . . . and I could see that people would pay to see those who could do it. A lot."

Linc is aware that the image of the surfer can give people a rush, and that this rush can be sold.

But this is precisely what Mitch hates. Before Mitch's enraged glare, Linc admits that he

> "made some mistakes with [Butchie]. All I could see was that him being a bad boy was good for business. I thought the image was the thing. What I see now—what it's taken me years to see—is that the thing itself—that's the thing. And I don't have to show them any more than that."

Mitch: "To get them to buy the thing that you're selling them."
Linc: "But what if I'm selling them the thing for itself?"
Sissy (Mitch's wife): "Yeah, it's like you're a fucking saint."
Shaun says: "I'd like to compete. I like it."
Giving in, but only for the love of Shaun, Mitch says to Linc: "No image."
Linc replies: "Just him. And some really great waves."

The character of Mitch, defending the purity of surfing from the dirty hucksters out to sully it by selling its image, is a prominent one in the history of the image of the surfer. And Linc is the quintessential ad man, giving voice to two related facts in the history of surfing: one, that the image of the surfer is wildly compelling, and two, that commercial forces understand that it's so compelling that selling it will make them tons of money. And the surfer image, especially the association with the mystical, that the show puts forth, is no accident. The show was co-created by *Deadwood* auteur David Milch and surf novelist Kem Nunn. Nunn is the name most associated with the genre of "surf noir", or the surf life as setting for heavy existential dramas to play out. In this series, the writers absolutely intended to deploy the image of surfing to mean the mystical, the free, and the site of existential drama.

In a short teaser for the show entitled "The Zen of Surfing," we can see exactly how intentional this portrayal of surfing is. The first frame of the teaser shows a quote from Genesis: "and the spirit of God was moving over the face of the water." The actors interviewed say things like, "the show is really about spiritual transformation," "redemption," "healing," and that "surfers embody this very odd contradiction—they are in many ways counter to society. The truth is that they are more connected to what's really important—nature, the earth, the rhythms of nature . . ." Another actor states that "surfing represents freedom, the cyclical nature of life . . . and a community." We hear that "if you think about surfing and the ocean and the waves, you can think about it in the literal sense, but I think it's really better in David's work to really say, well, what can it mean?" David Milch says explicitly that "the idea of the surfer's *submission to the wave* as the source of his or her pleasure was the kind of theme I wanted to engage . . ." So the themes intentionally deployed in this image of surfing are just the ones we've seen before. The image of the surfer is an archetype that even the *auteur* can't modify much. It's bigger than he is. He submits to it, and from that submission comes creativity.

However, the show's creators are free to put one or another angle on the image in a positive or negative light. Linc looks like a beady water rat, while Mitch is given the power to levitate. Nevertheless, this back and forth between authenticity or "soul" and the selling of the image is a major dynamic in the surfing world, and one that frequently gets played out within pop culture images of surfing like films and television shows. Instead of being partial to one side or another, though, we can see that this dynamic is precisely that between the "real" and "language." Language, the signifier, the image, constantly chases after the incredibly compelling memory of the "real", the unmediated, which is prelinguistic, fundamental to language and to the language of popular culture. Surfing's popular culture representation is particularly powerful precisely because surfing actually comes close to this pleasure beyond and before language—a prelinguistic unselfconsciousness, a full envelopment in the moment, total unfettered connection to the world. Surfing is a metaphor for this pure pleasure. So people chase surfing, just as we chase all pure pleasure that we unconsciously remember. People chase it with words, writing about surfing for a neverending market; they chase it with still images—photographing the surfer began simultaneously with the beginning of modern surfing at Waikiki; they chase it with moving images—surfing has been filmed since film began (a recently discovered reel shows surfers shot by Thomas Edison in 1906), and it's been a major Hollywood archetype from the start. The image reminds all of us of this unconsciously remembered pleasure and so tends to produce action in pursuit of it. Surfers are actually quite explicit in talking about their lives being organized around chasing this pleasure—what they call "the stoke," and what Freud, in a connection that grounds the argument of this book, calls "oceanic."

This is why we should not be concerned to debunk the image as an insufficiently accurate copy of the "real." Instead, we look at the image as a language that constantly chases after prelinguistic, unconscious pleasure. Like language, cultural representations can never fully access the contents of this remembered "real" pleasure, this "true" experience—but they never stop trying. Just as language never stops reaching for the experience of that unconsciously remembered past. This is why cultural representations matter—they speak to the memories and desires that truly animate us, they (the popular ones, the ones that keep coming up anyway) point in the direction of our collective desire. And understanding this collective desire (not as "true" or "false" but knowing its contents) is necessary to understand the ways that people attempt to bring their lives a little closer to it. "True" or not, surfing's popular culture representations point in one way or another to the mythical, primitive past that exists in all of our unconscious psyches. The memory of pure gratification, pure connection, pure pleasure, gets accessed when we behold the image of the beachcomber. Its truth lies not in its accurate or inaccurate representation of "reality" but in its power as an enduring archetype of freedom.

Now, it tends to be surfers, like Mitch, who claim "authority" to debunk the commercially disseminated image of the surfer from the "authentic" perspective of the "true" surfer. One example among many is the eloquent Thad Ziolkowski, who writes in a review of a recent crop of documentary films about surfing, like *Step Into Liquid* and *Riding Giants*, that the corporate underwriting of these films undermines their ability to truly "represent" surfing. Writers like Ziolkowski tend to critique popular culture representations of surfing as inauthentic, from the supposedly privileged point of a real surfer who knows the reality of surfing against which these images can be measured. However, the truth is that every surfer is as subject to "surfing" being defined by its popular culture image as are non-surfers. The moment the surfer gets off the board and onto the page, he or she is participating in the creation of the image of surfing, subject to everything that's come before, part of the same process of image creation that we've been tracing in the present work. "Real" surfers, as we've seen, produce fantasy too.

This image of the surfer is not only composed of the board rider on the wave, although that's still the most prominent. The image of "surfing" invokes a whole host of historical memories, crafted partly from history and partly from desire, that appeal to this primitive layer of the psyche. It's not just *John From Cincinnati*, either, that plays to nostalgic memory this way. As we've seen, a great deal of commercially produced surf culture of today is nostalgic to the core and evokes the lost paradise—a hybrid of Waikiki Beach and mid-century Malibu, in the contemporary incarnation. When commercial culture invokes the repressed memory of freedom and abundance in the archetype of the beach bum, the consequences can threaten the work discipline that depends for its existence on the disavowal of this very possibility. The history of surf culture and its image bears this out; it's been profoundly inspirational of pleasure-seeking collective behavior, both commercial and subcultural.

The fact that popular culture is so much more the visible hand of capital in our society, too often blinds progressives from seeing that the commercial side of capitalism is precisely what broadcasts subterranean values all over the nation, and the globe—songs that glorify drug use, films that tantalize the libido and bring to life the satisfaction of fantasy desires, and always, *always*—the surfer. The image of freedom from all sorts of repression, the image of people collectively resisting austerity and insisting on constituting time on their own terms. Employers can break a union, as we've seen all too universally. But this, a culture of freedom and play—this you can't break, not so easily anyway. And the fact that a more relaxed culture is a weapon against capitalist exploitation is only its secondary benefit. What's primary is that it's not only the means, but the end, the ultimate goal—a life lived in the moment, with pleasure. As the surfers say, stoked.

Notes

NOTES TO CHAPTER 1

1. I am indebted to Carin Crawford's unpublished Master's thesis for giving me the idea for this title. She quotes from Todd Gitlin's (1987) *The Sixties*: "Most American political attitudes are not neatly laid out on a simple left-right continuum; they are hybrid varieties, self-contradictory at their core. They have not yet found their language. The most prevalent use of `radical' meanwhile, is as a Southern California surfer's term for a particularly good wave," calling this prominent dismissal of the possibility of anything political about surf culture "a sad commentary on the state of recent cultural history." Crawford, Carin, "Waves of Transformation," unpublished Master's thesis, http://www.lajollasurf.org/wavesof.html.
2. Freud, Sigmund, *The Interpretation of Dreams* (New York: Avon Books, 1965), 573.
3. See R. L. Rutsky, "Surfing the Other: Ideology on the Beach," *Film Quarterly* 52 (Summer 1999): 12–23, Krista Comer, "Taking Feminism and Regionalism Toward the Transnational Third Wave," in *A Companion to the Regional Literatures of America*, edited by Charles Crow (Malden, Mass: Blackwell, 2003), 111–128, and "Wanting to be Lisa: Generational Rifts, Girl Power, and the Globalization of Surf Culture," in *American Youth Cultures*, edited by Neil Campbell (New York: Routledge, 2004), 237–265, as well as Nick Ford and David Brown, *Surfing and Social Theory: Experience, Embodiment, and the Narrative of the Dream Glide* (New York: Routledge, 2006). I happily join these authors in re-reading the surf image in light of its subversive tendencies.
4. May, Kirse Granat, *Golden State, Golden Youth: The California Image in Popular Culture, 1955–1966*, (Chapel Hill: University of North Carolina Press, 2002).
5. Rutsky, in a parallel reading of *Beach Party* movies and *Gidget*, puts it beautifully: " . . . to see these films solely in terms of conformity, reassurance, or escapism . . . overlooks the degree to which the appeal of these films also depends on elements of sexual, cultural, and ideological difference that can never be simply or entirely normalized . . . Indeed, in these films, the appeal of surfing and surf subculture is often based on the attractiveness of non-conformist, irreverent, and anti-bourgeois attitudes . . . [and] is, moreover, linked to the allure of non-Western cultures, derived in large part from surfing's own Pacific Island origins." Rutsky's piece also reads the significance of this primitivism in the surf image, which will be treated in Chapter 2, as characterized not only by racist stereotypes but also by the desire to transcend the repressive social structures of the West. R. L. Rutsky, "Surfing the Other: Ideology on the Beach," *Film Quarterly*, 52 (Summer 1999): 13.

6. Jock Young, *The Drugtakers: The Social Meaning of Drug Use* (London: Paladin, 1971).
7. Herbert Marcuse, *Eros and Civilization: A Philosophical Inquiry into Freud* (Boston: Beacon Press, 1955).
8. Theodore Roszak, *The Making of a Counter Culture* (Berkeley: University of California Press, 1968).
9. Ford and Brown, in *Surfing and Social Theory*, continually refer to the "dream glide" of surfing as an overcoming of the Western mind-body dualism, and fascinatingly, to the potential of scholarship on surfing to overcome the split between representation and non-representation, narrative and embodied experience. Nick Ford and David Brown, *Surfing and Social Theory: Experience, Embodiment, and the Narrative of the Dream Glide* (New York: Routledge, 2006).
10. In Krista Comer's "Wanting to be Lisa," and in *Surfer Girls in the New World Order* (Duke, forthcoming) the author also reads the surf image (and, even more, the subcultural reality) as subversive, especially of traditional gender roles, but sees the growth of surf culture not as a consistent effect of the broadcasting of alluring images but as a more historically specific set of events. What she calls the two "break-out moments" of surf culture and its image—the mid-twentieth century and the post-1989 period—correspond to the popular cultural articulation of mass Cold War national sensibilities and a new way of conceptualizing post-1989 globalized subjectivities, respectively. I am intrigued by this analysis, especially of the impact of post-1989 political and economic globalization on surf culture's massive and growing presence across the globe today. For Comer, the deterritorialized flows constituting globalization may make the surf image and experience particularly resonant in the current period. However, I argue that ebb and flow notwithstanding, the surfer has been the most consistent and prominent bohemian image in all of twentieth-century popular culture (and its mass popularity far predated the early sixties explosion). I see this as evidence of an important, always available consistency in the content of mass fantasy.
11. Subcultures and countercultures are not identical, but analytically and historically, in the case of surfers, they are interchangeable for our purposes of analyzing images in popular culture.
12. David Brooks, *Bobos in Paradise: The New Upper Class and How They Got There* (New York: Simon and Schuster, 2000).
13. Birmingham's Simon Frith later makes some interesting moves in the direction of seeing political potential in commodified leisure (he'd always been more sympathetic to commercial culture than Hebdige or the editors of *Resistance Through Rituals*). In discussing rock, Frith maintains that "rock's commodity form can't be denied . . . but the problem is to what extent its commercial function determines its cultural meaning." Cultural meaning rests with the context of cultural products, rather than the text, and the context of punk and other music is the context of leisure. For Frith, "it is in this context that the bohemian tradition in rock (as in cultural history generally) needs explaining: bohemians articulate a particular kind of leisure critique of the work ethic. They are cultural radicals . . ." The politics of culture only make sense "if we're better at using the concept of leisure to understand that *leisure commodities are not necessarily conducive to good behavior . . .* " In this way, the system-subverting tendencies of leisure are helped on by capitalists themselves. Frith invokes Marx's observation that "employers have quite different attitudes to their own workers, whose needs they attempt to limit, and to other people's, whose needs they attempt to extend." If we define class

struggle as the fight against work and for higher wages, it seems that leisure and leisure commodities (like surfboards, for instance), through which most subcultures take form, are much more significant than most cultural critics tend to understand. Simon Frith, "Music for Pleasure," *Screen Education* 34 (1980): 51–61.

14. Ellen Willis, *Beginning to See the Light: Sex, Hope, and Rock and Roll* (Hanover, NH: Wesleyan University Press, 1992),: xvi.
15. Daniel Bell, *The Cultural Contradictions of Capitalism* (New York: Basic Books, 1976), 75.
16. Harry Cleaver, *Crisis of the Keynesian Era,* http://www.eco.utexas.edu/~hmcleave/304Lfall.html.
17. Cleaver, in Negri, *Marx Beyond Marx: Lessons on the Grundrisse* (Brooklyn: Autonomedia, 1991), xxiv. Especially important to my discussion is Cleaver's recent contention that ocean waves are the most apt metaphor for the signs of cultural resistance afoot within the now-globalized and increasingly connected working class (which for him includes both the waged and the unwaged). He elaborates: "Currents are masses in motion . . . Everything is in motion, nothing is stable, deterritorialization is virtually constant, there is no "safe haven", no "secure foundation" other than familiarity with the ever rushing, ever changing flow. Yet nomadic whales sing and dolphins play as they traverse thousands of miles of ocean. *All of these characteristics are evocative of the behavior of those forces in opposition to capitalism* . . . They are fluid, often changing and only momentarily forming those solidified moments we call "organizations" . . . some currents of opposition are quite visible, on the surface as it were, sometimes steady, sometimes turbulent. When they connect reinforcing each other the social equivalent of rogue waves and gyres are the swirling turbulence of public struggle . . . But, it is worth remembering that oppositional movements on the surface of society are like the surface currents of the oceans—they only involve a small percentage of the total mass. *Most currents of opposition run deep*, below surface appearances . . . when such deep currents surface in surprising, massive upwellings of social struggle they can nourish wider conflict and change the world . . . In every case the biggest mystery and the hardest thing to explain have been what was going on in those invisible, deep, but rich currents of struggle that made possible and led to their sudden, explosive and world changing upwelling. *Thus the importance of the various kinds of study that have sought to understand these largely invisible forces*, e.g., analyses of everyday life . . . [and] of *certain aspects of popular culture.*" Harry Cleaver, "Deep Currents Rising: Notes on the Global Threat to Capitalism," in *Subverting the Present, Imagining the Future: Insurrection, Movement, Commons* (New York: Autonomedia, 2007) emphasis mine, https://webspace.utexas.edu/hcleaver/www/DeepCurrentsRisingFinal2.htm (accessed September 29, 2009).
18. In fact, the very globalization that has proven so devastating for workers may actually amplify the dynamic I'm laying out here, since fantasy images, like capital and workers, flow across national boundaries too (with divergent local receptions, certainly). As Marx famously says in the *Communist Manifesto*: "And how does the bourgeoisie get over these crises? On the one hand by enforced destruction of a mass of productive forces; on the other, by the conquest of new markets, and by the more thorough exploitation of the old ones. That is to say, by paving the way for more extensive and more destructive crises, and by diminishing the means whereby crises are prevented." Karl Marx and Friedrich Engels, *Manifesto of the Communist Party* (Peking: Foreign Languages Press, 1970).

19. Stephen Duncombe, *Dream: Re-Imagining Progressive Politics in an Age of Fantasy* (New York: The Free Press, 2007), 40 and 26–27.
20. In their analysis of the narrative history of surfing, Ford and Brown call this "surfing's aetiological myth" and argue that "the narrative of surfing's beginnings in the islands of the Pacific is imbued with notions of a pantheistic spirituality, courage and harmony with nature . . ." Nick Ford and David Brown, *Surfing and Social Theory: Experience, Embodiment, and the Narrative of the Dream Glide* (New York: Routledge, 2006), 29.
21. For additional treatments of imaginaries of the ocean and the roots of their appeal, see Ford and Brown, especially Chapter 2, "The Enchanted Sea," Christopher Connery, "The Oceanic Feeling and the Regional Imaginary," in Rob Wilson and Wimal Dissanayake, eds., *Global/Local*, (Durham: Duke University Press, 1996) and Phillip Steinberg, *The Social Construction of the Ocean* (Cambridge: Cambridge University Press, 2001).
22. See Stanley Aronowitz and William DiFazio, *The Jobless Future: Sci-Tech and the Dogma of Work* (Minnesota: University of Minnesota Press, 1995); Aronowitz, *Just Around the Corner: The Paradox of the Jobless Recovery* (Philadelphia: Temple University Press, 2005); and Jeremy Rifkin, *The End of Work* (New York: G. P. Putnam's Sons, 1996).
23. Karl Marx and Friedrich Engels, *Manifesto of the Communist Party* (Peking: Foreign Languages Press, 1970).
24. The image of the surfer, from its inception, has proven alluring and inspirational in an international context as well. For instance, as we'll see in Chapter 2, beach boy, Olympian, and cultural icon Duke Kahanamoku demonstrated surfing as he traveled the world, and wherever he surfed, locals took it up and a surf subculture developed.

NOTES TO CHAPTER 2

1. James Cook, *The Voyages of Captain James Cook, Vol. II, Round the World* (London: W. Smith Publisher, 1842), 216.
2. Although there's obviously no written evidence of this, it's assumed that the Polynesians who took to the Pacific and settled in Hawaii are actually the world's first surfers.
3. The main reference for this tends to be the work of anthropologists Finney and Houston, in James D. Houston and Ben Finney, *Surfing: A History of the Ancient Hawaiian Sport* (Rohnert: Pomegranate Art Books, 1996).
4. This is also passed on in the oral folklore tradition of contemporary surfers (a tradition of "talking story" on the beach which is itself a translation from the ancient Hawaiian culture): see Tanis Thorne, "Legends of the Surfer Subculture, Part One," *Western Folklore* 35(3) (July 1976): 209–217, and "Legends of the Surfer Subculture, Part Two," *Western Folklore* 35(4) (October 1976): 270–280.
5. Haunani-Kay Trask, *From a Native Daughter: Colonialism and Sovereignty in Hawaii* (University of Hawaii Press: Honolulu, 1993), 4.
6. The allure of the "primitive" and the imagination of "paradise," and the image of surfing that spoke of these things, transcended the American context. In fact, in the Japanese tourist imagination Hawaii is remarkably similar to that in the American one—surfing, hula, beach boys, slack-key music, freedom from toil, easy sexuality, relaxation, consumption—and figures just as prominently in Japan, if not more prominently. The images have mirrored one another throughout the twentieth century, even though Hawaiiana had to go underground in Japan during and immediately after the war. For

instance, Hawaiian music groups changed their names but not their music. The dynamic of playing on the longing for a primitive paradise among moderns is not just a European one—it's played out almost identically in Japan, too. See Yujin Yaguchi and Mari Yoshihara, "Evolutions of 'Paradise': Japanese Tourist Discourse about Hawai`i," *American Studies* 45(3): 81–106.

7. Karl Marx, *The Economic and Philosophic Manuscripts of 1844* (New York: International Publishers, 1964).
8. Roszak, *The Making of a Counter Culture.*
9. Max Weber, *The Protestant Ethic and the Spirit of Capitalism* (New York: Routledge, 1992).
10. In many ways, the long education that most of us endured was training in just this simple, but ever-difficult lesson. How did we learn to delay gratification? To accept that the majority of our lives would be spent doing the bidding of someone else? That although the natural imperative of the libido is to live pleasurably now, the new reality is to be one in which pleasure comes only after necessary work is done, afterschool, on the weekends, etc.? School, of course. It's no accident that in the US, it was the Puritans who instituted compulsory public education.
11. Gavan Daws, *Shoal of Time: A History of the Hawaiian Islands* (Honolulu: University Press of Hawaii, 1974), 65.
12. William Bates, *Sandwich Island Notes, by a Haole* (New York, Harper & Bros., 1854), quoted in Daws, *Shoal of Time,* 65.
13. William Ellis, *Polynesian Researches* (London: Fisher, Son & Jackson, 1836).
14. Thrum, quoted in Drew Kampion, *Stoked! A History of Surf Culture* (Salt Lake City: Gibbs Smith, 2003), 34.
15. Keauokalani, quoted in Daniel Duane, *Caught Inside: A Surfer's Year on the California Coast* (New York: North Point Press, 1996), 85.
16. Bingham, quoted in Duane, *Caught Inside,* 85.
17. Bingham, quoted in Daws, *Shoal of Time,* 64.
18. Lueras, Leonard. *Surfing: The Ultimate Pleasure.* (New York: Workman International, 1984), 54.
19. Hiram Bingham, *A Residence of Twenty-One Years in the Sandwich Islands.* (New York: S. Converse, 1848),127.
20. Trask, *From A Native Daughter,* 6.
21. Bingham, *A Residence of Twenty-One Years in the Sandwich Islands,* 471.
22. Kampion, *Stoked,* 36.
23. Dibble, quoted in T. G. Thrum, *A History of the Sandwich Islands*, (Honolulu: T.G. Thrum, 1909): 120.
24. Bingham, quoted in Finney and Houston, *Surfing: A History of the Ancient Hawaiian Sport,* 54.
25. William S. Ruschenberger, *Narrative of a Voyage Round the World, Vol. II* (New York: Cornell University Press, 1838), 373.
26. Tinker, quoted in Daws, *Shoal of Time,* 90.
27. Trask, *From a Native Daughter,* 6.
28. Isabella Bird, *Six Months among the Palm Groves, Coral Reefs, and Volcanoes of the Sandwich Islands* (New York: G. P. Putnam's Sons, 1876), 137.
29. Daws, *Shoal of Time,*100–101.
30. Ibid, 105.
31. Nathaniel B. Emerson, "Causes of the Decline of Ancient Polynesian Sports," *The Friend* L no. VII (1892): 57–60.
32. E. P. Thompson, "Time, Work-Discipline, and Industrial Capitalism," *Past and Present: Journal of Historical Studies* 38 (1967):56–97.
33. Ibid, emphasis mine.

34. *Hawaii: Paradise of the Pacific*, Yearbook(Honolulu: Hawaii Promotion Committee, 1913).
35. Mark Twain, *Roughing It* (Berkeley: University of California Press, 1972), 526.
36. Timothy De La Vega, *200 Years of Surfing Literature: An Annotated Bibliography*. (Hawaii, T. De La Vega, 2004), 16.
37. Isabella Bird, *Six Months among the Palm Groves, Coral Reefs, and Volcanoes of the Sandwich Islands* (New York: G. P. Putnam's Sons,1876), 72–73.
38. Ibid, 150.
39. Ibid, 167.
40. Ibid, 134.
41. Hawaii Visitors and Convention Bureau, Corporate History, www.hvcb.org.
42. Ibid.
43. Significantly, 10,000 Japanese workers (who'd been imported to the islands by whites in the late 1800s) were paralyzing business with a general strike at that time. So Ford's "racial harmony" was really a way to maintain white supremacy in Hawaii, and his strategy was to "repopulate" Hawaii with white people. The discourse of Americanization of the islands and fear of Japanese influence was so powerful, that in a sense, Ford rode the wave of the anti-immigrant sentiment that was sweeping America (which expressed itself on the islands as anti-Japanese) to promote surfing and tourism/relocation to Hawaii by whites. He was just one guy, but the moment was right for what he was tapping into—he gained powerful allies who were also constantly harping about the Japanese threat to American hegemony in Hawaii. Although for them, the "threat" was both a real fear of Japanese imperialism in the Pacific, and a phony code for class war on the Japanese who made up much of the islands' sugar worker population.

    Once the islands were annexed by the US, American labor law came into effect and the Japanese began experimenting (not very successfully, thanks to the existence of even lower-status groups of ethnic workers, like Filipinos and Chinese, who could be played off of one another) with the American strike weapon, in 1909 and again in 1920. The islands' capitalists responded with racist tirades that masked their class interests in crushing the strikes. In 1920 especially, during the height of anti-immigrant sentiment in American culture, the planters who were being struck emphasized that the strike was part of a deliberate conspiracy on the part of the Japanese to "Japanize" the islands. The *Star-Bulletin* editorialized that if the "agitators" were to be victorious, they would be "as completely the masters of Hawaii's destiny as if they held title to the land and the growing cane. They would be the autocratic dictators of Hawaii's industrialism . . . Hawaii would be as thoroughly Japanized, so far as its industrial life is concerned, as if the Mikado had the power to name our governor and direct our political destiny . . . Never lose sight of the real issue: is Hawaii to remain American or become Japanese? A compromise of any nature or any degree with the alien agitators would be a victory for them and an indirect but nonetheless deadly invasion of American sovereignty in Hawaii. The American citizen who advocates anything less than resistance to the bitter end against the arrogant ambition of the Japanese agitators is a traitor to his own people" (quoted in Daws, *Shoal of Time*, 305).

    Like most capitalist "nationalism," the American patriotism of the haole planters was phony—they were agnostic at best when it came to annexation, because under it they'd lose the contract labor laws that benefited them more than the ending of sugar tariffs would have/did. Sugar planters needed cheap labor more than anything else, so they wanted to bring in as many workers from other places as possible—whites wouldn't take the wages they paid. This was why the United States Commissioner General of Immigration said in 1920 that "either the planters were insincere in their declared desire to Americanize the islands or else their efforts are at crosspurposes with their ambitions." This was because the planters were asking the US government to limit the number of Japanese immigrants but replace those numbers with Chinese immigrant workers (quoted in Daws, *Shoal of Time*, 307).

44. A. H. Ford, "Our_Japanese_Territory," *Colliers* 43, July 24, 1909, 12–13.
45. Lorrin A. Thurston,"What Hawaii Really Means to Southern California," *Los Angeles Times*, January 1, 1925, E2.
46. Alexander Hume Ford, "Riding the Surf in Hawaii," *Collier's* 43, August 14, 1909, 17.
47. Charmian London, quoted in Valerie Noble, *Hawaiian Prophet: Alexander Hume Ford* (Smithtown, NY: Exposition Press, 1980), 45.
48. Charmian London, *Our Hawaii,* quoted in Kampion, *Stoked*, 38.
49. Jack London, *The Cruise of the Snark* (New York: Macmillan, 1918), 78.
50. Kampion, *Stoked,* 39.
51. In an early affirmation of the relationship between the ocean, freedom, and commercial success, it was a Sydney newspaperman trying to sell papers who organized, and heavily publicized on the front pages, the first occurences of civil disobedience.
52. Lueras, *Surfing: the Ultimate Pleasure,* 77.
53. Grady Timmons, *Waikiki Beachboy* (Honolulu: Editions Limited, 1989): 27.
54. Ibid, 30.
55. Ibid, 15.
56. Malcolm Gault-Williams, *Legendary Surfers, Volume I: 2500 B.C. to 1910 A.D.*, Chapter 2, self-published manuscript, (c) 2005. www.legendarysurfers.com/surf/legends/ls07z_**duke**.html, 5.
57. Timmons, *Waikiki Beachboy,* 16. This insight is confirmed by the fact that both the detractors and the admirers of the beach boys agree on the basic outlines of their lifestyle. Timmons recounts that "a prominent Honolulu archivist I spoke with recalled that when he was a young man growing up in the fifties the beach boys were regarded as a joke—'a bunch of lazy male prostitutes who made their living off mainland divorcees.'" And in Henry Kim's master's thesis in Sociology on "The Waikiki Beach Boy: Changing Attitudes and Behavior," he notes that beach boys have been portrayed in "schizophrenic" terms—"at one moment he is a romantic throwback to ancient Hawaii; at the next, a social parasite." (Henry Kim, quoted in Timmons, *Waikiki Beachboy,* 17) The difference lies not in the outlines of the portrayal, but in the judgment of their lifestyle. Everyone agrees on what the beach boy lifestyle embodied—the disagreement comes with the evaluation. As usual, the evaluation of a relatively free lifestyle depends on whether the observer comes out of a Puritan mentality or a more liberated one.
58. Hawaii Visitors and Convention Bureau website. http://www.hvcb.org/corporate/history.htm.
59. I am indebted to the Bishop Museum archivist DeSoto Brown for the examples used in the following discussion, which are all included in his books and articles chronicling images of Hawaii.
60. DeSoto Brown, *Surfing: Historic Images from the Bishop Museum Archives* (Honolulu: Bishop Museum Press, 2006): 76–77.
61. Ibid, 68–69.
62. DeSoto Brown, *Hawaii at Play: Images of a Bygone Era* (Honolulu: Watermark Publishing, 2003), 30.
63. Ibid, 127.

64. *Hawaii: Paradise of the Pacific*, Yearbook (Honolulu: Hawaii Promotion Committee, 1913).
65. Brown, *Hawaii at Play*, 26.
66. Ibid, 22.
67. Ruth Taylor White, *Hawaii as the Camera Sees It*, (Honolulu: Honolulu Star-Bulletin, 1933). Imprint.
68. Brown, *Surfing*, 63.
69. Ibid, 51.
70. Brown, *Hawaii at Play*, 31.
71. Ibid, 10.
72. Ibid, 16.
73. Ibid, 21.
74. DeSoto Brown, "Beautiful, Romantic Hawaii: How the Fantasy Image Came to Be," *The Journal of Decorative and Propaganda Arts* 20 (1994): 264.
75. Ibid, 24.
76. Ibid, 113.
77. Ibid, 21.
78. Ibid, 22.
79. Brown, "Beautiful, Romantic Hawaii," 267.
80. Brown, *Hawaii at Play*, 13.
81. Ibid, 22.
82. Ibid, 23.
83. Ibid, 12.
84. Ibid, 15.
85. Ibid, 15.
86. Brown, *Hawaii at Play*, 37.
87. Ibid, 15.
88. Ibid, 13.
89. Ibid, 25.
90. Ibid, 20.
91. Ibid, 27.
92. Ibid, 11.
93. Ibid, 20.
94. Brown, *Surfing*, 40–41.
95. Reproduced in Gault-Williams, *Legendary Surfers, Volume I*, Chapter 2, 8.
96. "Living Dynamite is in Wait at Waikiki, Says Dorothy Mackaill," *Honolulu Star-Bulletin* , January 29, 1932, 4.
97. Reproduced in Brown, *Surfing*, 131.
98. Timmons, *Waikiki Beachboy*, 138.
99. Tony Todaro, "Waikiki's Famous Beach Boys," *Paradise of the Pacific*, Yearbook (Honolulu: Hawaii Promotion Committee, 1913).
100. Timmons, *Waikiki Beachboy*, 154.
101. Quoted in Timmons, *Waikiki Beachboy*, 103.
102. Ibid, 109.
103. Ibid, 138.
104. Ibid, 32.
105. Brown, *Surfing*, 78–79.
106. Frances Parkinson Keyes, "Aloha From Hawaii," *Good Housekeeping* 82, December 1925, 30–31.
107. H. H. Yost, "Rough Riders of the Surf," *Sunset* (Central West edition) 56, January 1926, 12–13.
108. G. Marvin, "Riding the Surf at Waikiki," *Outing* 64, April 1914, 24–35.
109. H. Coffin, "Riding the Waves at Waikiki," *Country Life* 64, September 1933, 56–57.

110. H. Wilde, "Waikiki Mirage," *Colliers* 106, September 14, 1940, 14–15.
111. Brown, *Surfing*, 90.
112. *Waikiki Wedding*, dir. by Frank Tuttle, Paramount Pictures, 1937.
113. Timmons, *Waikiki Beachboy*, 30.
114. Ibid, 85.
115. Brown, "Beautiful, Romantic Hawaii," 254.
116. Brown, *Hawaii at Play*, 26.
117. Ibid, 28.
118. Ibid, 112.
119. Ibid, 18.
120. James Michener, *Hawaii* (New York: Ballantine, 1982).
121. Michener, *Hawaii*, 891.
122. Ibid, 912.
123. Ibid, 1013.
124. Ibid, 905.
125. Ibid, 907.
126. Ibid, 918.
127. Ibid, 918.
128. Ibid, 928.
129. Ibid, 927.
130. bell hooks, "Eating the Other" in *Black Looks: Race and Representation* (Boston: South End Press, 1992).
131. Marianna Torgovnick, *Gone Primitive: Savage Intellects, Modern Lives* (Chicago: University of Chicago Press, 1991.
132. Sigmund Freud, *Civilization and its Discontents* (New York: W. W. Norton, 1989).
133. Torgovnick, *Gone Primitive*, 17.
134. Ibid, 18.
135. Tom Wolfe, "Radical Chic," in *Radical Chic and Mau-Mauing the Flak Catchers* (New York: Farrar, Strauss, and Giroux, 1970).
136. Norman Mailer, "The White Negro," in*Advertisements for Myself* (Cambridge, Mass: Harvard University Press, 1992), 306.
137. In arguing for an existentialist relation to the moment as the essence of Hip, Mailer makes clear that it's not French existentialism that he's talking about, but a particularly American brand that "sees every man and woman as moving individually through each moment of life forward into growth or backward into death." This is to be distinguished from the "civilized" existentialism of the French: "Only the French, alienated beyond alienation from their unconscious, could welcome an existential philosophy without ever feeling it at all . . ." Ibid, 341.
138. The sexually submissive, non-aggressive nature of the Hawaiian surfer was clearly part of the reason that during such a racist moment in American history, interracial "sex on the beach" was to a large extent tolerated at a time that a similar volume of black–white unions on the mainland would have provoked race riots.
139. Stanley Aronowitz, *False Promises: The Shaping of American Working-Class Consciousness* (Durham: Duke University Press, 1992): 58.

NOTES TO CHAPTER 3

1. Tom Blake, *Hawaiian Surfboard*, (Honolulu: Paradise of the Pacific Press, 1935). Note the publisher, which also published the magazine of the same name and was overtly promoting Hawaii.

2. Tom Blake, "Waves and Thrills at Waikiki," *National Geographic* 67, May 1935, 597—604.
3. Blake, *Hawaiian Surfboard*, 40.
4. Ibid, 40–41.
5. Gary Lynch, quoted in Kampion, *Stoked*, 45.
6. Ibid, 45.
7. Gary Lynch, *Tom Blake: Surfing 1922–1932* (Santa Barbara: T. Adler Books, 2000): 67.
8. Gary Lynch and Malcolm Gault-Williams, *Tom Blake: The Uncommon Journey of a Pioneer Waterman* (Corona Del Mar, California: Croul Family Foundation, 2001): 102.
9. Thomas Zahn, "Surf Boarding from Molokai to Waikiki," *Paradise of the Pacific*, March 1954, 26; quoted in Lynch and Gault-Williams, *Tom Blake*, 184.
10. Lynch and Gault-Williams, 71.
11. Blake, *Voice of the Wave*, 1968, quoted in Lynch and Gault-Williams, 205–206.
12. Ibid, 225.
13. "San Onofre Fast Turning Into Another Waikiki," *Los Angeles Times*, August 30, 1954, 2.
14. Kampion, *Stoked*, 49.
15. Craig Stecyk, in Introduction, *Surfing San Onofre to Point Dume 1936–1942: Photographs by Don James* (San Francisco: Chronicle Books, 1996). This book was originally published by T. Adler Books.
16. Lynch and Gault-Williams; *Tom Blake*, 120, 121, 115, 116, 117.
17. "Riders of Sunset Seas," *Los Angeles Times Sunday Supplement*, January 18, 1931, 0.
18. Roy Rosenzweig, *Eight Hours for What We Will: Workers and Leisure in an Industrial City, 1870–1920* (New York: Cambridge University Press, 1983).
19. "Venice Girls Ride Surf-Boards With as Much Skill as Boys," *The Los Angeles Times*, June 20, 1911, Section III p. 1.
20. "Riding Surf Board Thrills," *The Los Angeles Times*, July 14, 1912, Section VII p. 10.
21. "Surf-Board Riding is Some Sport," *The Los Angeles Times*, July 13, 1919, Section VI p. 1.
22. "Hold Everything!" *The Los Angeles Times*, August 18, 1923, 15.
23. "Surf Rider Awaits Tidal Wave," *The Los Angeles Times*, June 17, 1934, B4.
24. Lynch and Gault-Williams, *Tom Blake*, 122.
25. "Surf Riding on California Beach is a Favorite Summertime Sport," *Life* 9, August 26, 1940, 50–52.
26. "How Southern California's Most Photographed Girl Keeps Her Figure," *The Los Angeles Times*, February 20, 1938, H2.
27. Hamilton, Andy, "Surfboards, Ahoy!" *The Los Angeles Times*, September 19, 1937, J6.
28. John Heath "Doc" Ball, *Early California Surfriders* (Ventura, California: Pacific Publishing, 1995), originally published in 1946 as *California Surfriders*.
29. "Surf Boarders Capture California," *National Geographic* 86, September 1944, 355–362.
30. E. Cherrington, "Surf-Board Rider," *American Mercury* 47, June 1939, 234.
31. Arms, L. L., "Humper!" *Christian Science Monitor Magazine*, November 7, 1942, 6.

32. Ibid, 173–174.
33. Ibid, 182.
34. It's precisely this refusal that Birmingham theorists trace in the British working-class youth subcultures they study. However, for them, this symbolic or ideological resistance is ultimately swallowed up and fed into the process of reproduction, either through the diffusion of punk dislocation of meaning and subjectivity into consumer culture, a process Hebdige traces, or through the related process of the development of capital through its own contradictions. This process is analyzed by Paul Willis in his story of the "lads," working-class boys who refuse the subjection of work and discipline in school, but by that very process reproduce their own working-class subordination. See Dick Hebdige, *Subculture: The Meaning of Style* (London: Methuen, 1979); and Paul Willis, *Learning to Labor: How Working-Class Kids Get Working-Class Jobs* (New York: Columbia University Press, 1981).
35. Jacques Lacan, "The Mirror Stage as Formative of the Function of the I," in *Ecrits: A Selection* (New York: Norton, 1977).
36. Louis Althusser, "Ideology and Ideological State Apparatuses," in *Lenin and Philosophy* (New York: Monthly Review Press, 1971): 185.
37. Ibid, 131.
38. "Riding Waikiki's White Horses," *Review of Reviews* 79, April 1929, 151–152.
39. James, *Surfing San Onofre to Point Dume,* 11.
40. Ibid, 18.
41. *Doc Ball: Surfing's Legendary Lensman*, dir. by Carl Ackerman, Carl Ackerman Productions, 1999.
42. Don James, *Prewar Surfing Photographs* (Santa Barbara: T. Adler Books, 2004).
43. Ibid, 5.
44. Ibid, 5.
45. *Doc Ball: Surfing's Legendary Lensman.*
46. James, *Prewar Surfing Photographs,* 5.
47. James, *Surfing San Onofre to Point Dume,* 11.
48. Ibid, 12.
49. Ibid, 12.
50. Ibid, 13.
51. Ibid, 14.
52. *Doc Ball: Surfing's Legendary Lensman.*
53. Ibid.
54. Marshall Sahlins, "The Original Affluent Society," in *Stone Age Economics* (Chicago: Aldine-Atherton, 1972).
55. James, *Surfing San Onofre to Point Dume,* 110. Surfers have proven enduringly ambivalent and frequently hostile to this aspect of their image. In a recent example, the town of Cardiff, near San Diego, erected in 2007 a statue of a graceful male surfer that was immediately (and correctly) deemed effeminate and gained the nickname "Fairy Mary." The surfer outcry, especially on the Internet, against the town and the sculptor, has been considerable.
56. Ibid, 92.
57. Ibid, 34.
58. *Doc Ball: Surfing's Legendary Lensman.*
59. James, *Surfing San Onofre to Point Dume,* 50.
60. Ball, *Early California Surfriders,* 47.
61. Lueras, *Surfing: the Ultimate Pleasure,*109.
62. *Doc Ball: Surfing's Legendary Lensman.*

63. Ibid.
64. Marcuse, *Eros and Civilization*,19.
65. C. R. Stecyk III and Drew Kampion, *Dora Lives: The Authorized Biography of Miki Dora* (Santa Barbara: T. Adler Books, 2005).
66. Ibid, 19.
67. Ibid, 31.
68. Ibid, 22.
69. Ibid, 16.
70. Ibid, 2–3.
71. Stecyk, C. R., "Malibu: Curse of the Chumash, *Surfer Magazine*, July 1976, quoted in Kampion, *Stoked*, 70.
72. Stecyk and Kampion, *Dora Lives*, 52.
73. Ibid, 60–62.
74. Ibid, 63.
75. Ibid, 82.
76. Ibid, 43.
77. Ibid, 12.
78. Ibid, 32.
79. Ibid, 54.
80. Ibid, 30.
81. Ibid, 105.
82. Ibid, 24.
83. Ibid, 50.
84. Ibid, 65.
85. Ibid, 67.
86. Sheila Weller, "Malibu's Lost Boys," *Vanity Fair* no. 552, August 2006, 166–179.
87. Stecyk and Kampion, 118.
88. Ibid, 173.
89. Ibid, 171.
90. Ibid, 176.
91. Leroy Grannis, *Surf Photography of the 1960s and 1970s*, Jim Heimann, ed., Los Angeles: Taschen, 2006.
92. Ron Church, *Surf Contest* (Santa Barbara: T. Adler Books, 2006).
93. Ibid, 25.
94. Ibid, 88.
95. Ibid, 10.
96. Ibid, 78.
97. Grannis, *Surf Photography of the 1960s and 1970s*, 23.
98. Jeff Divine, *Surfing Photographs from the Seventies Taken by Jeff Divine* (Santa Barbara: T. Adler Books, 2005).
99. Ibid, 1–2.
100. Ibid, 5.
101. Ibid, 7–8.
102. Ibid, 9.

NOTES TO CHAPTER 4

1. Kampion, *Stoked*, 27.
2. Tom Wolfe, *The Pump House Gang* (New York: Farrar, Strauss, and Giroux, 1968).
3. Ibid, 3.
4. Ibid, 19–20.

5. Ibid, 27.
6. Ibid, 24–25.
7. Ibid, 9.
8. John Irwin, "Surfing: the Natural History of an Urban Scene," *Urban Life and Culture*, 2(), (1973), 133–46.
9. Elizabeth Hayt, "On These Waves, Everyone's a Local," *The New York Times*, July 8, 2007, E1.
10. Jim Murray, "Boys With Green Hair," *The Los Angeles Times*, June 30, 1961, C1.
11. Larry Liebman, "Surfers Spilled on Wave of Ire," *The Los Angeles Times*, May 12, 1963, A16.
12. "They Go Down to the Sea on Surf Boards," *The Los Angeles Times*, May 29, 1960, J1.
13. "Surfing Brings Big Crowd of Tide Riders to Area Beaches," *The Los Angeles Times*, April 29, 1962, CS1.
14. Trebay, Guy, "Back to the Beach," *The New York Times*, June 1, 2006, E1.
15. "Restrictions Pile Up As Surf Sport Grows," *The Los Angeles Times*, August 17 1960, C6.
16. "To Surf or Not to Surf? Answer Sought at Sunset Beach Next Week," *The Los Angeles Times*, March 3, 1963, OC1.
17. "Surf Riding Controls to be Enacted," *The Los Angeles Times*, September 20, 1959, WS1.
18. "Surfers to Challenge Summer Regulations," *The Los Angeles Times*, March 14, 1966, OC8.
19. "Request for Surfer Ban to Be Aired," *The Los Angeles Times*, February 24, 1963, OC1.
20. "Beach Group Opposes Inland Freeway Route," *The Los Angeles Times*, April 5, 1962, A8.
21. "To Surf or Not to Surf? Answer Sought at Sunset Beach Next Week," *The Los Angeles Times*, March 3, 1963, OC1.
22. "10 to 15% of Newport Surfers Obtain Licenses; Deadline Friday," *The Los Angeles Times*, June 29, 1966, OC9.
23. "Zoning Settles Battle of Beaches," *The Los Angeles Times*, August 5, 1962, SG1.
24. "Holidays Contest to Bar 'Surf Bums'," *The Los Angeles Times*, May 21, 1961, CS4.
25. Kovitz, Ray, "Surfers: Good Kids or Gangs of Rowdies? Parents, School Authorities Claim Sport Creating Discipline Problems," *The Los Angeles Times*, April 23, 1961, CS1.
26. "Parents to Fight School's Ban on Their Long-Haired Son," *The Los Angeles Times*, March 26, 1967, CS1.
27. Kovitz, Ray, "Surfers: Good Kids or Gangs of Rowdies? Parents, School Authorities Claim Sport Creating Discipline Problems," *The Los Angeles Times*, April 23, 1961, CS1.
28. "Police Off to Early Start in Try to Upgrade Teen-Age Beach Manners," *The Los Angeles Times*, June 9, 1963, CS1.
29. "Beach Residents Seek Crackdown on Surfers," *The Los Angeles Times*, January 17, 1965, CS3.
30. Grant, Gordon, "Bums No More: A Once-Tarnished Image of Surfers Has a New Shine," *The Los Angeles Times*, September 21, 1969, OC1.
31. Emmons, Steve. "Huntington Beach Attracts Trouble," *The Los Angeles Times*, April 28, 1969, D1.

32. "Court Test of License Law Considered by Surfing Group," *The Los Angeles Times*, May 25, 1967, OC1.
33. "City Rules the Waves, but Many Surfers Still Object," *The Los Angeles Times*, July 28, 1966, OC1, emphasis mine.
34. Seymour Beubis, "Harbor Planners to Consider Surfers," *The Los Angeles Times*, February 6, 1969, WS1.
35. As Carin Crawford describes in her unpublished Master's Thesis, "Waves of Transformation," (available at http://www.lajollasurf.org/wavesof.html), surf clubs on the California coast were part of the "Coastal Alliance," a grassroots coalition that successfully campaigned for Proposition 20, a referendum that established the California Coastal Commission in 1973. The Commission was a regulatory agency whose jurisdiction superseded the local agencies that for decades had been so easily bought off by the oil and development interests that were both polluting beaches and making them increasingly inaccessible to the public. Charged with protecting both ecology and public access, the establishment of the Commission was an enormous victory for the grassroots coalition in its battle with the rich and influential companies that vehemently opposed Proposition 20 and outspent the advocates by a margin of 4 to 1. Proposition 20 was the biggest and most successful of many struggles that constituted a newly activist surf community. Others included fighting the Army Corps of Engineers on several prominent harbor-dredging projects in California, as well as similar struggles to save beaches in Hawaii and in Florida.
36. Will Carless, "Park Toll Road Plan Rejected in California," *The New York Times*, February 8, 2008, A12.
37. Drew Kampion, "Trestles," *Surfer* 10(5), quoted in Sam George, ed., *The Perfect Day: 40 Years of Surfer Magazine* (San Francisco: Chronicle Books, 2001), 42.
38. "Pendleton Beach—a Good Start," (editorial) *The Los Angeles Times*, April 5, 1971, A6.
39. The most famous exception is Gordon "Grubby" Clark, who in 2004 threw the entire surf industry into crisis when he shut down his foam factory rather than bowing to environmental regulations. Many small board manufacturers, though, have taken the resulting shortage of foam surfboard blanks as an opportunity to find more environmentally friendly ways to manufacture light and durable boards.
40. Pierce Julius Flynn, "Waves of Semiosis: Surfing's Iconic Progression," *The American Journal of Semiotics* 5 (3&4), (1987): 397–418.
41. Glen Hening, "Pierce Flynn: Surfers and Their Symbols" *Groundswell Society Third Annual Publication*, (Oxnard, California: Groundswell Society, 2001), 186–187.
42. "Dredging Protester Stands by Surfing Stunt," February 9, 2008, ABC news Australia online. http://www.abc.net.au/news, accessed February 10, 2008.
43. David Helvarc, "Making Waves," *Sierra* (May/June 2005): 22–28.
44. Howard Slusher, "Surfing Helps Youth Express Individuality," *The Los Angeles Times*, March 3, 1968, 12.
45. "Command Generation," *Time* 88, July 29, 1966, 50–54.
46. "Sunset Along the Strip," *Time* 88, December 2, 1966, 69.
47. "Short and the Long of It," *Time* 86, October 1, 1965, 54.
48. "Hunt of the Sun," *Time* 88, July 8, 1966, 6.
49. "Life Revisits the Ski Bums (and Finds that Now They Are Beach Bums),"*Life* 29, August 28 1950, 116–118+.
50. "Aspen's Awful Problem: Surfers on Skis," *Life* 58, March 12, 1965, 42–44+.

51. C. Phinizy, "Riders of the Surging Sea," *Sports Illustrated* 18, February 18, 1963, 26–30.
52. "Surf's Up," *Time* 82, August 9, 1963, 49.
53. "Riding the Crest of Surfing's Wave," *Life* 61, September 9, 1966, 37–38+.
54. Bonfante, J. "Is J. J. Really King of the Surf?" *Life* 60, June 10, 1966, 81–82.
55. "Surfer's Cross," *Time* 87, April 22, 1966, 81.
56. D. K. Webster, "They Ride the Wild Water," *The Saturday Evening Post* 230, June 14, 1958, 3839+.
57. J. Severson, "Riding the World's Wild Giants," *The Saturday Evening Post* 235, July 14, 1962, 20–25.
58. J. Siegel, "Surf, Wheels, and Free Souls," *The Saturday Evening Post* 239, November 19, 1966, 32–37.
59. Phil Edwards, "You Should Have Been Here an Hour Ago" [excerpt], *The Saturday Evening Post* 240, July 1, 1967, 32–39.
60. "Mad Happy Surfers," *Life* 51, September 1, 1961, 47–53.
61. E. Burdick, "They Ride the Big Surf," *Reader's Digest* 83, July 1963, 224–230.
62. "Shooting the Tube," *Time* 83, January 10, 1964, 57.
63. "That Wall of Water," *Time* 79, February 16, 1962, 36.
64. G. Greene, "Take a Surfer Out of the Surf (And What Have You Got?)" *Ladies' Home Journal* 84, October 1967, 172–174+.
65. R. W. Johnston, "You Can Always Surf on It," *Sports Illustrated* 35, December 6, 1971, 102–103.
66. R. W. Johnston, "Shark Huntress of Mooloolaba," *Sports Illustrated* 43, December 8, 1975, 82+.
67. "The Knee and the Board," *Time* 85, May 7, 1965, 75.
68. "The Isla Vista Uprising," *Time* 95, March 9, 1970, 19–20.
69. Tanis Thorne, "Legends of the Surfer Subculture, Part One," *Western Folklore* 35(3), (July 1976): 209–217.
70. Daniel Duane, *Caught Inside: A Surfer's Year on the California Coast* (New York: North Point Press, 1996),59.
71. *Riding Giants,* dir. by Stacey Peralta, Agi Orsi Productions, 2003.
72. "Riding the Wild Waves," *Life* 54, May 24, 1963, 56–69+.
73. W. Bolster, "All Aboard the Tunnel Express," *Sports Illustrated* 46, May 30, 1977, 32–36.
74. D. Levin, "Doo Wa Diddie Squiggly Wigglies: Get Lost!" *Sports Illustrated* 31, December 8, 1969, 22–23.
75. C. Kirkpatrick, "The Closest Thing to Being Born," *Sports Illustrated* 34, February 22, 1971, 60–64+.
76. Daniel Duane, *Caught Inside*, 98.
77. Ibid, 115.
78. Quoted in Ben Marcus, ed., *Surfing and the Meaning of Life* (St. Paul, MN: Voyageur Press, 2006),45.
79. Ibid.
80. Duane, *Caught Inside,* 114.
81. Ibid, 211.
82. "Surf's Up," *Time* 82, August 9, 1963, 49.
83. J. Maisel, "High Surfdom," *Sports Illustrated* 20, May 18, 1964, 60–65.
84. "The King at Twenty-Four," *Newsweek* 62, August 26, 1963, 71.
85. "New Wave," *Newsweek* 68, October 17, 1966, 64+.
86. "Surf's Up: The Wet-Set Revolution," *Newsweek* 70, August 14, 1967, 52–56.
87. M. C. Cronin, "Surf Safety School," *Parks & Recreation* 2 (July 1967): 16–17+.

88. G. D. Hunsaker, "Explorers in the Surf," *Recreation* 58 (June 1965): 286–287+.
89. Ibid, 51.
90. Rogin, G., "An Odd Sport, and an Unusual Champion," *Sports Illustrated* 23, October 18, 1965, 94–98+.
91. Quoted in Fred Hemmings, *The Soul of Surfing is Hawaiian* (Hong Kong: Sports Enterprises Inc., 1997), 96.
92. Ibid, 110.
93. Ibid, 76.
94. Ibid, 116.
95. Ibid, 117.
96. Nat Young, *The History of Surfing* (Palm Beach: Palm Beach Press, 1983),110.
97. Nat Young, Letter, *Tracks*, October, 1970, 7, quoted in Douglas Booth, "Ambiguities in Pleasure and Discipline: The Development of Competitive Surfing," *Journal of Sport History* 22(3), (Fall 1995): 195.
98. The competitive aspect of surfing resurged in the eighties and has become a major piece of surf culture since then, but I think that Booth is incorrect to say that the rise of a competitive circuit has "disciplined" the more countercultural aspects of surf culture. The contests take place all around the world, participating in the image of the surf tribe as collective and nomadic, always in search of great waves. If you watch the coverage of these contests on, for instance, Fuel TV, which is devoted to surfing and other "extreme" sports, you'll see clearly that nobody is taking the stuff all that seriously. (This was true of ABC's *Wide World of Sports* coverage of international contests beginning in the sixties, as well.) The surf companies get advertising and the surfers make money, and everybody's just mostly having fun and prodding one another on to better and better performances. And in the most prominent pop culture images of surf competitions, such as the 2002 film *Blue Crush*, surfers in competition with one another tend to be depicted as ready to help one another excel. They're portrayed as understanding that the "stoke" of riding waves is far above a "win" in a contest in terms of what's important.
99. Young, *The History of Surfing*, 117.
100. *Rainbow Bridge*, dir. by Chuck Wein, Antakharana Films, 1972.
101. http://www.youtube.com/watch?v=DZu_EkYAOKg, accessed March 7, 2010.
102. Reproduced in George, *The Perfect Day*, 84.
103. This point is powerfully depicted in the documentary, *History of Rock and Roll, Vol. 6*, dir. Obie Benz, Andrew Solt Productions/PBS, 1995.
104. "Desert Blooms with Surf," *Life* 68, March 6, 1970, 48–9, and C. Phinizy, "Instant Ocean: It Just Keeps Rolling Along," *Sports Illustrated* 31, November 10 1969, 74–8.
105. Brian Chidester and Dominic Priore, *Pop Surf Culture: Music, Film and Fashion from the Bohemian Surf Era* (Santa Monica: Santa Monica Press, 2008).
106. "The King at Twenty-Four," *Newsweek* 62, August 26, 1963, 71.
107. *Amazing Journey: The Story of the Who*, dir. by Paul Crowder and Murray Lerner, Spitfire Productions, 2007.
108. Ben Marcus, *Surfing, USA! An Illustrated History of the Coolest Sport of All Time* (St. Paul, MN: Voyageur Press, 2005),97.
109. For the following discussion, I have relied on Matt Warshaw's brilliant 2005 compilation of surf movie posters, *Surf Movie Tonite! Surf Movie Poster Art, 1957–2004*, (San Francisco: Chronicle Books, 2005).

110. Ibid, 56.
111. Ibid, 65.
112. Ibid, 67.
113. Ibid, 72.
114. George, *A Perfect Day,* 35.
115. Warshaw, *Surf Movie Tonite!,* 91.
116. Ibid, 93.
117. This is the blurb on the film's iconic poster.
118. R. Vaughan, "Splashy, Surf-Soaked Sleeper," *Life* 61, November 25, 1966, 19.
119. Thad Ziolkowski, "Chairmen of the Boards," *Artforum International* 42(10), (Summer 2004): 47–50.
120. *The Endless Summer,* dir. by Bruce Brown, Bruce Brown Films, 1966.
121. The eloquent Daniel Duane puts this dynamic nicely: "It makes an appealing vision of global community forged by Californian fun . . . both sides engage in a joyous nonconversation. Play transcends not just culture, but language itself." Duane (1996): 180. This insight is reminiscent of Johan Huizinga's discussion of the nature of play in the seminal *Homo Ludens*. In that work, Huizinga posits play as the foundation of all ritual and thus all culture—for him, play precedes and transcends all oppositions, such as that between the serious and the non-serious, the real and the un-real. In both games and ritual, everyone knows that what's happening isn't "real" or "serious," but in order for play to take place, it has to simultaneously be taken as utterly "real" and dead "serious." For Huizinga, play is *the* single cultural universal, and the footage in *Endless Summer* bears out this insight. Johan Huizinga, *Homo Ludens* (New York: J & J Harper Editions, 1970).
122. Sigfried Kracauer, *From Caligari to Hitler: A Psychological History of the German Film* (Princeton: Princeton University Press, 1947), 6–7, emphasis mine.
123. *Step Into Liquid,* dir. by Dana Brown, Top Secret Productions, 2003; *Riding Giants,* dir. by Stacey Peralta, Agi Orsi Productions, 2004.
124. "Surf's Up," *Time* 82, August 9, 1963, 49.
125. *Gidget,* dir. by Paul Wendkos, Columbia Pictures, 1959.
126. Frederick Kohner, *Gidget: The Little Girl with Big Ideas* (New York: Berkley Books, 2001), 119.
127. Ibid, 66.
128. Ibid, 50.
129. Krista Comer, whose work on Gidget as a feminist character encourages "university feminism" to reconsider its dismissal of the role pleasure, desire, and what she calls "countercultural subjectivity" play in generating feminist politics, goes even further than I do in ascertaining the radical implications of *Gidget*; for her, the film's ending is not quite as domesticating as it appears. In her reading, it's significant that Gidget ends the film outdoors rather than in the domestic frame, "playing at the edge of national femininity . . . the conditions of possibility are present for her enunciation as an international and a transnational subject." Krista Comer, "Taking Feminism and Regionalism Toward the Transnational Third Wave," 111–128.
130. Ibid, 140–142.
131. Ibid, 154.
132. Joseph Breen, enforcer of the Hollywood Production Code from 1934–1954, was a Roman Catholic Priest but a Puritan at heart. His most recent biographer, Thomas Doherty, says that he "embodied the restraint, repression, and rigidity of a personality type known as the 'Victorian Irish.'" Ada Calhoun, "Hollywood Chronicle," review of *Hollywood's Censor: Joseph I.*

Breen and the Production Code Administration, by Thomas Doherty. *The New York Times Book Review*, December 2, 2007, http://www.nytimes.com/2007/12/02/books/review/Calhoun-t.html, accessed December 2, 2007.

133. Kohner, *Gidget*, 48–49.
134. *Gidget Goes Hawaiian*, dir. by Paul Wendkos, Columbia Pictures, 1961.
135. Interview in Marcus, *Surfing, USA*, 110.
136. *Beach Party*, dir. by William Asher, American International Pictures, 1963.
137. *Bikini Beach*, dir. by William Asher, American International Pictures, 1964.
138. Interviewed in *Riding Giants*.
139. *Ride the Wild Surf*, dir. by Don Taylor, Columbia Pictures, 1964.
140. D. Jenkins, "Bleachies, Beachies and Blasters on a Summer-in at Waikiki," *Sports Illustrated* 27, July 24, 1967, 48–54.
141. "The Sixties: Decade of Tumult and Change," *Life* 67(26), December 26, 1969, 110–111.
142. *Apocalypse Now*, dir. by Francis Ford Coppola, Zoetrope Studios, 1979.
143. Interview in Marcus, *Surfing, USA*, 124.
144. *Fast Times at Ridgemont High*, dir. by Amy Heckerling, Refugee Films, 1982.
145. Donna Gaines, *Teenage Wasteland: Suburbia's Dead-End Kids* (New York: Pantheon Books, 1991).

NOTES TO CHAPTER 5

1. Benjamin Hunnicutt, *Work Without End: Abandoning Shorter Hours for the Right to Work* (Philadelphia: Temple University Press, 1988); and *Kellogg's Six-Hour Day*, (Philadelphia: Temple University Press, 1996).
2. Juliet Shor, *The Overworked American: the Unexpected Decline of Leisure* (New York: Basic Books, 1992).
3. Kathy Peiss, *Cheap Amusements: Working Women and Leisure in Turn-of-the-Century New York* (Philadelphia: Temple University Press, 1986), 6–8.
4. Nan Enstad, *Ladies of Labor, Girls of Adventure: Working Women, Popular Culture, and Labor Politics at the Turn of the Century* (New York: Columbia University Press, 1999): 10–15.
5. Scott Norwood, *Labor's Flaming Youth: Telephone Operators and Worker Militancy 1878–1923* (Urbana: University of Illinois Press, 1990): 11–13.
6. Robin D.G. Kelley, *Race Rebels: Culture, Politics, and the Black Working Class* (New York: The Free Press, 1994).
7. Ibid, 9.
8. John Rawls, *A Theory of Justice* (Cambridge, Mass: Belknap Press of Harvard University Press, 1971).
9. John Rawls, "The Priority of the Right and Ideas of the Good," *Philosophy and Public Affairs* 17(4), (Fall 1988): 275 note.
10. Philippe Van Parijs, *Real Freedom For All: What (If Anything) Can Justify Capitalism?* (New York: Oxford University Press, 1995).
11. Philippe Van Parijs, "Why Surfers Should Be Fed: the Liberal Case for an Unconditional Basic Income," *Philosophy and Public Affairs* 20(2), (Spring 1991): 101–131.
12. Alan Law, "Surfing the Safety Net," *International Review for the Sociology of Sport* 36 Issue 1 (March 2001): 25.
13. Ibid, 29.
14. Freud, *Civilization and its Discontents*, 91–92, emphasis mine.

15. Jonathan Cutler, *Labor's Time: Shorter Hours, the UAW, and the Struggle for American Unionism* (Philadelphia: Temple University Press, 2004).
16. It's important to distinguish between the price of labor-power and its value. According to Marx, the value of labor-power is determined by what it took to "produce" it—that is, sustenance plus skill. This quantitative value is distinct from price—commodities, including labor-power, can sell at prices above or below their actual quantitative value due to fluctuations in supply and demand.
17. Jock Young, "The Hippie Solution: an Essay in the Politics of Leisure," in *Politics and Deviance,* Ian Taylor and Laurie Taylor, eds. (Baltimore: Penguin Books, 1973).
18. An entire panicked field of sociology, called Leisure Studies, emerged at this time. There was some interesting work done, but the field mostly expressed bourgeois fears about the degraded nature of working-class leisure.
19. Lawler, Kristin, "Capitalism and Counterculture: the View from the Wall Street Journal," unpublished paper.
20. Max Weber, *The Protestant Ethic and the Spirit of Capitalism* (New York: Routledge, 1992): 157.
21. "A Vast Uncertainty," *The Wall Street Journal,* November 3, 1966, 18.
22. "Salesmen of Sloth," *The Wall Street Journal,* October. 14, 1959, 18.
23. "No Surprise to Moses," *The Wall Street Journal,* December 22, 1969, 12.
24. "The Wellsprings of Anarchy," *The Wall Street Journal,* June 3, 1968, 14.
25. "The Value of Inhibition," *The Wall Street Journal,* July 22, 1969, 20.
26. Weber, 119.
27. *John from Cincinnati,* created by David Milch and Kem Nunn, HBO Productions, 2007.
28. *North Shore,* dir. by William Phelps, Finnegan/Pinchuk Productions, 1987.

Bibliography

BOOKS AND ARTICLES

"A Vast Uncertainty," *The Wall Street Journal*, November 3, 1966, 18.

"Aspen's Awful Problem: Surfers on Skis," *Life* 58, March 12, 1965, 42–50.

"Champion of the Heavies," *Time* 85, January 8, 1965, 35.

"Command Generation," *Time* 88, July 29, 1966, 50–54.

"Desert Blooms with Surf," *Life* 68, March 6, 1970, 48–49.

Hawaii: Paradise of the Pacific, Yearbook. Honolulu: Hawaii Promotion Committee, 1913.

Hawaii Visitors and Convention Bureau (formerly the Hawaii Tourism Bureau) website http://www.hvcb.org/corporate/history.htm.

"Humper!" *Christian Science Monitor Weekly Magazine Section*, November 7, 1942, 6+.

"Hunt of the Sun," *Time* 88, July 8, 1966, 6.

"Life Revisits the Ski Bums (and Finds That Now They Are Beach Bums),"*Life* 29, August 28, 1950, 116–120.

"Living Dynamite is in Wait at Waikiki, Says Dorothy Mackaill", *Honolulu Star-Bulletin*, January 29, 1932.

"Mad Happy Surfers," *Life* 51, September 1, 1961, 47–53.

"New Wave," *Newsweek* 68, October 17, 1966, 64+.

"No Surprise to Moses," *The Wall Street Journal*, December 22, 1969, 12.

"Riding the Crest of Surfing's Wave," *Life* 61, September 9, 1966, 37–38+.

"Riding the Wild Waves," *Life* 54, May 24, 1963, 56–69+.

"Riding Waikiki's White Horses," *Review of Reviews*, 79, April 1929, 151152.

"Salesmen of Sloth," *The Wall Street Journal*, October 14, 1959, 18.

"Shooting the Tube," *Time* 83, January 10, 1964, 57.

"Short and the Long of It," *Time* 86, October 1, 1965, 54.

"Sunset Along the Strip," *Time* 88, December 2, 1966, 69.

"Surf Boarders Capture California," *National Geographic* 86, September 1944, 355–362.

"Surfer's Cross," *Time* 87, April 22, 1966, 81.

"Surf Riding on California Beach is a Favorite Summertime Sport," *Life* 9, August 26, 1940, 50–52.

"Surf, Snow, Sex, and Protest," *Time* 85 April 2, 1965, 61.

"Surf's Up," *Time* 82, August 9, 1963, 49.

"Surf's Up: The Wet-Set Revolution," *Newsweek* 70, August 14, 1967, 52–56.

"That Wall of Water," *Time* 79, February 16, 1962, 36.

"The Isla Vista Uprising," *Time* 95, March 9, 1970, 19–20.

"The King at Twenty-Four," *Newsweek* 62, August 26, 1963, 71.

"The Knee and the Board," *Time* 85, May 7, 1965, 75.
"The Sixties: Decade of Tumult and Change," *Life* 67(26), December 26, 1969, 110–111.
"The Value of Inhibition," *The Wall Street Journal*, July 22, 1969, 20.
"The Wellsprings of Anarchy," *The Wall Street Journal*, June 3, 1968, 14.
Althusser, Louis. "Ideology and Ideological State Apparatuses," in *Lenin and Philosophy*. New York: Monthly Review Press, 1971.
Aronowitz, Stanley. *False Promises: The Shaping of American Working Class Consciousness*. New York: McGraw Hill Book Company, 1973.
Aronowitz, Stanley. *The Crisis in Historical Materialism*. Minnesota: University of Minnesota Press, 1990.
Aronowitz, Stanley and William DiFazio. *The Jobless Future: Sci-Tech and the Dogma of Work*. Minnesota: University of Minnesota Press, 1995.
Aronowitz, Stanley. *Just Around the Corner: The Paradox of the Jobless Recovery*. Philadelphia: Temple University Press, 2005.
Arms, L.L., "Humper!" *Christian Science Monitor Magazine*, November 7, 1942, 6+.
Ball, John Heath, photographer. *Early California Surfriders: A Collector's Edition of Rare Photographs Covering Classic California Longboard Surfing in the Thirties and Forties*. Ventura, California: Pacific Publishing, 1995 (first published as "California Surfriders", 1946.)
Bell, Daniel. *The Cultural Contradictions of Capitalism*. New York: Basic Books, 1976.
Bingham, Hiram. *A Residence of Twenty-One Years in the Sandwich Islands*. New York: S. Converse, 1848.
Bird, Isabella L. *Six Months among the Palm Groves, Coral Reefs, and Volcanoes of the Sandwich Islands*. New York: G. P. Putnam's Sons, 1876.
Blake, Tom. *Hawaiian Surfboard*. Honolulu: Paradise of the Pacific Press, 1935.
Blake, Tom. "Waves and Thrills at Waikiki," *National Geographic* 67, May 1935, 597–604.
Bolster, W. "All Aboard the Tunnel Express," *Sports Illustrated* 46, May 30, 1977, 32–36.
Bonfante, J. "Is J. J. Really King of the Surf?" *Life* 60, June 10, 1966, 81–82.
Booth, Douglas. Ambiguities in Pleasure and Discipline: The Development of Competitive Surfing, *Journal of Sport History* 22(3), (Fall 1995): 189–206.
Brooks, David. *Bobos in Paradise: The New Upper Class and How They Got There*. New York: Simon and Schuster, 2000.
Brown, DeSoto. "Beautiful, Romantic Hawaii: How the Fantasy Image Came to Be," in *The Journal of Decorative and Propaganda Arts* 20, (1994): 252–271.
Brown, DeSoto. *Hawaii at Play: Images of a Bygone Era*. Honolulu: Watermark Publishing, 2003.
Brown, DeSoto. *Surfing: Historic Images from the Bishop Museum Archives*. Honolulu: Bishop Museum Press, 2006.
Burdick, E. "They Ride the Big Surf," *Reader's Digest* 83, July 1963, 224–230.
Caffentzis, George. "The Work-Energy Crisis and the Apocalypse," in Midnight Notes Collective, eds., *Midnight Oil: Work, Energy, War 1973–1992*, New York: Autonomedia, 1992.
Calhoun, Ada. "Hollywood Chronicle," review of *Hollywood's Censor: Joseph I. Breen and the Production Code Administration*, by Thomas Doherty. *The New York Times Book Review*, December 2, 2007, http://www.nytimes.com/2007/12/02/books/review/Calhoun-t.html, accessed December 2, 2007.
Cherrington, E. "Surf-Board Rider," *American Mercury* 47, June 1939, 234.
Chidester, Brian, and Dominic Priore. *Pop Surf Culture: Music, Film and Fashion from the Bohemian Surf Era*. Santa Monica: Santa Monica Press, 2008.

Church, Ron. *Surf Contest*. Santa Barbara: T. Adler Books, 2006.

Cleaver, Harry. "Crisis of the Keynesian Era." http://www.eco.utexas.edu/~hmcleave/304Lfall.html

Cleaver, Harry. *Reading Capital Politically*. Austin: University of Texas Press, 1979.

Cleaver, Harry. "Deep Currents Rising: Notes on the Global Threat to Capitalism" in *Subverting the Present, Imagining the Future: Insurrection, Movement, Commons*. New York: Autonomedia, 2006, https://webspace.utexas.edu/hcleaver/www/DeepCurrentsRisingFinal2.htm

Coffin, Harold. "Riding the Waves at Waikiki," *Country Life* 64, September 1933, 56–57.

Cohen, Albert K. *Delinquent Boys: The Culture of the Gang*. New York: The Free Press, 1955.

Comer, Krista. "Taking Feminism and Regionalism Toward the Transnational Third Wave," in *A Companion to the Regional Literatures of America*, edited by Charles Crow, Malden, Mass.: Blackwell, 2003.

Comer, Krista. "Wanting to be Lisa: Generational Rifts, Girl Power, and the Globalization of Surf Culture," in *American Youth Cultures*, edited by Neil Campbell, New York: Routledge, 2004.

Comer, Krista. *Surfer Girls in the New World Order*. Duke University Press, forthcoming.

Connery, Christopher. "The Oceanic Feeling and the Regional Imaginary," in Rob Wilson and Wimal Dissanayake, eds., *Global/Local*. Durham: Duke University Press, 1996.

Cook, James. *The Voyages of Captain James Cook, Vol. II, Round the World*. London: W. Smith Publisher, 1842.

Crawford, Carin. "Waves of Transformation," unpublished Master's thesis, available at http://www.lajollasurf.org/wavesof.html.

Cronin, M. C. "Surf Safety School," *Parks & Recreation* 2 (July 1967):16–17+.

Daws, Gavan. *Shoal of Time: a History of the Hawaiian Islands*. New York: Macmillan, 1968.

Deagan, J. P. "Cool on a Hot Curl," *The New York Times Magazine*, August 22, 1965, 72–73.

De La Vega, Timothy. *200 Years of Surfing Literature: An Annotated Bibliography*. Hanapepe, Kauai, Hawaii: T. De La Vega, 2004.

Divine, Jeff. *Surfing Photographs from the Seventies Taken by Jeff Divine*. Santa Barbara: T. Adler Books, 2005.

Duane, Daniel. *Caught Inside: A Surfer's Year on the California Coast*. New York: North Point Press, 1996.

Duncombe, Stephen. *Dream: Re-Imagining Progressive Politics in an Age of Fantasy*. New York: The Free Press, 2007.

Edwards, P. "You Should Have Been Here An Hour Ago" [excerpt], *The Saturday Evening Post* 240, July 1, 1967, 32–39.

Ellis, William. *Polynesian Researches*. London: Fisher, Son & Jackson, 1836.

Emerson, Nathaniel B. "Causes of the Decline of Ancient Polynesian Sports," *The Friend* (Honolulu) L, VIII (1892).

Emory, Kenneth Pike. *Ancient Hawaiian Civilizations*. Honolulu: the Kamehameha Schools, 1933.

Enstad, Nan. *Ladies of Labor, Girls of Adventure: Working Women, Popular Culture, and Labor Politics at the Turn of the Century*. New York: Columbia University Press, 1999.

Flynn, Pierce Julius. "Waves of Semiosis: Surfing's Iconic Progression." *The American Journal of Semiotics* 5(3&4), (1987): 397–418.

Ford, Alexander Hume. "Our Japanese Territory," *Colliers* 43, July 24, 1909, 12–13.

Ford, Alexander Hume. "Riding the Surf in Hawaii," *Collier's* 43, August 14, 1909, 17.
Ford, Nick and David Brown. *Surfing and Social Theory: Experience, Embodiment, and the Narrative of the Dream Glide.* New York: Routledge, 2006.
Frank, Thomas. *The Conquest of Cool: Business Culture, Counterculture, and the Rise of Hip Consumerism.* Chicago: University of Chicago Press, 1997.
Freud, Sigmund. *The Interpretation of Dreams.* New York: Avon Books, 1965.
Freud, Sigmund. *Civilization and its Discontents.* New York: W. W. Norton, 1989.
Frith, Simon."Music for Pleasure," *Screen Education* 34 (1980): 51–61.
Gabbard, Andrea. *Girl in the Curl: A Century of Women in Surfing.* Seattle: Seal Press, 2000.
Gaines, Donna. *Teenage Wasteland: Suburbia's Dead-End Kids.* New York: Pantheon Books, 1991.
Gault-Williams, Malcolm. *Legendary Surfers, Volume I*, Chapter 2: 2500 B.C. to 1919 A.D., (c) 2005. Self-published manuscript available at www.legendarysurfers.com/surf/legends/ls07z_duke.html, 1999.
George, Sam, ed. *The Perfect Day: 40 Years of Surfer Magazine.* San Francisco: Chronicle Books, 2001.
Gitlin, Todd. *The Sixties:Years of Hope, Days of Rage.* New York: Bantam Books: 1987.
Goffman, Erving. *Stigma: Notes on the Management of Spoiled Identity.* New York: Simon and Schuster, 1963.
Gramsci, Antonio. *Selections from the Prison Notebooks.* New York: International Publishers, 1971.
Grannis, Leroy. *Surf Photography of the 1960s and 1970s*, ed. by Heimann, Jim. Los Angeles: Taschen, 2006.
Greene, G. "Take a Surfer Out of the Surf (And What Have You Got?)" *Ladies' Home Journal* 84, October 1967, 172174+.
Hall, Stuart and Tony Jefferson, eds. *Resistance Through Rituals.* London: Routledge, 1975.
Hebdige, Dick. *Subculture: the Meaning of Style.* London: Methuen, 1979.
Heimann, Jim, ed. *Icons: Surfing: Vintage Surfing Graphics.* Los Angeles: Taschen, 2004.
Hemmings, Fred. *The Soul of Surfing is Hawaiian.* Hong Kong: Sports Enterprises Inc., 1997.
Helvarc, David. "Making Waves," *Sierra* (May/June 2005): 22–28.
Hening, Glen. "Pierce Flynn: Surfers and Their Symbolsî (includes an interview by Glen Hening). In *Groundswell Society Third Annual Publication.* Oxnard, California:
Groundswell Society, 2001.
hooks, bell. *Black Looks: Race and Representation.* Boston: South End Press, 1992.
Houston, James D. and Ben Finney. *Surfing: A History of the Ancient Hawaiian Sport.* Rohnert: Pomegranate Art Books, 1996.
Huizinga, Johan. *Homo Ludens.* New York: J & J Harper Editions, 1970.
Hunnicutt, Benjamin. *Work Without End: Abandoning Shorter Hours for the Right to Work.* Philadelphia: Temple University Press, 1988.
Hunnicutt, Benjamin. *Kellogg's Six-Hour Day.* Philadelphia: Temple University Press, 1996.
Hunsaker, G. D. "Explorers in the Surf," *Recreation* 58 (June 1965): 286–287+.
Irwin, John. "Surfing: the Natural History of an Urban Scene," *Urban Life and Culture,* Volume 2(2), (1973): 133–46.

James, Don. *Surfing San Onofre to Point Dume, 1936–1942*. Santa Barbara: T. Adler Books, 1996.

James, Don. *Prewar Surfing Photographs*. Santa Barbara: T. Adler Books, 2004.

Jenkins, D. "Bleachies, beachies and blasters on a Summer-in at Waikiki," *Sports Illustrated* 27, July 24, 1967, 48–54.

Johnston, R. W. "You Can Always Surf on It," *Sports Illustrated* 35, December 6, 1971, 102–103.

Johnston, R. W. "Shark Huntress of Mooloolaba," *Sports Illustrated* 43, December 8, 1975, 82+.

Kampion, Drew. *Stoked! A History of Surf Culture*. Salt Lake City: Gibbs Smith, 2003.

Kelley, Robin D. G. *Race Rebels: Culture, Politics, and the Black Working Class*. New York: The Free Press, 1994.

Keyes, Frances Parkinson. "Aloha From Hawaii," *Good Housekeeping* 82, December 1925, 30–31.

Kirkpatrick, C. "The Closest Thing to Being Born," *Sports Illustrated* 34, February 22, 1971, 60–64+.

Kohner, Frederick. *Gidget: The Little Girl with Big Ideas*. New York: Bantam Books, 1957.

Kracauer, Sigfried. *From Caligari to Hitler: A Psychological History of the German Film*. Princeton: Princeton University Press, 1947.

Lacan, Jacques. "The Mirror Stage as Formative of the Function of the I," in *Ecrits: A Selection*, New York: Norton, 1977.

Law, Alan. "Surfing the Safety Net: 'Dole Bludging', 'Surfies' and Governmentality in Australia," *International Review for the Sociology of Sport* 36(1), (March 2001): 25–40.

Levin, D. "Doo Wa Diddie Squiggly Wigglies: Get Lost!" *Sports Illustrated* 31, December 8, 1969, 22–23.

London, Jack. *The Cruise of the Snark*. New York: Macmillan, 1918.

London, Jack. "A Royal Sport," *The Woman's Home Companion* (1907) reprinted in Matt Warshaw, ed., *Zero Break: An Illustrated Collection of Surf Writing 1777–2004*, New York: Harcourt, Inc., 2004.

Lueras, Leonard. *Surfing: The Ultimate Pleasure*. New York: Workman International, 1984.

Lynch, Gary. *Tom Blake: Surfing 1922–1932*. Santa Barbara: T. Adler Books, 2000.

Lynch, Gary and Malcolm Gault-Williams. *Tom Blake: The Uncommon Journey of a Pioneer Waterman*. Corona Del Mar, California: Croul Family Foundation, 2001.

Mailer, Norman. "The White Negro," in *Advertisements for Myself*, Cambridge, Mass: Harvard University Press, 1992.

Maisel, J. "High Surfdom," *Sports Illustrated* 20, May 18, 1964, 60–65.

Marcus, Ben, ed. *Surfing and the Meaning of Life*. St. Paul, Minn: Voyageur Press, 2006.

Marcus, Ben. *Surfing, USA! An Illustrated History of the Coolest Sport of All Time*. St. Paul, Minn.: Voyageur Press, 2005.

Marcuse, Herbert. *Eros and Civilization: A Philosophical Inquiry into Freud*. Boston: Beacon Press, 1955.

Marvin, George. "Riding the Surf at Waikiki," *Outing* 64, April 1914, 24–35.

Marx, Karl. *The Economic and Philosophic Manuscripts of 1844*. New York: International Publishers, 1964.

Marx, Karl. *Capital: A Critique of Political Economy*. Moscow: Progress Publishers, 1965.

Marx, Karl and Friedrich Engels. *Manifesto of the Communist Party*. Peking: Foreign Languages Press, 1970.
May, Kirse Granat. *Golden State, Golden Youth: The California Image in Popular Culture 1955–1966*. Chapel Hill: University of North Carolina Press, 2002.
Michener, James. *Hawaii*. New York: Random House, 1959.
Muggleton, David and Rupert Weinzierl, eds. *The Post-Subcultures Reader*. New York: Berg Publishers, 2004.
Negri, Antonio. *Marx Beyond Marx: Lessons on the Grundrisse*. Brooklyn: Autonomedia, 1991.
Noble, Valerie. *Hawaiian Prophet: Alexander Hume Ford*. Smithtown, NY: Exposition Press, 1980.
Norwood, Scott. *Labor's Flaming Youth: Telephone Operators and Worker Militancy 1878–1923*. Urbana: University of Illinois Press, 1990.
Peiss, Kathy. *Cheap Amusements: Working Women and Leisure in Turn-of-the-Century New York*. Philadelphia: Temple University Press, 1986.
Phinizy, C. . "Riders of the Surging Sea," *Sports Illustrated* 18, February 18, 1963, 26–30.
Phinizy, C. "Instant Ocean: It Just Keeps Rolling Along," *Sports Illustrated* 31, November 10, 1969, 74–78.
Rawls, John. *A Theory of Justice*. Cambridge, Mass: Belknap Press of Harvard University Press, 1971.
Rawls, John. "The Priority of the Right and Ideas of the Good," *Philosophy and Public Affairs* 17(4), (Fall 1988): 251–276.
Rifkin, Jeremy. *The End of Work*. New York: G. P. Putnam's Sons, 1996.
Rogin, G. "An Odd Sport, and an Unusual Champion," *Sports Illustrated* 23, October 18, 1965, 94–98+.
Rosenzweig, Roy. *Eight Hours for What We Will: Workers and Leisure in an Industrial City, 1870–1920*. New York: Cambridge University Press, 1983.
Roszak, Theodore. *The Making of a Counter Culture*. Berkeley: University of California Press, 1968.
Rutsky, R. L. "Surfing the Other: Ideology on the Beach." *Film Quarterly* 52 (Summer 1999): 12–23.
Sahlins, Marshall. "The Original Affluent Society," in *Stone Age Economics*, Chicago: Aldine-Atherton, 1972.
Severson, J. "Riding the World's Wild Giants,"*The Saturday Evening Post* 235, July 14, 1962, 20–25.
Shor, Juliet. *The Overworked American: the Unexpected Decline of Leisure*. New York: Basic Books, 1992.
Siegel, J. "Surf, Wheels, and Free Souls," *The Saturday Evening Post* 239, November 19, 1966, 32–37.
Stecyk, C. R. III and Drew Kampion. *Dora Lives: The Authorized Biography*. Santa Barbara: T. Adler Books, 2005.
Steinberg, Phillip. *The Social Construction of the Ocean*. Cambridge: Cambridge University Press, 2001.
Stratton, Jon. "Youth Subcultures and Their Cultural Contexts," *Australian and New Zealand Journal of Sociology* 21(2), (1985): 194–218.
Thompson, E. P. "Time, Work-Discipline, and Industrial Capitalism," *Past and Present: Journal of Historical Studies* 38 (1967): 56–97.
Thorne, Tanis. "Legends of the Surfer Subculture, Part One," *Western Folklore* 35(3), (July 1976): 209–217.
Thorne, Tanis. "Legends of the Surfer Subculture, Part Two," *Western Folklore* 35(4), (October 1976): 270–280.
Thurston, Lorrin A. "What Hawaii Really Means to Southern California," *Los Angeles Times*, January 1, 1925, E2.

Timmons, Grady. *Waikiki Beach Boy*. Honolulu: Editions Limited, 1989.

Todaro, Tony. "Waikiki's Famous Beach Boys," in *Paradise of the Pacific Yearbook*, Honolulu: Hawaii Promotion Committee, 1913.

Torgovnick, Marianna. *Gone Primitive: Savage Intellects, Modern Lives*, Chicago: University of Chicago Press, 1991.

Trask, Haunani-Kay. *From a Native Daughter: Colonialism and Sovereignty in Hawaii*. Honolulu: University of Hawaii Press, 1993.

Trebay, Guy. "Back to the Beach," *The New York Times*, June 1, 2006, E1.

Tronti, Mario, "The Strategy of the Refusal," in *Operai e Capitale*, Turin: Einaudi, 1961. (translation used: http://www.geocities.com/cordobakaf/tronti_refusal.html).

Twain, Mark. *Roughing It*. Berkeley: University of California Press, 1972.

Van Parijs, Philippe, "Why Surfers Should be Fed: The Liberal Case for an Unconditional Basic Income," *Philosophy and Public Affairs* 20(2), (Spring 1991): 101–131.

Van Parijs, Philippe. "*Real Freedom for All: What (If Anything) Can Justify Capitalism?*" New York: Clarendon Press, 1995.

Vaughan, R. "Splashy, Surf-Soaked Sleeper," *Life* 61, November 25, 1966, 19.

Warshaw, Matt. *Zero Break: An Illustrated Collection of Surf Writing 1777–2004*. New York: Harvest Books, 2004.

Warshaw, Matt. *The Encyclopedia of Surfing*. New York: Harcourt, 2003.

Warshaw, Matt. *Surf Movie Tonite! Surf Movie Poster Art, 1957–2004*. San Francisco: Chronicle Books, 2005.

Weber, Max. *The Protestant Ethic and the Spirit of Capitalism*. New York: Routledge, 1992.

Webster, D. K. "They Ride the Wild Water," *The Saturday Evening Post* 230, June 14, 1958, 38–39+.

Weller, Sheila. "Malibu's Lost Boys," *Vanity Fair* 552, August 2006, 166–179.

White, Ruth Taylor. *Hawaii as the Camera Sees It*. Honolulu: Honolulu Star-Bulletin, 1933.

Wilde, H. "Waikiki_Mirage," *Colliers* 106, September 14, 1940, 14–15.

Willis, Ellen. *Beginning to See the Light: Sex, Hope, and Rock and Roll*. Hanover, NH: Wesleyan University Press, 1992.

Willis, Ellen. "Escape from Freedom: What's the Matter with Tom Frank? (And the Liberals Who Love Him)," *Situations* I(2), (Winter 2006): 5–20.

Willis, Paul. *Learning to Labor: How Working-Class Kids Get Working-Class Jobs*. New York: Columbia University Press, 1981.

Wolfe, Tom. *The Pump House Gang*. New York: Farrar, Strauss, and Giroux, 1968.

Wolfe, Tom."Radical Chic," in *Radical Chic and Mau-Mauing the Flak Catchers*, New York: Farrar, Strauss, and Giroux, 1970.

Yaguchi, Yujin and Yoshihara, Mari. "Evolutions of 'Paradise': Japanese Tourist Discourse about Hawai`i'," *American Studies* 45(3), (2005): 81–106.

Yost, H. H. "Rough Riders of the Surf," *Sunset (Central West edition)* 56, January 1926, 12–13.

Young, Jock. *The Drugtakers: The Social Meaning of Drug Use*. London: Paladin, 1971.

Young, Jock. "The Hippie Solution: An Essay in the Politics of Leisure" in *Politics and Deviance*, Taylor, Ian and Laurie Taylor, eds. Baltimore: Penguin Books, 1973.

Young, Nat. *The History of Surfing*. Palm Beach: Palm Beach Press, 1983.

Young, Nat. *Nat's Nat and That's That: A Surfing Legend*. Angourie, Australia: Nymboida Press, 1998.

Ziolkowski, Thad. "Chairmen of the Boards," *Artforum International* 42(10), (Summer 2004): 47–50.

NEWSPAPERS

The Los Angeles Times
The Wall Street Journal

FILM/TELEVISION

Amazing Journey: The Story of the Who, dir. by Paul Crowder and Murray Lerner, Spitfire Productions, 2007.

Apocalypse Now, dir. by Francis Ford Coppola, Zoetrope Studios, 1979.

Beach Party, dir. by William Asher, American International Pictures, 1963.

Bikini Beach, dir. by William Asher, American International Pictures, 1964.

Blue Hawaii, dir. by Norman Taurog, Paramount Pictures, 1961.

Doc Ball: Surfing's Legendary Lensman, dir. by Carl Ackerman, Carl Ackerman Productions, 1999.

Fast Times at Ridgemont High, dir. by Amy Heckerling, Refugee Films, 1982.

Gidget, dir. by Paul Wendkos, Columbia Pictures, 1959.

Gidget Goes Hawaiian, dir. by Paul Wendkos, Columbia Pictures, 1961.

History of Rock and Roll, Vol. 6, dir. Obie Benz, Andrew Solt Productions/PBS, 1995.

John from Cincinnati, created by David Milch and Kem Nunn, HBO Productions, 2007.

North Shore, dir. by William Phelps, Finnegan/Pinchuk Productions, 1987.

Rainbow Bridge, dir. by Chuck Wein, Antakharana Films, 1972.

Ride the Wild Surf, dir. by Don Taylor, Columbia Pictures, 1964.

Riding Giants, dir. by Stacey Peralta, Agi Orsi Productions, 2004.

Step Into Liquid, dir. by Dana Brown, Top Secret Productions, 2003.

The Endless Summer, dir. by Bruce Brown, Bruce Brown Films, 1966.

Waikiki Wedding, dir. by Frank Tuttle, Paramount Pictures, 1937.

Index

Camp Pendleton, 100, 121–122

29891343R00125

Made in the USA
San Bernardino, CA
31 January 2016